Soulfaring

Celtic Pilgrimage
Then and Now

Cintra Pemberton, O.S.H.

MOREHOUSE PUBLISHING

(SPCK)

Morehouse Publishing
P.O. Box 1321
Harrisburg, PA 17105

Society for Promoting Christian Knowledge
Holy Trinity Church
Marylebone Road
London, NW1 4DU

Morehouse Publishing is a division of The Morehouse Group.

Printed in the United States of America

Cover design by Dana Jackson
Cover image: Carved Stone Station of the Cross, Inishmurray Island
          CORBIS/Michael St. Maur Sheil

Library of Congress Cataloging-in-Publication Data

Pemberton, Cintra.
        Soulfaring : Celtic pilgrimage then and now / Cintra Pemberton.
            p.   cm.
        Includes bibliographical references.
        ISBN 0-8192-1780-8
        1. Christian pilgrims and pilgrimages—British Isles.
        2. Christian pilgrims and pilgrimages—History. I. Title.
        II. Title: Soulfaring.
        BX2320.5.B65P45   1999
        263'.04241—dc21   99-23925
                                                                          CIP

British Library Cataloguing-in-Publication Data
        A catalogue record for this book is available from the British Library.
        ISBN 0-281-05276-X

For Pemmie and John

Contents

Foreword

THIS BOOK GIVES US a vivid picture of one of the most unexpected and promising religious movements of our time, the revival of pilgrimage. It takes us across great distances of space and time, from one side of the Atlantic to the other, from 1999 back into the remote past. Once you embark on these pages, I suspect that you will want to follow them to the end, as you find yourself taken to a great variety of places, great and small, in western Britain and Ireland.

Soulfaring is a friendly, welcoming book to read and deals with the many varied aspects of the subject of pilgrimage. It begins by exploring Celtic spirituality and the nature of sacred space, and moves on through the consideration of the history of the development of the practice of pilgrimage through the Christian centuries. Then, just in case you should feel cheated, Cintra throws in a remarkable chapter that underlines the extraordinary diversity of pilgrimage places today (Canterbury, Knock, Pennant Melangell, Lough Derg, and others) all of them full of promise of a new life that will lead us into the third millenium.

The second part of the book, "A Pilgrimage Journal," is surely its heart. As you read on and come to visit all the places Cintra explores, you will find that you are getting to know a very interesting and practical, yet deeply prayerful, companion. One of the joys of these pages is the way in which Cintra takes us into her confidence and tells us not only of her own experience of the places she visits but also about the discoveries she has made about how a pilgrimage should be arranged and organized.

One of the secrets of pilgrimage, Cintra writes, is not to attempt to do too much too quickly; better to go to a few places and really have time to savor the unique flavor of each one. Another of the secrets is to be found in her practical concern for such things as weather and climate. Here in Britain and Ireland we are constantly meeting winds coming in from the Atlantic bringing rain with them. These Atlantic winds, sometimes mild and friendly, sometimes stormy and threatening, are part of the climate of our world. But if they make our countries damp they also give us thousands of holy wells, some famous like St. Winifred's Well at Holywell, and others, such as Tobar na Mult, that are still largely known only in local memory and affection.

Above all you will observe how Cintra is constantly concerned that her companions should never become tourists just looking on from outside, but should be real pilgrims who enter into direct contact with the people who live at or around the pilgrimage sites. These personal contacts leading to shared worship and meals are a particular feature—and a very important one—of the pilgrimages she organizes.

As you read through *Soulfaring* you will get to know the author better. She is, in many ways, a person of our own times. She has her moments of depression; think of that cave near Whithorn. She has other times of skepticism and questioning, even when it comes to holy wells. She has her moments of elation and discovery when everything seems to come together, when the group of people who have come across the Atlantic as companions suddenly find themselves bonded into one, when the pilgrims discover themselves to be not only one with one another but with the angels and archangels and all the company of heaven.

Looked at from a British perspective, where the practice of pilgrimage in England, Scotland, and Wales effectively came to an end at the time of the Reformation, this gradual twentieth-century rediscovery of the ancient holy places is a strikingly counter-cultural phenomenon. It is something that no one in 1900 could have foreseen, a movement that seems to have grown spontaneously, bit by bit, without any central organization or direction.

As Cintra writes: "Countless Christian sacred places are reasserting themselves as places of live-giving peace, places that radiate a healing presence and a great sense of welcome to all.... People are going on pilgrimage again, walking, cycling, and riding together, visiting ancient holy places, but seeing them in a new light and finding in the pilgrimage experience renewed spiritual strength and nourishment.... Men and women who would never have expected to become twentieth-century pilgrims have found themselves drawn to ancient pilgrim places and have found in them not some devotional luxury, but a clarity and a vision which are necessary for truly human life."

I count it a privilege to have had some small part in the pilgrimages that these pages record; and I have greatly valued the opportunity of contributing this Foreward to Cintra's remarkable book.

CANON A. M. ALLCHIN

Acknowledgments

WITHOUT ESTHER DE WAAL'S guidance and mentorship during the year I was on sabbatical in Wales and her subsequent participation in the pilgrimage programs, it is unlikely I would have gotten caught up in Celtic spirituality in the first place. And it is certain that without her suggestions I could never have moved into a new area of ministry, that of leading prayer and study pilgrimages overseas. From this new ministry developed the Order of St. Helena's Pilgrimages: Explorations of Celtic Spirituality.

Without the scores of Welsh, Irish, Scottish, and Manx people who have encouraged, befriended, and given of themselves so freely to me—far too many to name individually—the Order of St. Helena would never have been able to offer our annual pilgrimage programs and my life would be considerably poorer.

Without the hundreds of American people who have shared a pilgrimage with me, many of them on two, three, four, five, or even six different programs, the pilgrimages themselves would have been far less stimulating and rewarding—and much less fun.

Without generous scholarship assistance and free use of the library at St. Deiniol's in Hawarden, North Wales, I could never have set aside the time or found the resources to actually write the book.

Without the editorial skill and scrutiny of my editor, Debra Farrington at Morehouse, my readers would have had to suffer through interminably long sentences, irrelevant non sequiturs, and loquacious digressions.

There are, additionally, certain individuals who over several years have given to me so generously of their time, energy, hospitality, and friendship that I would like to mention them by name: thanks to Glyn Conway of Chester, England; Nona Rees of St. David's, Wales; and Saunders and Cynthia Davies of Criccieth, Wales.

Special thanks are also due to my good friends Donald Allchin of Bangor, North Wales, and Peter Harbison of Dublin, not only for writing the Foreword and Afterword respectively, but also for their early reading of the manuscript and for their suggestions and encouragement.

Most of all, without the ongoing and unremitting love, support, prayers, and reassurance of my housemates, Sisters Linda Julian, Mary Lois, and Mary Michael, I would have given up long ago. To each of them in particular, as well as to all the above, I say a heartfelt thank you.

Introduction

DEEPLY RELIGIOUS PEOPLE are pilgrim people; that is, they are always on the move, on an interior if not a literal journey, always seeking that which will draw them closer to their God, seeking that which is Holy. The tradition of pilgrimage is thus as old as humanity and is to be found among people of all faiths and all belief systems. Studies in anthropology confirm this as they uncover prototypical aspects of sacred journeys common to all humankind. Recent years have also witnessed a greatly increased enthusiasm for pilgrimage, reflecting a contemporary hunger for spiritual renewal. Given the advantages and convenience of modern travel, it is hardly surprising that people are responding to their natural urges to find for themselves the Holy in places previously known only through tradition, others' experiences, or books. Chaucer's words are as true today as they were in the fifteenth century:

> Whan that Aprille with his shoures soote...
> [comes,]
> Than longen folk to goon on pilgrimages[1]
> (When April comes... folk long to go on pilgrimages)

In December of 1991, the Reverend James McReynolds of the Teleios Foundation invited me to lead a pilgrimage overseas with a focus on Celtic spirituality. Even though I had never done anything like that before—had never even been on an organized tour myself—I leapt at the opportunity, and in late January I flew over to Wales to make arrangements. Thanks to help and encouragement from both Esther deWaal and Donald Allchin, I was introduced to Welsh people who showered me with their Welsh hospitality—people who became friends immediately and who have remained so. I studied as frantically as one does for a major exam in order to learn which sites to visit; I pored over maps and read endless articles. I was also a regular visitor to the Wales Tourist Board in New York and devoured their help as well.

At that stage I had little idea of the spiritual riches to be found through the pilgrimage experience. I think I was driven by my own "longing to go" because of a deep unhappiness in my life at that time. Further, I am a natural teacher with an unflagging energy to share with others those things which interest me, and Celtic Wales certainly fit into that category. Finally, my vocation as a religious sister carries a commitment to spread the good news of the Gospel of Christ. For more than twenty years I had been leading quiet days and retreats throughout the church, preaching sermons, and talking to people about their spiritual lives, so it seemed to me that a pilgrimage would simply be an extension of that ministry. To be truthful, however, I must also add that the proverb "Fools rush in" has often rung true in my life, and I think accepting the invitation to lead a travel program for which I had had no previous training or experience whatsoever exhibited a kind of foolishness. Nevertheless, I rushed right in and have never regretted it.

That first program to South Wales in 1992 had a kind of magic quality that I unhesitatingly attribute to the Holy Spirit. Not only did all the details of planning the trip come together within a few weeks, but registrations poured in with a rapidity that astonished me. Even while we were in the midst of the trip itself, my fellow pilgrims were asking me about adding another itinerary to North Wales the next summer. So delightful and successful was that first program that I have continued to design, organize, and lead pilgrimages to the Celtic countries ever since. South Wales was first, but the next year I did add a Pilgrimage to North Wales, then a year or so later to the eastern part of Ireland, then to western Ireland, and finally to Scotland and the Isle of Man. Other than the making of airline arrangements, I have never worked through a professional travel agency, much preferring to do all the scouting and contracting myself.

In all cases with my pilgrimages, the geographical area covered by a given program is very small, for I feel it important to settle in to a place for several days and appreciate fully its particular ambiance, to meet people who live and work and pray there, and to have time to assimilate the experience before moving on to something else. The result of this kind of an approach to pilgrimage, both for me and for the people who travel with me, is a deep and rich experience of a given locale—much deeper and richer than can be gained by visiting a number of widely separated sites in a short period of time. To walk the streets of St. David's after all the tour buses and day visitors have left, enjoying the tranquility of the cathedral in twilight, is an experience not easily forgotten. Similarly, Iona becomes a totally different place after the last ferry has left for Mull, leaving behind on the island only those in residence.

One other aspect of the limited geography is the chance to meet local residents and to spend more time with local lecturers and guides. Continuing conversations with them over meals or in the pub enriches our experience enormously. So my pilgrims get short-changed in the sense that they do not see the number of places that many other packages offer, but the people who have traveled with me seem to feel the trade-off is worth it. Again and again I am told how their lives have been greatly enriched by their pilgrimage experience, particularly by the Welsh or Irish or Scottish or Manx people they have met.

These experiences have profoundly affected my life also, for they have raised within me all kinds of questions regarding the church and its mission and ministry today. Some of these will surface in the essays that follow. The information I have gained, the astonishing variety of places I have visited, and the people I have met on both sides of the Atlantic have been to me blessing beyond measure. In addition to leading the pilgrimages, I have had the privilege of conducting many workshops and being a guest lecturer in the field of Celtic spirituality all over the United States, and this book is the cumulative result of all these experiences.

The word *Celtic* technically refers only to those peoples who share a common linguistic background, speakers of Irish or Scots Gaelic, Manx, Welsh, Cornish, or Breton. *Celtic studies* usually means scholarship pertaining to the countries where those languages are (or were) spoken. However, the term has come to be used in broader and broader contexts today, creating certain inevitable difficulties.

The resurgence of interest in anything Celtic today is amazing. We find all kinds of things with that label: Celtic music, Celtic gift shops, Celtic clothing, Celtic basketball, Celtic restaurants, Celtic laundries—even Celtic Crunch ice cream. If a new commodity today is marked "Celtic," it is sure to sell. Each year sees the publication of new books on both sides of the Atlantic, and unfortunately many of them are superficial and glib approaches to a complex area of investigation. Sadly, there is a frequent tendency to equate Celtic spirituality with exclusively Irish spirituality, and this does great injustice not only to Ireland but to the other Celtic areas as well, for each of the Celtic countries has its own rich heritage. The huge proliferation of material under the heading of "Celtic spirituality" flooding the market in recent years therefore needs to be approached with caution.

There is among many students and scholars appropriate objection to the term *Celtic spirituality*, and there are good reasons for this. There exists a long and rich tradition of spirituality among the pre-Christian (pagan) Celts. We know this through their rich tradition of myths and stories and their archaeological remains. Therefore the term is ambiguous; does it refer to pre-Christian spirituality or to Christian spirituality or to both? At the same time, using the term does a distinct injustice to the marked distinctions between the different Celtic countries. Many of our brothers and sisters from the Celtic lands are decidedly uncomfortable at being lumped together as one homogeneous lot. A fair comparison comes when we in the United States assume all Native American tribes to have a common spirituality, as if the Seminoles in Florida and the Chinook in Washington and the Navajo in the Southwest were all alike. However, even while recognizing its inadequacy, as a term of convenience, I shall continue to use the now generally accepted term *Celtic spirituality*, fervently hoping that my many Celtic friends will forgive me for doing so.

Pilgrimage is a complex area to explore, and the huge quantity of literature available—on the phenomenon of pilgrimage in all major religions, the history of pilgrimage in all its aspects, the designation of sacred space, the multiplicity of pilgrimage sites and pilgrimage practices, the rituals (religious and otherwise) that may take place at a particular site, even the definition of pilgrimage itself, to say nothing of personal accounts of pilgrimages—is enormous and daunting. Simon Coleman and John Elsner, in their excellent book *Pilgrimage Past and Present in the World Religions*[2], make reference to an international conference on pilgrimage held in London in 1988 in which historians, geographers, anthropologists, and theologians gathered, with the hope of drawing the disciplines together into an increased understanding of pilgrimage. Sadly, however, dissension was rife, and reaching agreement was impossible. Pilgrimage is simply too big a topic with too many different ramifications and too many different interpretations to be reduced to the simplicity I am attempting here. Yet, with that limitation stated, I nevertheless offer my own understanding of pilgrimage and contemporary pilgrimage to the Celtic countries in particular, as a way of deepening our spiritual lives. This is what I mean by "exploring Celtic spirituality."

I make no claim whatsoever to be an academic. The essays in the first half of this book do draw on extensive reading and a moderate amount of historical research, but they are written primarily for lay people with a casual interest in the history of pilgrimage and a curiosity about pilgrimage in general and Celtic spirituality in particular. Serious scholars may find the material interesting, but for in-depth material, I refer them to the extensive bibliography included in the Appendix.

The second half of the book is more informal and personal, describing certain selected pilgrimage sites and offering some meditative reflections on them. These insights are my own, but I have been much influenced by the hundreds of women and men who have shared a pilgrimage with me and the scores of lecturers I have had the privilege of meeting and hearing. It is hoped that glimpses of these holy sites will whet the appetite of my readers to visit the places themselves, or barring that, at least to get a good internal picture of what they look like and a small sense of what it might be like to visit them.

On the opening night of every one of my pilgrimage programs, I tell my groups that deciding what to leave out in putting the programs together is far and away the most difficult part of their design. Wales, Ireland, Scotland, and the Isle of Man have among them literally thousands of interesting places to visit, and having to choose among them is very difficult indeed. Putting the second part of this book together was no different. I limited myself to only fifteen sites out of a choice of several hundred that I myself have visited and/or taken pilgrimage groups to—and that limitation was a challenge in and of itself. At the same time I also wanted to include a wide variety of places, some very well known, such as Iona and St. David's, but also some others totally unknown (at least to people in the United States), places such as Tobar na Mult and Pistyll. It will be obvious that some of the best-known Celtic sites in Ireland and Britain are not included here, and that is because the really famous ones are thoroughly described elsewhere. For example, for an armchair visit to Glendalough, the book written by Michael Rodgers and Marcus Losack entitled *Glendalough: A Celtic Pilgrimage*[3] is excellent, and anything I might write about Glendalough would only duplicate what they have already made available.

So if Chaucer is right that folk long to go on pilgrimages, perhaps this book will have appeal. It has been fun to write; I hope it will be equally enjoyable to read.

Part One

Celtic Spirituality and Pilgrimage

Celtic Spirituality, Background

THE SPIRITUALITY OF the early church in Ireland and parts of Britain is often described as Celtic, and there is much interest in it today. Considering the restlessness and spiritual hunger that pervades the contemporary church, it is easy to find in this early understanding of Christianity an approach to the gospel that holds much appeal: there is a deep respect for the feminine, a great love of mysticism, storytelling, and poetry, a recognition of the sacredness of all creation, and a ready acknowledgment of the interrelatedness of all that is, seen and unseen. However, each of the Celtic countries (Ireland, Scotland, Wales, the Isle of Man, Cornwall, and Brittany), although linked by a common linguistic background, has its own distinct history, language, and culture, and it would be foolish to assume that spirituality, Celtic or not, is the same for all of them. Dr. Ian Bradley, in his recent book on Columba (*Columba: Pilgrim and Penitent*, 1996)[4], for example, points out with considerable emphasis that the spirituality of Columba on the Isle of Iona is not at all the bright creation-centered spirituality that is found in Wales, and he compares the poetry from the Celtic period of those two areas to illustrate the difference.

Since Ireland and Northern Scotland were untouched by Roman occupation, naturally their history is different from that of Wales and Cornwall, which were overcome first by Rome and later by England. The Isle of Man, as a small island, also has its own story, in large part governed by its isolation and vulnerability in the middle of the Irish Sea. The Viking invasions of the ninth and tenth centuries influenced all the coastal areas, but the Viking influence on Mann is particularly prevalent, as can be seen in the magnificent Manx carved crosses.

Somewhat later, throughout the many turbulent centuries of English oppression, particularly on mainland Britain, much of the rich Celtic heritage in the form of early Celtic monasteries, high crosses, and other sacred sites was either systematically destroyed or devastated by endless wars. What is now referred to as Celtic spirituality was subtly pushed underground or even outright destroyed.

Each of the Celtic areas thus grew and developed in a different way, each responding to its distinct historical and geographical context, and their individual spiritualities reflect these differences.

We have little information about life in the early Christian centuries in the Celtic countries; the second through ninth centuries are called the Dark Ages with some justification. However, increased knowledge in several disciplines, particularly sophistication in archaeological methods of investigation and dating, plus the incredible availability of and rapid access to new information, has changed the picture dramatically. Most important of all is the intense interest in the period, particularly in the last few decades. A whole generation of serious scholars has undertaken new research and has learned the old and middle Irish and Welsh languages; this has made available for the first time materials, especially early poetry, formerly hidden in the murk of the Dark Ages. To these scholars we indeed owe a great deal, and thankfully the Dark Ages are now considerably less dark. (In fact, in some circles it is no longer politically correct to call these centuries dark; the preferred title is Early Middle Ages.) Archaeology, anthropology, history, geography, and language studies have all influenced the study of Celtic spirituality, and all have helped identify the distinguishing characteristics of the spirituality of the different Celtic countries.

A Different Understanding

Certain aspects of Celtic spirituality, however, are common to all the Celtic countries, and the one which is perhaps most significant is its understanding of the Christian gospel independent from that taught by Rome. Roman Christianity tended to be authoritarian, hierarchical, and male dominated, rational and strongly legalistic, with a powerful need for control and uniformity and an under-standing of governance inherited from the dying Roman Empire.

Generally speaking, the Celtic understanding of church leader-ship was somewhat different, stemming from a rural and agrarian communal culture. Not unlike Native Americans or indigenous Africans or Australians, Celtic peoples had little concept of land ownership or taxes or tithes and little liking for cities, all of which were introduced into the Celtic lands by the Romans and further established by the Normans. Rules of primogeniture among the Celts were nonexistent; leadership tended to pass to the most qual-ified (or the mightiest in battle) among the many tribes. Emerging logically from the communal and tribal system were the great Celtic monasteries, and the leaders of these monasteries and thus of Celtic Christianity were not necessarily ordained. It was unusual to have a bishop as the head of a Celtic monastery. Bishops were necessary for administration of the sacraments, particularly of ordination, but in the Christian church in the Celtic lands the real leadership—and power—lay in the hands of the abbots of the monasteries.

A serious pitfall in such comparisons of Celtic Christianity with Roman Christianity is the inevitable tendency to make value judgments of Roman versus Celtic. Such an attitude is singularly inappropriate. The Roman genius for organization and for intel-lectual synthesis is of great value to the church, even as is the Celtic love of mysticism, imagination, poetry, and fluid bound-aries. We need both.

A second pitfall, most likely stemming from today's disillusion-ment with the Romanized Christianity that we have inherited, is to assume that the Celtic world view arising from what we are calling Celtic Christianity is somehow superior to our own. Some even go so far as to suggest that a return to Celtic values is an important goal for the contemporary church.

Both of these attitudes stem from a gross oversimplification of what we are calling Celtic spirituality. They exhibit a superficiality and a longing to find easy answers to the church's problems of today. Any study of any aspect of Celtic spirituality must be careful to avoid both of these traps.

The Communion of Saints

The Communion of Saints takes on a new and profound meaning when visiting holy places long associated with holy people. Such places may be great cathedrals dedicated to major saints or apostles, but in the Celtic world they are more likely to be tiny churches, sacred shrines and isolated holy wells dedicated to obscure saints. Who today has heard of St. Teilo, St. Illtud, St. Maughold, St. Brynach, St. Ita, St. Beuno, St. Gobnet, St. Non, or St. Manchán? How many people have done the pilgrim rounds at Tobar na Mult in southwest Ireland or stopped in at the tiny church of Llanaelhaearn in northwest Wales? Yet, when visiting and praying in these holy places while in the company of fellow pilgrims, with other seekers of the Holy, one feels the presence of unknown saints profoundly. One has the sense of being in the presence of holy persons, even though perhaps nameless, who lived in a particular place at a particular time and left their particular mark. Though they lived long in the past, today they are alongside us in the great Communion of Saints.

The Communion of Saints also includes those who live and pray today at the sites visited. We can feel immediately the holiness of a place like Tintern Abbey, and we can feel the centuries of prayer that took place there in the Middle Ages. For the past four hundred years, though, Tintern has been a ruin (albeit a beautiful one), and the custodians are faithful civil servants. Regular worship and times of prayer are no longer a routine part of its existence; rather Tintern is a pilgrimage site of considerable historic interest with a lovely visitor center and an admission fee. This is very different from the great cathedrals such as St. David's, which regularly hold several services each day, as they have for hundreds of years. It is also different from parish churches that are holy sites while still remaining the ordinary places of worship for the local community; and it is different from hidden shrines and holy wells that are still visited and still hold spiritual meaning for those who know how to find them. The people who care for such sites are also part of the Communion of Saints.

Meeting the people who care for the sites, whether state employees or local clergy or shopkeepers or local residents, is very important. Personal interaction with other people at the place of pilgrimage is a vital aspect of a pilgrimage experience. How else can one truly seek one's self and search for the Holy, without intentionally interacting with other people? When we are able to invite local residents to share a picnic or dinner or tea with us, thereby breaking bread together, both we and they are greatly enriched. And not infrequently, lasting relationships are formed. Such interactions are truly Incarnational, truly a finding of the Holy, and both pilgrim and local resident are changed within.

The Outer Journey

In effect, the pilgrim's journey begins even before the pilgrim leaves home; it begins with the decision to undertake a pilgrimage in the first place. Many intentional pilgrimage groups prepare for the journey by engaging in times of shared prayer, reading, and in some cases even involvement with the local church congregation. The activities leading up to departure are important, and the more the pilgrim-to-be engages in preparatory prayer and study, the more likely the "search for the Holy" will be successful.

Pilgrimage typically is made in the company of other pilgrims, with the entire group serving as *anamcháirde* (soul friends) to one another, searching together for that which is Holy. Today's pilgrims may not make up stories to tell to one another throughout the day to help the time pass by, as did Chaucer's pilgrims, but pilgrimage groups typically share their spiritual experiences along the way informally and pray together regularly. The old saying that "the family that prays together stays together" is also true with pilgrims— the bonding that takes places in a praying group of pilgrims with a common focus is very powerful indeed.

The first gathering of the pilgrim band is an important part of the pilgrimage experience: when pilgrim meets pilgrim, the shared search for the Holy begins. Even the first conversations are likely to touch on spiritual topics and inner journeys. Subsequent travel, site visits, guide presentations, lectures, prayer times, meals, postcards sent home, souvenirs bought, tokens or mementos of the trip, and even the return journey are all part of the cumulative pilgrimage experience. Each kind of interaction between pilgrims traveling together is important.

On the journey itself, the use of pilgrimage time is tremendously important. Athough visiting holy places in a prayerful attitude is perhaps to be assumed, the amount of time allowed for such visits is significant. A once-over-lightly stop at a holy site followed by a hurried return to the coach for transportation to another site for another once-over-lightly stop is not likely to give the would-be pilgrim a chance to drink deeply of the spiritual riches to be found there. Generous time needs to be allowed at each holy place. Although this may mean visiting fewer holy sites, it also means pilgrims will be able to savor the particular spiritual quality, or numen, of each place. Such use of time will greatly enhance the overall pilgrim experience.

The Inner Journey

Pilgrims must always be aware of the inner journey taking place simultaneously with the outer journey. Sharing lodging, meals, and transportation is meaningful, but each pilgrim also needs a certain amount of solitude, time, and space to assimilate experiences. For some people, periods of silence are golden opportunities for individual reflection. Other time needs to be available for liturgical worship, reading, and journaling, as well as for keeping in touch with family and friends at home. For a successful pilgrimage experience, the outer journey must never be so filled with activity that the inner journey is crowded out.

Praying together is vital. By prayer I do not necessarily mean recitation of the Daily Office or daily Eucharist, although these are important. To me, the prayer that helps a group of pilgrims grow closer to one another is the one that furthers the inner journey. Such a prayer will address the vulnerability that comes through sharing one's thoughts, observations, and insights, for from these come a recognition of the holy dwelling within one another. From such also comes a particular kind of bonding, for one person's thoughts often trigger another's; individuals find they have much more in common than they realized. Thus we all learn and grow

together. The Welsh word *bendithion*, means "the sharing of bless-
ings"—ultimately it is *bendithion* that distinguishes the pilgrim
from the tourist and ties together the outer with the inner journey.

Pilgrim prayer appropriately includes common intercessions for
needs of the world, the church, our loved ones, and above all, common thanksgiving. One of my favorite intercessions, offered repeatedly, is a thanksgiving for all who have made each trip possible, and
I like to remember those at home who are feeding the dog, watering
the houseplants, bringing in the mail, taking care of young or elderly ones, covering our usual responsibilities and jobs, and so forth.
I am always acutely aware that very few people (if any) are so independent that they do not need help from others while they are away.

In common intercessions voiced aloud, pilgrims are usually
quick to mention the more obvious thanksgiving for one another,
for our coach drivers, for good weather, and for all those who have
lectured to us, guided us around sites, opened their churches to us,
invited us into their homes, and fed us. Surely a successful pilgrimage means the combined (but usually independent) efforts of
many, many people who have given generously of their own gifts.
Corporate thanksgiving is essential to a true pilgrimage experience,
and growth in prayer, in all its aspects, will always further the inner
journey—*bendithion*.

The Search for the Holy

True pilgrimage in any age is always a search for that which is Holy,
and the kind of search engaged in reflects that age's understanding
of God and the world. We cannot be totally sure of the Celtic
understanding of God, but the earliest references and documents
lead us to believe that for the Celts God was very immanent, very
close, overwhelmingly present all around them. The numinous
qualities perceived in certain places in the natural world were
revered and respected. When Christianity arrived, the physical
place where one would die and see God face to face tied in with earlier Celtic beliefs and was thus extremely important. Because of the
clear gospel mandate to go into the world and make disciples, missionary outreach was also seen as a vital element in the search for

the Holy. As Celtic pilgrimage developed, the search for the Holy always included journeys to significant holy places, the personal journey toward a meeting with God, a real striving to imitate Jesus, and a firm commitment to evangelism. Today, a pilgrimage with a Celtic focus will still contain these elements, with contemporary understanding of evangelism meaning ecumenical outreach.

Theology today inclines toward an increasingly holistic and inclusive understanding of the gospel (things we may appropriately associate with Celtic spirituality), with a diminution of the barriers of dualisms that have plagued the church for so long. There is a renewed commitment to seeking and serving Christ in all people, and there is renewed interest and energy in pilgrimage. People are seeking God through visiting and praying in holy places long associated with sanctity. For those of us who live in the English-speaking world, this often means a pilgrimage to one of the ancient Celtic sites in Ireland or Great Britain.

Holiness of place and the Communion of Saints, past and present, reflect the modern church's more inclusive theology with wider arms outstretched in love and hospitality. We are greatly enriched by visiting holy places in the company of other seekers of the Holy, praying together and actively engaging with one another. We are further blessed when we can interact with those who live and worship regularly in recognized holy places. Our world has become very small, and with today's means of travel, almost every place on earth is accessible. It is right to want to see, experience, and learn about the world we live in.

Tourist or Pilgrim?

One can justifiably ask whether there is a difference between a tourist and a pilgrim, and while most people readily will answer yes, few can clearly articulate exactly what that difference is. When I ask my pilgrim groups what they perceive the difference to be, the answers are always varied—fascinating and wide-ranging—but a totally satisfactory and generally accepted answer has yet to surface. The viewpoint most often expressed seems to be that pilgrimage includes sharing a common focus with one's fellow travelers, but even that is incomplete. Surely it is also much more than that.

People traveling together on a modern tour coach covering mile after mile on paved highways, comfortably seated in upholstered reclining seats and looking out of huge windows, will engage in conversations according to the kind of program they are sharing. Sometimes tourists who have come together only because they have chosen a particular itinerary cannot get beyond superficial conversation, because there is little held in common. Conversation among traveling companions who share a common focus, such as the theater, gardens, stately homes, golf, historical sites, or whatever, is likely to be deeper. The more substantive conversations can become, regardless of the nature of the journey, the more likely travelers will discover the Holy and have pilgrimage experiences.

There is no intention here to denigrate general tours or special interest journeys, for they undoubtedly bring deep satisfaction to many people and meet needs on many different levels. People do return home broadened and refreshed, probably with more knowledge and a deeper understanding of their chosen field, having thoroughly enjoyed their experience. The ones I have been on myself have been very rich experiences.

A spiritual pilgrimage is nevertheless different. Along with a common goal, shared interests, and the desire to visit specific sites, there is the deeper goal—growth of the inner self and the total existential experience itself. Thus the primary focus of a pilgrimage is the interior growth resulting from an exterior journey. According to anthropologists, authentic pilgrimage is commonly described as a universal search for the self, and such a search undoubtedly involves much more than common or shared interests—it involves a search for the Holy and a willingness to engage in activities promoting spiritual growth. As such, an intense pilgrimage may thus be very hard work.

Pilgrimage also means other people—people on a similar, perhaps parallel, spiritual journey. I once saw a map of the different routes for pilgrims going to Santiago de Compostela in northwest Spain; there were sea travelers landing at one place, several routes crossing the Pyrenees at various points, another path from the south, and then all roads joining together and moving as a body to the shrine itself. It reminded me of a map of a great river, the Mississippi perhaps, with many tributaries ultimately converging into one mighty stream.

Is it fair to say that a pilgrimage *is* people? People as opposed to a topic? After hearing hundreds of descriptions of the difference between a tourist and a pilgrim, I find myself describing it by saying that a tourist visits to *see*, to take in, to learn about, to buy souvenirs from a certain place and then move on; but a pilgrim comes to *offer oneself* and to share personally with the people who live and work there in order to further inner growth.

I must admit that sometimes when I travel I do not want to be on pilgrimage. I do not want to further my inner journey, I am not traveling with an interest in personal growth, and I am not searching for the Holy. I am simply on vacation and I want to be 100 percent tourist, sightseeing and enjoying whatever there is to enjoy, with or without traveling companions. Often after I have led a two-week pilgrimage, I go somewhere I have never been before for relaxation, perhaps simply out of curiosity. I enjoy the sights I see and the people I meet, but I do not think of myself as being on a pilgrimage. I am traveling simply for the joy of traveling.

The line between tourist and pilgrim can sometimes be very fluid. Occasionally someone says, "I started out as a tourist, but after a few days I realized I had become a pilgrim." When this happens, it usually is a result of a shift in the person's inner focus; what may have begun as curiosity or an intent for increased education or some other goal has become unmistakably an experience of the Holy. This can happen on a conventional tour or in any other kind of travel, and the person is deeply enriched by the shift.

An example: recently I visited the Outer Hebrides on my own, as a casual tourist. As part of my personal tour, I went to see the Arnol Blackhouse on the Isle of Lewis, owned and operated by Historic Scotland. No one else was visiting at that time, and I struck up a casual conversation with the site keeper. Soon we were talking about what life in Scotland was like one hundred, two hundred, years ago when such houses were commonplace, and I told her about my interest in early Christian history and Celtic spirituality and pilgrimage and so forth. All the while I was smelling the fragrant smoke from the peat fire and hearing in my inner ear the great prayer poems of the *Carmina Gadelica*. This young woman had grown up on Lewis in that very village and could tell me about

Hebridean life in the early part of this century as she had heard it from her own grandmother and great grandmother. I greatly value and was enriched by that conversation, and I know I will remember the Arnol Blackhouse vividly as a result.

Perhaps I should add that we so enjoyed the conversation that neither of us noticed I had not paid for the book I had selected. About forty-five minutes later, some twenty miles away along the narrow single lane road, I realized my oversight and returned. Not only did I pay for my book, but this time the site keeper introduced me to her younger sister, who was playing with Blicky, her favorite hen, and we had a cup of tea together. In that experience, I had started out as a tourist, but totally unexpectedly, I realized I had stumbled upon the Holy—so perhaps I had been on pilgrimage after all.

Soulfaring

Finding the Holy comes to each of us in astonishingly different, often totally unpredictable ways, so today's pilgrimage is greatly enhanced by including a rich variety of locations and experiences. Visiting extremely well-known sites—such as Clonmacnois or Newgrange in Ireland, St. David's Cathedral in southwest Wales, Lindisfarne in Northumbria, Iona in Scotland, or other such places—is important. All these are tourist sites as well as pilgrim sites, so they tend to have many people around, plus visitor centers, souvenir shops, and tea rooms. Seeing these places may be very meaningful for those seeking the Holy, and in no way should visits to them be denigrated.

However, equally profound spiritual experiences may come from visiting less well-known and therefore less-frequented sites. Being less well-known does not make a place any less holy. In fact, when one can experience a remote holy site alone (or with only one's own travel companions), and thus find peace and solitude without the distraction of other visitors, the experience may be profoundly life-changing.

In such unknown places, my groups typically have Eucharist, often outdoors. Late in the afternoon the ruins of Basingwerk

Abbey are all but deserted, and three of the site keepers from the adjoining Greenfield Valley join us there for Eucharist and shared prayer. We all then walk together up to the local pub for a pint and dinner. On another occasion, we have Evensong together in Dolwyddelan, a fifteenth-century church hidden away in the folds of Snowdonia, with members of the tiny parish joining us for afternoon tea, for worship, and then for dinner. At Mellifont Abbey in Ireland we celebrate the Eucharist in the remains of the medieval Chapter House. These are all pilgrim experiences, not tourist ones.

St. Augustine said, "Truly our hearts are restless until they find their rest in you, O God," and he is right. While human restlessness may at times be uncomfortable, ultimately it is a gift straight from God and one for which we must be truly thankful. We search for God because God is constantly, endlessly, searching for *us*. In the Garden of Eden, we hear God call to the two who had sinned, "Where are you?" In the New Testament, we read the story of the Good Shepherd, who left the flock in order to search for the one who had wandered, an enactment of God's asking each of us the same question: Where are you? In our search for the Holy, we must remember that God is not only looking for us, but also is inviting us into the Godlife. We read in John 1:38–39:

> When Jesus turned and saw [the disciples] following, he said to them, "What are you looking for?" They said to him, "Rabbi" (which translated means Teacher), "where are you staying?" He said to them, "Come and see."

It thus follows that when we ask the same question of God, "Where are you?" the answer is always the same: Come and see.

To go on pilgrimage in the late twentieth century is unquestionably, at one level, to be a tourist (*i.e.*, one who travels around), but at a much deeper and more life-changing level, it is to travel in such a way that our restlessness (or perhaps we might call it our wanderlust) is always searching for God, even as God is searching for us. On our pilgrimage, we are all soulfarers together. Each of us makes the conscious choice to seek the Holy, which means responding to God's invitation: Come and See.

Sacredness of Place

There the angel of the LORD appeared to Moses in a flame of fire out of a bush; he looked, and the bush was blazing, yet it was not consumed. Then Moses said, "I must turn aside and look at this great sight, and see why the bush is not burned up." When the LORD saw that he had turned aside to see, God called to him out of the bush, "Moses, Moses!" And he said, "Here I am." Then [God] said, "Come no closer! Remove the sandals from your feet, for the place on which you are standing is holy ground." (Exodus 3:2–5)

WHEN GOD SPEAKS to us from a burning bush and tells us a place is holy, we have little question that we stand on sacred ground. But what actually makes a site sacred? As with the distinction between tourist and pilgrim, answers are many and varied. Noel Dermot O'Donoghue suggests that any sacred *place* is sacred *space*; he then defines sacred space as "where we see the angels."[5] Perhaps that is as good a definition of sacred space as can be found. Where we see the angels is where we encounter God, where we experience Incarnation, where there is a point of intersection between God and humankind.

Identifying Sacred Space

One can argue that all places are sacred, or at least potentially so, because points of intersection between God and humans can be literally anywhere. But human experience over countless centuries has taught us that certain places all over the world have a peculiar quality, a liminality, where encounter with the Holy is immediate, even overwhelming. These are the places where we feel an inner pull to take off our shoes, either literally or figuratively.

13

Surely the locations of various prehistoric sacred sites (such as the thousands of dolmens, cromlechs, stone circles, incised stones, and burial chambers found throughout Britain and Ireland) were not accidental. Whether situated at places of outstanding natural beauty, such as in oak groves, on mountaintops, on islands, or at certain points along presumed leylines, most of these locations have a particular numinous quality that is still recognizable today. In many parts of the world, disturbing these ancient holy places is unthinkable. Farmers, for instance, are known to plow in decidedly inconvenient patterns rather than remove an ancient standing stone from the middle of a field.

When God broke into human history about two thousand years ago through Jesus' birth and ministry, it was not long before Jerusalem became a sacred place—surely a point of intersection between God and humankind. (It had already been sacred for Jews.) A little later it would also become sacred for Muslims, so that today the Holy Land is a center for three of the world's great religions. Even to the nonbelieving curiosity seeker, the sense of the sacredness of the Holy Land is palpable. Disputed as the territory may be, and as strife-torn as its history has been, Jerusalem, with its surrounding area, is undisputedly sacred space. It is a place of intersection between God and humankind; it is a place where we see the angels, and it is with good reason that some of the places are visited barefoot.

There are other points of intersection between God and humankind that have occurred because of particular human experiences. Certain people seem to have been particularly in touch with God, and their locales or monasteries became holy places. Visiting the island of Skellig Michael off the southwest coast of Ireland, where a small community of monks lived an incredibly austere life in the ninth century, for instance, is very profound.

Whatever one believes about miraculous apparitions, thousands— perhaps millions—of people believe that the Virgin Mary appeared at Guadalupe (in Mexico) in 1531, at Knock (County Mayo, Ireland) in 1879, at Medjugorje (former Yugoslavia) in 1981, and at countless other places revered as Marian shrines. We cannot dismiss these occurrences as insignificant: these places are sacred in the hearts and minds of the believers because they are places where people do see the angels and encounter the Holy.

Experiences other than specifically religious ones can also make a space sacred. One feels a great sense of reverence and awe when walking through a military cemetery such as Arlington or a historical park such as Gettysburg, or visiting the Holocaust Memorial in Washington or countless other similar places where the sacrifice of human lives is memorialized. Some people call a place like Elvis Presley's home near Memphis, Tennessee, a pilgrimage site. Because Elvis had such an enormous influence on people, they flock to Graceland to taste something of his spirit and to encounter what for them is holy. Visits to these places may be moving pilgrimage experiences. All are places that touch the human psyche at very deep levels, and whether one describes a visit there as seeing the angels or finding the Holy, they are, for many people, points of intersection with God.

Sacred Places in Britain and Ireland

Sacred places exist all over the world, but any number of writers, residents, and travelers have observed in Britain and Ireland and on the islands edging their coasts certain qualities that make the sacred spaces found there unique.

Weather and Wells

The first quality to be considered is the weather. The winds of the Gulf Stream come across the Atlantic and sweep these islands; the warm air then collides with the cold winds descending from the polar regions. Such a mingling inevitably has meteorological implications. The "green and pleasant land" of England (and the rest of Britain) and the "forty shades of green" of Ireland are the inevitable result. One does not travel to those islands without raincoat, umbrella, and "wellies"—always prepared for rain. In some of the western parts of Ireland and Britain, rainfall can be as much as sixty to eighty inches per year, compared to the eastern United States, where even the highest figures are rarely above forty inches.

Such wetness produces literally thousands of springs, where water emerges spontaneously from the earth. Some experts estimate that there are three thousand springs in Ireland alone; Francis Jones who has studied the wells (i.e., natural springs) in Wales estimates more than one thousand there. To primitive peoples, water emerging thus from the earth was a great mystery, and they deemed certain of these natural springs to be holy wells. They believed that in or near the wells lived various deities and gods who controlled much of human life, and so the people offered rituals and sacrifices to them.

When the Christian missionaries arrived, these springs were "Christianized" and conveniently converted into places of holy baptism. Continuing a sacred tradition already in place since time immemorial, Christians also considered wells as sacred places for healing, and many still do. Especially in Ireland, visits to certain holy wells involve participating in specified patterns or rounds of prayer, often done barefoot, thus acknowledging the holy ground. There is good scriptural basis for such an attitude. We read in John:

> Jesus said to [the woman], "Everyone who drinks of this water will be thirsty again, but those who drink of the water that I will give them will never be thirsty. The water that I will give will become in them a spring of water gushing up to eternal life." (John 4:13–14)

Holy wells are indeed springs of water gushing up to eternal life, offering water needed for survival as well as for religious reasons, and therefore they are sacred spaces.

Fog

Another meteorological phenomenon adding to the distinct weather patterns of Britain and Ireland is fog, which is also caused by the mingling of warm and cool air. Many psychologists have suggested that long periods of fog have significant influence on the human psyche, sometimes causing introversion and introspection, even depression and withdrawal, but always firing the imagination. Some years ago the play *Brigadoon*, set in a Scottish village, told the story of villagers who discovered in the dense fog of the Highlands a neighboring (magic?) village from a previous century. When the fog descended thickly, people from the two villages could mingle with one another, but once the fog lifted, the neighboring village vanished. Only when the fog set in could the boundary between the familiar and the unfamiliar be crossed.

Fog is not without mystery to us even today. To walk between the Calanais Stones on the Isle of Lewis in northwest Scotland or Stonehenge in the south of England in a dense fog can be an unnerving experience, to say the least. We can begin to understand the anxiety of Peter, James, and John who "were terrified as they entered the cloud" (Luke 9:34). Surely it is not coincidence that many sacred places in Britain and Ireland are to be found in areas where dense fog and low-hanging clouds are common.

As the Celtic peoples were converted to Christianity and exposed to the sacred Scriptures, the importance of God's presence in the cloud in their frequently cloudy country was especially significant, for the presence of cloud or fog is often equated with the presence of God. Throughout the story of the Exodus, God always goes before the Israelites "in a cloud by day." Clouds are referenced 161 times in the New Revised Standard Version of the Bible, almost without exception referring to the presence of God.

Early Celtic poetry draws on many mystical elements, including indigenous mythology, and some passages refer to the mysterious presence of fog:

> Hail to you, glorious Lord....
> May the seven days and the stars praise you,
> May the lower and upper air praise you...[6]

In this poem from the Welsh tradition, filled with symbolism and dating from the tenth century, experts agree that the entire poem is a cosmic and all-inclusive song of praise to God. In the lines above, many interpret the "lower air" as the air at ground level which we breathe, while the "upper air" refers to low clouds or fog hovering just above us. Where fog is, there God is.

Tides
Another consideration of importance is tide. Flowing around Ireland and Britain are some of the highest tides in the world, with

normal tidal exchanges sometimes reaching as much as thirty to forty feet. This fierce rush of so much water between islands and mainland twice daily gives all offshore islands a certain mystique, and it was especially intriguing to the Celtic peoples. Even today, with powerful diesel engines, boat operators cross those tidal currents with great caution, and many of the islands are accessible only when sea conditions are just right. Weeks may go by, for example, before a crossing and landing can be made to Skellig Michael off the southwest coast of Ireland. That early peoples crossed such treacherous waters in tiny skin-covered boats is astonishing, but the islands' very inaccessibility only added to their perceived holiness.

We can only speculate as to what early sailors from the Mediterranean area must have thought when they first encountered the fierce tides in the English Channel, the Irish Sea, and adjoining waters. Tides in the Mediterranean Sea rarely reach more than a few feet, so seamen originating there would not have experienced before anything like the tides of Britain and Ireland. Nowhere in the Scriptures, even with all the references to the sea, do we encounter references to tides. High tides would have been a completely new experience, one more aspect of the mystery of God and creation.

Boundary Places
When we look at spaces sacred to the Celtic peoples, we find that boundaries of all kinds are tremendously important, places of creative tension. For the very early peoples, long before the arrival of Christianity, such places were always "thin places," points of intersection between the gods and humans.

Burial sites indicate a particular kind of boundary, a portal between life and death. Such obvious boundaries between this world and the next were always holy places, places of interpenetration and intersection. There are thousands of prehistoric burial places in Britain and Ireland, sometimes found singly in isolated areas, others clustered closely in a particular area. Anglesey Island, for example, off the north coast of Wales, the Burren in County Clare, Ireland, and the Kilmartin Glen in Scotland all have an unusually high proportion of burial sites, be they court, portal, or wedge tombs, passage graves, dolmens, or burial mounds.

Hillforts, located on peninsulas or right at the very edge of cliffs, are dramatic boundary points between land and sea. Dun Aengus, for example, a hillfort on Inishmore in the Aran Islands, is on a promontory jutting out into the Atlantic, several hundred feet above the roaring of the waves. Recent excavations at the Isle of Whithorn in southwest Scotland have uncovered a Celtic hillfort, occupied and active during Christian times, surrounded by the sea on three sides.

Fog, or low-hanging cloud, as already pointed out, readily serves as a boundary between reality and imagination. Among people accustomed to living with the unknowable of fog, the development of a profound sense of mystery and mysticism, of sacred place, was inevitable.

Islands were among the most important of all boundary places. Visible from the land only when there were no fog banks, they were separated by the sea and accessible only when wind and tide and weather cooperated. A few islands are cut off from the mainland at high tide, such as Lindisfarne, off the northeast coast of England, and St. Michael's Mount, off the coast of Cornwall. These islands are deemed to be holy places because of their mysterious position in the sea. To this day, people—sometimes in bare feet—still walk across the wet sands at low tide to Lindisfarne, or Holy Isle, on prayerful pilgrimages. An island is neither mainland nor ocean nor lake, but rather is a point of creative tension between land and water.

Important crossing points were often the chosen location for royal forts and Christian monasteries alike. Clonmacnois, for example, founded by St. Ciaran in the middle of the sixth century, is situated where the main east-west ancient trackway across Ireland (following an esker, or natural ridge, above the bogs and peatlands) reaches a fording place on the Shannon River, the main north-south navigational artery. Clonmacnois is thus situated at what was in its time the most important crossroads in all Ireland, the boundary between north and south as well as that between east and west.

Some monastic foundations were at points seen as boundaries between *isolation and accessibility*. Islands and promontories have already been mentioned. Inland hilltops were also favored, as for example, Croagh Patrick in western Ireland, where archaeology has recently found remains of pre-Christian dwellings. Croagh Patrick was (and is) conspicuously visible for miles around, but it is relatively inaccessible because of the arduous climb to the top. It was easy to find a scriptural basis for Christianizing such a place, for references to encounters with God on a holy mountain are many—for example, in the Old Testament, the story of Moses receiving the Ten Commandments on Mount Sinai, and in the New Testament, the story of the Transfiguration.

Standing Stones and Stone Circles
In Ireland and the British Isles, standing stones and stone circles nearly always mark holy places. The astronomical alignments of many of the stone circles have been studied carefully, and to our modern mind the accuracy of celestial measurements taken up to four thousand years ago is staggering. Carnac in Brittany, Stonehenge in England, and Calanais in Scotland are only the most familiar and well known of literally hundreds of such places. Travelers in any of the Celtic countries are likely to find a number of stone circles to visit. Some are in isolated, obscure places in the countryside or on private ground; some can be found right beside modern paved roads. Many are in the protective care of national preservation organizations. Aubrey Burl's excellent *A Guide to the Stone Circles of Britain, Ireland and Brittany*[7] lists nearly four hundred sites worth visiting, and he acknowledges that there are undoubtedly hundreds more scattered about the landscapes.

Individual standing stones are considerably harder to discuss, for we know so little about them. Some scholars see them as having replaced sacred trees, especially in the naturally barren areas of moor and tundra, serving as a vertical link between earth and heaven. Many of the stones were erected by the pre-Christian Celts and were later marked with Christian crosses to "de-paganize" them.

Not all cross-inscribed stones, however, were pre-Christian. Many were set up in the Christian period and later, usually as memorial stones or grave markers. For us today they are important indicators of the presence of founder-saints and the spread of Christianity in the early centuries. The ones that are marked bilingually, that is, with both Latin and *ogham* (a fifth- and early-sixth-century form of writing unique to the Irish), are particularly helpful as evidence of the contacts between Gaul, Ireland, and Wales. Ultimately, however, we know little about why most of these stones were erected in the first place. Thousands of standing stones have remained, however, revered enough to be left undisturbed.

Recognizing Holy Ground

It is not unusual to find a Christian foundation established on top of an older pagan one. Aerial photography and work in historical geography have shown again and again the distribution of Christian monastic sites to be closely related to the distribution of earlier pagan sites. Sometimes this might have been due to the natural features of the land itself, such as an abundant supply of fresh water (as at Glendalough) or accessibility to the sea (as at Whithorn). In other places the superimposition seems to have been for no reason that we can discern. All we know is that what was designated as sacred space in pre-Christian times continued as sacred space in Christian times and continues so today.

Although we can look at patterns and trends, we shall never know exactly why early peoples chose one spot over another for their sacred places. We have developed theories that make sense to us in our day and that seem to be borne out by our observations and experience, but still, we can only guess at what reasoning went into the original selection. What we can be sure of, however, is that when a site was chosen five thousand years ago (or at any time since), it was a selection made with great care, one that has been revered for countless generations, in many cases to the present day.

In looking at pilgrimage, which is defined as a journey undertaken in search of that which is holy, we must look at sacred space in all its many contexts. A pilgrimage can be to *any* holy place, anywhere in the world. Most of the time pilgrims seek out those places that have been made holy by others before us. Still, we need to be open to the fact that new holy places may emerge at any time—we never know. Ultimately we must admit that when or where we will see the angels and why we seem to encounter God more readily in some places than in others will always be a mystery. We can expect to be as startled and overcome as Moses was when he saw the burning bush. Like Moses, we must recognize that we are standing on holy ground.

Pilgrimage in the Celtic Period

IF WE THINK BACK to two thousand years ago, when travel was staggeringly difficult and the physical hazards of the journey were life-threatening—a high percentage of those who traveled died en route—we have to ask, what was the incredible lure of pilgrimage? Without doubt, specifically Christian pilgrimage has its roots in the desire to visit and experience first-hand the places where Jesus, his apostles, and the saints lived, ministered, witnessed, and died, but pilgrimage in general has a far longer history. The urge of human beings to travel, whether out of curiosity or simply to be on the move, to expand inner horizons, is as old as humanity itself. Thus the risks and expense of a pilgrimage were neither new nor unique to early Christianity, but they were a continuation of the age-long process to search for the Holy, no matter what the cost.

The Celtic Christians had a passion for that search. Their concept of pilgrimage came from Jesus' own instruction to his disciples:

> If any want to become my followers, let them deny themselves and take up their cross and follow me. For those who want to save their life will lose it, and those who lose their life for my sake will find it. For what will it profit them if they gain the whole world but forfeit their life? Or what will they give in return for their life? (Matthew 16:24–26)

Because the ancient Celtic religion had held in it no fear of death but simply saw death as a crossing over to an otherworld, it was easy for the Celtic Christians to accept the call to follow Jesus with little regard either for one's personal safety or the geographical destination of the pilgrimage. Furthermore,

Foxes have holes, and birds of the air have nests; but the Son
of Man has nowhere to lay his head. (Luke 9:58)

Thus for the Celtic Christians, the Bible gave ample justification to
encourage pilgrimage.

The four major aspects of Celtic pilgrimage were missionary
outreach and evangelism, an apparently aimless wandering for
God, the search for one's place of resurrection, and the imitation of
Jesus through a fierce asceticism.

Missionary Outreach and Evangelism

Go therefore and make disciples of all nations, baptizing
them in the name of the Father and of the Son and of the
Holy Spirit, and teaching them to obey everything that I have
commanded you. And remember, I am with you always, to
the end of the age. (Matthew 28:19–20)

Missionary outreach in the form of pilgrimage during the Age of
the Saints (the fifth through the ninth centuries) was almost a
given, closely associated with the planting of new churches and
evangelizing non-Christian people. Such pilgrimages would typically begin when an established monastery seemed to be at capaci-
ty; at that point a small band, often twelve in number, would set out
to make a new foundation. As an example, many of the monastic
foundations on the Western Isles of Scotland, the remains of which
can still be seen today, were probably founded by monks from
Columba's primary foundation on the Isle of Iona.

The Celtic approach to evangelization was a peaceful process
without bloodshed, different from the more militaristic Roman
approach. John Finney, in his excellent book *Recovering the Past:
Celtic and Roman Mission* (1996),[8] presents a strong case for noting
the differences in understanding of mission and evangelism
between the Roman approach and the Celtic approach, the one
stemming from the patterns of the militaristic Roman Empire and
the other from a communal and tribal society. It has been suggested,

perhaps facetiously, that the Roman understanding of mission was to "invade and impose," while the Celtic understanding was to "infiltrate and osmose." What is undeniable is that as Christianity was spread in the Celtic countries by converted Celtic Christians— usually monks—martyrdom for the Christian faith was almost totally unknown.

Peregrini

Monk and nun pilgrim evangelists, called *peregrini*, combined a strong inner vision with outward mobility and a commitment to bring others to Christ. No other period in history has seen such widespread and successful missionary outreach. During the third to eighth centuries, while pilgrims on the European mainland were turning their eyes eastward to Jerusalem and Rome to worship at their holy places, Celtic pilgrims were turning their eyes in all directions to preach the gospel. Most of these men and women became founders of small Christian communities or monasteries based on a Celtic model. When a community grew too large, either the original founder or one of his or her followers ventured out to begin a new community. Brittany, Cornwall, Wales, Scotland, Mann, and Ireland were literally peppered with these Celtic foundations, and it is no exaggeration to say that most medieval churches in the Celtic countries were originally Celtic ecclesiastical settlements.

Probably the best known of the *peregrini* was Colmcille (as he is usually called in Ireland), or Columba (as he is usually called in Britain). Born of noble parentage in County Donegal in northwest Ireland, he was trained as a monk by Finnian of Moville and then by Finnian of Clonard, two of the most highly respected teachers in sixth-century Ireland. We are led to believe that Columba was a man of high integrity, with consummate skill as a leader, and passionate in his commitments. This last characteristic was to get him in trouble time and again, but it also helped him become one of Ireland's most famous sons (second only to Patrick), and Scotland's most famous missionary. Columba founded the monasteries of Derry and Durrow before he left Ireland in 563 to found his most famous monastery of all, Iona, off the west coast of Scotland. The monastery at Kells, often associated with Columba and from which possibly came the great Book of Kells, was probably not established until the ninth century by monks fleeing from Iona.

Columbanus, a generation later than Columba, was another of the great Irish *peregrini*. He saw the imitation of Jesus as a self-imposed exile as being the highest form of asceticism. He also took literally Jesus' words to go into the world and spread the gospel. This he did with tremendous energy, leaving his homeland and traveling to the Continent to found a string of monasteries, including Luxeuil in Gaul, St. Gall in Switzerland, and Bobbio in northern Italy.

Columba and Columbanus were not alone in their travels and missionary foundations. There were literally hundreds, perhaps thousands, of others, all pilgrims for Christ. Eleanor Duckett's book, *The Wandering Saints*,[9] discusses the major Celtic *peregrini*, describing their adventures and achievements.

We know that the Irish *peregrini* sailed far beyond their native shores and reached not only the Orkneys and Shetland off the north coast of Scotland, but also the Faroes, Iceland, and other remote islands as well. Dicuil, an Irish monk writing in the ninth century, gives first-hand testimony to these monastic settlements in formerly uninhabited areas. We also have evidence in Norwegian records of Christian monastic settlements in Iceland. After the Vikings arrived, the inhabitants abandoned their monasteries but left behind various treasures and artifacts as clues to their Irish background.

Wanderers for God

Whereas many early Christians on the Continent went on pilgrimage to a particular place (most notably Jerusalem or Rome), many Celtic pilgrims went on pilgrimage without a destination in mind. These men and women were called *gyrovagi* or *vagari* (from which comes our word "vagabond"); they were simply wanderers for God, without an obvious clear direction in their travels. Some of these *gyrovagi* ended up as hermits, settling down near a water supply and living a simple eremitic life. In the British Isles in particular, these hermits came to be considered as very holy people, much sought out for their wisdom. Countless other *gyrovagi* spent their lives simply wandering from settlement to settlement, accepting that followers of Jesus, like Jesus himself, had nowhere to lay their heads (Luke 9:58).

A real theology stood behind some of these apparently aimless travels, however, for many Celtic travelers saw the outward journey as a reflection of the inward journey toward union with God. Therefore, many of the *gyrovagi* actually did not wander without direction, but rather went on pilgrimage in search of their "place of resurrection"—that place set apart by God where each individual would eventually settle and spend the rest of his or her life. A geographic goal was not the purpose of pilgrimage. Rather, the point was to place oneself totally in the hands of God and to allow the mystery of God to determine one's life's direction. One of the best examples of this is the story of the three Irishmen who set sail in a boat without oars. They drifted aimlessly for seven days and finally came to shore in British Cornwall. The three pilgrims explained their presence to King Alfred of Wessex by stating that they had left Ireland purely for the love of God, allowing their boat to drift in whatever direction God might lead it—in this case, to the shores of Cornwall. There, presumably, they established a new monastery.

Eleanor Duckett gives a vivid description of what the life of these wanderers must have been like:

> They might be seen, sometimes in small companies of two or three, often alone, tramping along the lanes and trails, struggling through the forest, plunging through the stretches of bog and marsh, climbing the mountains. On their feet they wore sandals of hide; their monkish habit was of skins roughly sewn together, with a hood to protect them from cold and rain; in their hands they carried a staff, and from their shoulders hung the pack which held their small store of food, their cup, and the books of prayer for Mass and Office. Their food they begged from the peasants of the cottages they passed, who often willingly gave a meal to a holy man in return for his blessing upon them and their home.

In lonely and inhospitable places they sat in the evening to eat what they had gathered as they walked from fruit trees growing wild, from bark, from the leaves of some wholesome plant. At night they made a bed of boughs under the open sky; sometimes a cottager gave them a lodging upon the hay of his barn and a drink of milk from his cow before they left at dawn. A pool or a stream by the path on the moor or in the forest was welcome for washing away the stains of travel and—a worse evil—the plagues of itching stings and bites gathered in the sun, in the woods, or in their host's thatched barn amid the straw. Often they halted a while for the prayers of their monastic round of Office, and if the wayfarer was a priest, a flat rock made for him an altar on holy days.[10]

Such description should be ample to dispel any romantic notions about how these holy men and women actually lived in the Age of the Saints.

One of the best-known pilgrims in this wandering tradition was St. Brendan the Navigator (not to be confused with St. Brendan of Birr, also of Ireland and a friend and disciple of Columba). Brendan's wanderings were not on land but on the sea, and he is rightly called the Navigator. He was born in southwest Ireland probably near Tralee in the early sixth century. As a young child he was sent to St. Ita and placed in her foster care (a common Celtic practice). Later he became a monk and then an abbot, establishing Irish monastic foundations at Clonfert and Annadown (both in County Galway), Inishadroum (County Clare), and Ardfert (County Kerry). Travel was second nature to Brendan; stories tell of his visits to Columba on Iona and to other foundations in the Hebrides (Scotland) and of further visits both to Wales and to Brittany. Most scholars believe the Brendan stories are a conflation of many saints' stories, and these were merged together to promote the cult of Brendan in the ninth and tenth centuries.

The *Navigatio Brendani*[11] is among the best loved of the Irish saints' stories. Because of these tales, Brendan is best known not as a founder of monasteries, but as a *gyrovagus* who set out to follow God without plan, not on the land, but in a frail boat. His sea voyage was a pilgrimage of voluntary exile. Brendan and twelve of his companions set sail from the Dingle Peninsula, seeking God's "Island of Promise" at some vague location in the Atlantic Ocean, trusting totally in the mercy of God to lead them to their destination.

There are mixed opinions as to the historic authenticity of Brendan's sea voyage. His various adventures certainly fall in the category of the traditional Irish *imrama*, or travel tales (many of them portraying wonderful phantasmagoric adventures), but we also know that there is a real possibility that some of Brendan's adventures described in the *Navigatio* may well be true. Historian and geographer Tim Severin spent several years exhaustively researching records of medieval boats and sailing practices and the *Navigatio* itself. In 1976, backed predominantly by funds from the National Geographic Society, he built a vessel matching (as nearly as could be determined) the one Brendan is said to have had. Over two seasons (1976 and 1977) he and his crew sailed ever westward and eventually landed safely on the shores of Newfoundland.[12] The actual boat used in this journey is today on display in the museum at Craggauowen in County Clare, Ireland. To look at it makes one gasp with incredulity that such a small craft was actually able to sail more than three thousand miles across the north Atlantic Ocean.

Romantic as such total (irrational?) dependence on God may seem, and as often as such a viewpoint is presented in some books about Celtic spirituality, the reality is not quite that simple. The Celtic seafarers, Brendan included, were extremely experienced at reading the sky, the wind, sea currents, and weather patterns. When setting sail out into the unknown, the Celtic gyrovague sailors had great trust in God, to be sure, but they also had a far greater knowledge of the sea than is usually acknowledged. All these wanderers for God simply took off, on land or on sea, following some indescribable internal pull to wherever, but knowing clearly that the inner pull came from God and was to be followed, no matter where it might lead.

Seeking the Place of One's Resurrection

One's place of resurrection in the Celtic context was understood to be the place where one would eventually die and thus meet God face to face. The journey undertaken in this search could lead to anywhere, but there was a strong tendency to follow the setting sun and move ever westward. Many early pilgrimage routes thus led to the west coasts of the Celtic countries, or even more desirable, to habitable islands lying off the western coasts. There was a sense of God's having prepared a unique place for each individual's entry into the Kingdom of Heaven:

> In my Father's house there are many dwelling places. If it were not so, would I have told you that I go to prepare a place for you? (John 14:2)

Celtic pilgrims sought that special place. Being natural wanderers anyway, they just "hit the road," so to speak. This may be one reason for settlements on so many of the islands off the western coasts, a result of combining missionary outreach with a personal quest. Bardsey Island, for example, off the westernmost tip of the Llŷn Peninsula in North Wales had a reputation of being the "Island of 20,000 Saints" and was sought out by wandering Celtic pilgrims long before it became a popular pilgrimage site in the Middle Ages.

Anamchàirde

Closely related to the pilgrimage in search of one's resurrection was the pilgrimage to one's *anamchara*, or soul friend, who today we might call a spiritual director. The Celtic Christians were quick to recognize the importance of the shared spiritual journey, for, as is attributed to St. Brigid, "The person without an *anamchara* is like a body without a head." *Anamchàirde* were sought out as men and women of wisdom and great spiritual insight, willing to share their understanding of the faith with others. Not infrequently an *anamchara* might serve as a foster parent to some young child, such as Ita's nurturing of the young Brendan. Sometimes these *anamchàirde* were hermits who had set themselves up in some isolated place, imitating the desert hermits from the Mediterranean world. St. Kevin of Glendalough was one such example. After Kevin's monastic foundation had grown to adequate size and self-sufficiency, Kevin went off to an isolated spot to be alone. Today there are still a number of small settlements with the name Díseart (Ireland) or Dysert (Wales), which trace their foundation to one of these hermit *anamchäirde*.

Imitation of Jesus through Asceticism

Along with the love of wandering, whether on the sea or on the land and whether as intentional evangelism or in search of one's "place of resurrection," a life of fierce asceticism was one of the most distinctive features of this period of Celtic Christianity. Certainly it was practiced by both *gyrovagi* and *peregrini*. Its original idea was the imitation of the life of extreme simplicity thought to have been practiced by Jesus as exemplified in the Beatitudes.

Tales of the saints' self-mortification are likely to seem extreme to us today. St. David, "the Waterman," is reputed to have stood for hours in the waters of the Alun River chanting his psalms. There is even the tale of naked women being paraded in front of him to induce him to leave the chill of the river to find warmth, presumably in their arms. St. Cuthbert, too, stood in the frigid waters of the North Sea to say his prayers, and when he returned to the shore, sea otters came and dried him with their fur. Many are the reports of the Celtic monasteries having only bread, water, and a few vegetables as their normal diet. Extreme asceticism and bodily mortification were an accepted part of the Christian life for the early Irish *peregrini*. Their theology was sound: the Christian's life must be a constant warfare against self-will and gratification of the senses.

> You were taught to put away your former way of life, your old self, corrupt and deluded by its lusts, and to be renewed in the spirit of your minds. (Ephesians 4:22–23)

Another explanation for the rise of such asceticism is that it was a kind of imitation of the great martyrs. Nowhere in the records of the evangelization and Christianization of the Celtic countries do we find examples of actual martyrdom, such as were so common in the Mediterranean countries prior to the Edict of Milan. Instead there emerged a different concept, in all likelihood arising from the reading of the lives of the martyrs and a longing to imitate them. Three types of martyrdom were possible for the Celtic peoples: red martyrdom was dying for the faith, as did countless hundreds in the Mediterranean world; white martyrdom was leaving home and country for the sake of love of Christ, as did the *gyrovagi* and *peregrini*; and green martyrdom was staying at home and giving up one's life in total subjection to Christ. Since people did not ordinarily suffer for Christ to the point of death and not everyone could travel to faraway places, many opted to subdue the body and its sensual pleasures by ascetic acts of bodily mortification: the green martyrdom. Such understanding of bodily sacrifice has its basis in the Scriptures:

> We know that our old self was crucified with [Christ] so that the body of sin might be destroyed, and we might no longer be enslaved to sin. (Romans 6:6)

> For the grace of God has appeared, bringing salvation to all, training us to renounce impiety and worldly passions, and in the present age to live lives that are self-controlled, upright, and godly, while we wait for the blessed hope and the manifestation of the glory of our great God and Savior, Jesus Christ. (Titus 2:11–13)

To subdue the flesh was to crucify the old self to Christ, to deliberately put away all those things that delude and corrupt the body. This was the call of Christ: to love a life that was self-controlled, upright, and godly. Asceticism was perceived to be a holy martyrdom, a daily dying to the self for the sake of the gospel.

> I have been crucified with Christ; and it is no longer I who live, but it is Christ who lives in me. And the life I now live in the flesh I live by faith in the Son of God, who loved me and gave himself for me. (Galatians 2:19b–20)

The ascetical life was an important part of the Christian life. Columbanus taught his followers that only by stripping oneself of all the desires and possessions that bind a person to the present world could one truly be in Christ. To that end he was hard not only on himself but on his followers as well. In his *Rule*[13] for his monks he insists that they work until they drop, arise before their sleep is finished, eat only what is given to them (which was very little), maintain silence in face of injustice (to turn the other cheek), and above all be obedient to their superior. In spite of such harshness, Columbanus attracted followers wherever he went, and his *Rule* and ascetic practices were not far different from those of his contemporaries in the sixth century and his successors in the seventh and eighth.

David, at his monastery in southwest Wales, also insisted on a life of extreme hardship for his monks. They ate only bread, vegetables, and water and pursued a life of demanding physical labor. Nevertheless, David, too, attracted a large band of followers. The important thing was to find the best way to follow Jesus: if one could not be physically martyred, one traveled; if that was not possible, one chose the harsh ascetic life. All combined together to make one's life a pilgrimage.

Early Christian Settlements

The monastic foundations established by the *peregrini* were not chosen at random. Historical geographer E. G. Bowen[14] has researched extensively the settlements of the major Celtic saints along all the coasts of the Irish Sea. John Marsden[15] has made a similar study of settlements in the Outer and Inner Hebridean islands further north. Both have examined prehistoric settlement patterns as they pertain to the natural prevailing winds, tides, and sea currents, and both make a convincing case for recognizing that Christian settlements were based on the same natural criteria. The hagiographic stories of the Middle Ages repeatedly tell of a saint's having settled in a particular location because he or she had received a heavenly message—a dream or a vision; nevertheless, behind each choice lay some important practical considerations.

In addition to the ready availability of sea routes, there is ample evidence that Roman roads continued in use in Wales and southern Scotland until as late as the seventh century. Many of the land-based Celtic missionaries traveled and made their monastic settlements along these roads, often moving inland from their initial foundation near the coast. Today, the hundreds of places in Wales beginning with the prefix *llan* bear witness to these early communities. Now *llan* generally implies "church" (for example, Llanbadarn means the church of St. Padarn), but historically the *llan* was simply a circular enclosure indicating a monastic settlement, which would always have included a church. Llanbadarn, then, actually means the monastic settlement of St. Padarn, who was one of the many wandering saints with foundations throughout Mid Wales.

The presence of bilingual *ogham* stones (upright stones marked with a form of writing unique to early Christian Ireland) is one of the clearest indications of the frequent intercourse between all the Celtic areas in the fourth, fifth, and sixth centuries. The beautifully carved stones at Nevern in southwest Wales, the Kirkmadrine and Whithorn stones in Galloway (Scotland), and a number of stones on the Isle of Man are good examples. All show the cultural artistic influence of one country on another, particularly on Ireland, and all document the frequent travels of the Celtic saints.

Circular churchyards today are nearly always indicative of an early Celtic foundation, and these early settlements were typically named after their founders. St. David's primary foundation is still called in Welsh, Tyddewi, meaning Dewi's (David's) House (or church), but his secondary settlements are typically called Llandewi (meaning a monastic settlement of David). Both Bowen and Marsden have made careful studies of the place names of settlements and see them as possible indications of a given saint's evangelism and influence. However, they both caution care in assigning too much significance to church dedications as such, as church dedications can rarely be precisely dated.

Pilgrimage, then, in the Celtic countries during the Age of the Saints was markedly different from that practiced on the Continent during the same period, and it was even more different from the patterns that were to develop during the subsequent Middle Ages. Celtic pilgrimage was inextricably linked to evangelism, to a free wandering "for the sake of Christ," to missionary outreach, or to self-imposed exile including a rigid self-discipline. Pilgrimage was a journey in search of the "place of one's resurrection" and a relentless spreading of the Christian gospel in every direction by way of monastic foundations.

Pilgrimage in the Middle Ages

IN ORDER TO UNDERSTAND the transition from the concept of pilgrimage during the Celtic period to our understanding of pilgrimage today, it is necessary to look briefly at the understanding and practice of pilgrimage during the Middle Ages. While many of the early Celtic peoples went on pilgrimage without a geographic goal in mind, in the Middle Ages geography was critically important. Rome and Jerusalem were visited regularly. Additionally, places such as Santiago de Compostela in northwest Spain and other more local sites began to develop and attract pilgrims. Most, if not all, of these places were associated with particular saints or miracles.

With the rise of church authority and huge increase in ecclesiastical power, the search for one's place of resurrection lost its relevance: the church was the beginning and end of all. There was even less interest in a life of simplicity and asceticism as western civilization regained its equilibrium after the Dark Ages. Trade routes were reestablished in all directions, and opulent living, to the extent that one could afford it, was much to be desired. The Celtic concept of pilgrimage died out, greatly helped in its demise by the rise of monasteries, particularly Benedictine, and by the expanding authority of the medieval church.

The Importance of Saints

With the gradual emergence of the feudal system, there also arose a new understanding of society that in turn introduced a new concept of pilgrimage. Feudalism was built on a hierarchical understanding of relationships; each lord, no matter how great or how minor, was utterly committed to the protection of those subordinate to him and equally committed to homage to his own overlord. It followed that God was the greatest of the spiritual overlords, with countless levels of lesser beings (some of whom came to be called saints) between lowly mortals and God.

Life was very hierarchical in the religious as well as the secular world. Within this context, all saints were seen to be kinds of holy spiritual overlords with varying degrees of closeness to God and varying degrees of "influence" with God. Saints were thought to be willing and able to provide assistance in time of need. These saints were thought to have special influence in the court of heaven, able to plead with God for favors.[16] Miracles of every conceivable kind happened; they ranged from visionary appearances to inexplicable healings, favors granted, mystical experiences, and more. Places at which favors had been granted (presumably God-given) or miracles performed quickly became pilgrimage sites. Pilgrims journeyed to a particular saint's site for a variety of reasons, such as to ask for healing or help, to offer thanksgiving, or perhaps to undertake a penance for wrong doings.

The Importance of Relics

The increased focus on saints brought with it the desire to collect relics, at first any items that saints had come in contact with, and a little later, actual body parts. Most recorded miracles from the twelfth to the sixteenth centuries were directly related to relics, which in and of themselves were believed to be holy and which caused miracles to happen. For people of the Middle Ages this practice was theologically sound, based on a variety of passages from the Bible, including these:

> Then suddenly a woman who had been suffering from hemorrhages for twelve years came up behind [Jesus] and touched the fringe of his cloak, for she said to herself, "If I only touch his cloak, I will be made well." (Matthew 9:20–21)

> God did extraordinary miracles through Paul, so that when the handkerchiefs or aprons that had touched his skin were brought to the sick, their diseases left them, and the evil spirits came out of them. (Acts 19:11–12)

Consequently, what had once belonged to or been touched by a holy person—even by that person's shadow—became holy in and of itself and was a true and authentic representation of that saint.

> They even carried out the sick into the streets, and laid them on cots and mats, in order that Peter's shadow might fall on some of them as he came by. (Acts 5:15)

Pope Gregory the Great in the fourth century wrote that all things necessary for worship in the church were to include not only the usual vessels and vestments, but also relics of the holy apostles and martyrs. The Second Council of Nicaea in 787 decreed that "no new church shall be consecrated without relics." Traffic in relics quickly became enormous; it even became fashionable and commendable to *steal* relics (*furta sacra*). The moral dilemma was conveniently explained away by the argument that because the saints were so powerful, they would never allow their relics to be stolen unless they were in favor of the relocation.

Soon the supply-and-demand syndrome set in, and by the high Middle Ages there were relics of every conceivable kind, from pieces of the true cross to bones. Also greatly treasured were other body parts, such as a tooth of the Virgin Mary; the ear of Malchus, which was cut off at the time of Jesus' arrest (John 18:10), fingers, arm and leg bones, and in some cases even blood. Scraps of clothing and garments of all kinds that had been associated with saints were greatly treasured. Chartres Cathedral today still enshrines in a modern reliquary the famous *Sancta Camisia Maria*, the garment supposedly worn by Mary when she gave birth to Jesus.

Inevitably came the increase in spurious relics, and well-traveled pilgrims learned to be skeptical about some of them. The great Boccacio in the *Decameron*[17] has one of his characters, Father Cipolla, announce that he has been on pilgrimage to Jerusalem and brought back with him, among other things, one of the feathers dropped by the Archangel Gabriel at the time of the Annunciation. In another case, a sixteenth-century pilgrim visiting in France saw several different heads of John the Baptist. When he commented on this, he was told, "Ah yes, the one you saw that day was the skull of John as a young man. Ours here at this monastery is his skull after he was fully advanced in years and wisdom."

Another amusing story about people's belief in relics involves a famous preacher of the late twelfth century, Fulk de Neuilly. He had a reputation for great sanctity, and the crowds who flocked to hear him would often try not just to *touch* his clothing, but to tear off a piece of it. On one occasion, he frustrated the efforts of his listeners by announcing that his own clothes had not been blessed, but that he was about to bless the clothing of a bystander, which he proceeded to do. No sooner had de Neuilly made the sign of the cross over the bystander than the unfortunate man had every stitch stripped off him, leaving him stark naked!

In the Middle Ages, saints were deemed powerful mediators to the throne of God, and prayers to a saint at that saint's shrine (with or without that saint's relics) were seen as a way to have petitions granted. Individual saints tended to have their own cults or devotees. It is known, for example, that Henry V made a pilgrimage to St. Winefride's Holy Well in North Wales following the battle of Agincourt in 1415. He went to ask St. Winefride's intercessions on his behalf, that her prayers might help persuade God to grant further victories to the English. (And the victories *did* go to the English. Who is to say that they were not the result of St. Winefride's petitions? The people of fifteenth-century England undoubtedly believed they were.)

Other Kinds of Pilgrimage

Not all pilgrims were concerned with relics and miracles. There are also countless stories on record of people who went on pilgrimages as acts of thanksgiving, perhaps for the birth of a child, or for preservation from some terrible calamity. We know from the writings of Erasmus that a man named Ogygius went to Santiago de Compostela because his mother-in-law had vowed that if her daughter bore a male child, Ogygius would visit the shrine of St. James and express gratitude. Kings often went on pilgrimages of thanksgiving after successful endeavors, and pilgrimages of thanksgiving following safe delivery from sea calamities were very common.

Besides petition and thanksgiving, the two kinds of prayers that most frequently and fervently found their way into the ears of the saints were prayers of penitence for wrongdoing and prayers for healing. One of the most famous penitential pilgrimages was Henry II's long walk from Canterbury to the shrine of St. David in St. David's Cathedral (southwest Wales) after the murder of Thomas à Becket (1170). Reputedly he wore a hair shirt and walked the last several miles barefoot, with the entire pilgrimage being a public as well as private act of penitence and reparation. He seems to have chosen the shrine of St. David because of David's reputation as a peacemaker.

Supplication for healing was extremely common, and it is in this regard that the relics come close to being idols in and of themselves. Miracles related to them abound. "If I can just touch the fringe of his cloak..." as the Scripture suggests (Luke 8:43–44) translated readily into "If I can just touch the bones, or the finger, or the garment, I shall be healed." This may seem rather farfetched, or even repugnant to us today, but we must try to appreciate the medical desperation that our medieval forbears endured. Today, at least in the West, when we are sick, we go to a doctor and know that we are going to receive highly sophisticated treatment; we have miracle drugs to combat current illnesses and infections and amazing inoculations against terrible diseases. Most of us live with the expectation that when we have an accident or get sick, we will get well. And most of us do, most of the time, but it was not so during the Middle Ages. The desperate searches for alleviation of pain and for cures are beyond our present-day comprehension. Typical medieval thinking went along these lines: "If St. Winefride can heal my blinding headaches, then I will surely make every effort to visit her shrine at Holywell, bathe in her holy waters, and above all, plead with her to pray for me to Almighty God, with whom she has a special relationship—and I will get well."

Perhaps surprisingly, to our modern mindset, many people did get well. Miracle cures *do* seem to have taken place at numerous shrines and places of healing (just as miracle cures, beyond medical explanation, still take place today). So the reputation of pilgrimage sites particularly associated with healing grew as did the numbers of pilgrims visiting the holy sites. Even today, thousands of people continue to visit healing shrines such as Knock in Ireland, Lourdes in France, or Fatima in Portugal.

Interestingly, the sites most frequently associated with healing were flowing springs, and the cures usually involved some kind of a ritual or liturgy that included bathing in the waters. A correlation with the sacrament of baptism is immediately apparent, baptism implying cleansing as well as healing and imparting new life in Christ. Many places in the Celtic countries had a long association with healing, and the sanctity of such places continued into the Middle Ages. St. Cybi's Well on the Llŷn Peninsula in North Wales was originally a Celtic foundation, and during the twelfth to six-teenth centuries it was a terribly busy place. There was a small hos-tel attached to the well where the pilgrims could have a kind of bed-and-breakfast while they "took the cure." Remains of the causeway leading to the well, fully a thousand years old, the cot-tage next door to the well chamber, and the nearby latrine, can still be seen today.

In some parts of the world, visiting holy wells to pray for heal-ing remains a common practice. With our modern tendency to dis-believe in miracles, and modern technology's attempt to gain more insight into them, the waters of a number of holy wells in Britain and Ireland have been scientifically analyzed, and indeed, in many cases, the mineral content does seem to indicate medicinal and cur-ative properties.

Near Ballyvourney in County Cork, Ireland, is a holy well, St. Gobnait's, where pilgrims still walk the Stations of the Cross and then bathe in the waters of the well for healing. Only a few years ago, a young boy living in the area accidentally drank weed killer. While his life hung by a thread and his family waited anxiously at the hospital, friends and neighbors in the community went to St. Gobnait's Shrine and Well and prayed for the child's healing. When the young boy recovered, many people attributed his healing not only to medical science but also to the prayers at the shrine of St. Gobnait.[18]

Another kind of pilgrimage that was often undertaken was the judicial pilgrimage. Unlike the penitential pilgrimage, which was a voluntary act of reparation for sin, the judicial pilgrimage was imposed by an outside authority, most frequently the church. Instead of being sent to prison, the offender was sent on a very long pilgrimage, perhaps to the Holy Land. On the face of it, the pilgrimage was meant to atone for sins. At the practical level, however, it was a shrewd way of getting the malefactor out of the area for quite a long time, and given the rigors of travel, perhaps forever. Such a mandatory pilgrimage inevitably required the offender to bring back tangible evidence of having completed the journey, and this coincided nicely with the emergence of specific tokens that were unique to given pilgrimage sites.

Pilgrimage Symbols and Tokens

Very early on, pilgrims assumed a distinctive garb that allowed them to be identified wherever they might be on their travels. This garb assured the travelers both hospitality and safety. They typically wore a plain tunic, perhaps with a large cross sewn on the breast or back, with a leather belt, a staff, and a scrip, or purse. Depictions of pilgrims as found in engravings and stained glass windows always show this clothing which was in effect a uniform. Those who have engaged on a long and arduous journey, or on one that was particularly meaningful, quite naturally want to have a badge or token saying "I did it," or "I was there." Today cameras and film for snapshots proliferate, but the medieval pilgrims, lacking photographic equipment, either wore specific badges, brooches, pins, or medals or carried small flasks or ampullae to validate their journeys.

Specific symbols were associated with specific sites. The scallop shell associated with Santiago de (St. James of) Compostela is perhaps the best-known example. Early pilgrims to Compostela simply picked up shells off the beach as a symbol of their having been there. Alternately, they had a scallop shell embroidered on their tunic. Not long ago in County Galway an ancient grave was discovered, and in it was a scallop shell, a clear indication that the deceased had been on pilgrimage to Compostela. Many illustrations of pilgrims with scallop shells are to be found in medieval illuminated manuscripts and in stained glass windows. As the popularity

of Compostela as a pilgrimage site grew to international propor-
tions, the shell became a symbol of pilgrimage more generally,
although to this day it remains particularly associated with
Santiago de Compostela.

Overuse and Abuse

We might be tempted to say today that the huge pilgrim traffic to
holy sites was a "racket" (and certainly there were abuses), but pilgrimage to holy shrines was a major part of the way people lived
and believed. As pointed out above, in the Middle Ages, the great
Age of Pilgrimage, people's understanding of their place in society
was a very hierarchical one, where one's overlord was responsible
for protection of those under him, and one was obligated to honor
and obey the overlord. People prayed to God through the saints,
preferably at a shrine where some physical reminder of a particular
saint was held. Because God was seen as too far away and inaccessible for ordinary mortals, the saints, who had more immediate
access to God, would intercede on their behalf. Such was the driving motivation for pilgrimage during the Middle Ages.

Unfortunately, like so much else in human history, things that
start out clean and pure all too often become contaminated, and
overuse becomes abuse. Thus it was with pilgrimages, shrines, and
relics in the Middle Ages. More and more miracles were reported
from increasingly dubious relics, meaning more shrines were
opened; increasingly, a financial commitment was required of the
pilgrims once a shrine was reached. In many of the great medieval
pilgrimage sites, the stone coffer to receive the offerings from
the pilgrims repeatedly had to be redesigned so that greedy hands
were not able to remove what humble hands had dropped in. The
slanted slot chest in which coins slide down a slope into the chest,
and no hand can get into at all, was invented in the Middle Ages
and is still in use today.

The importance of the income from pilgrims' offerings cannot
be overestimated. Pilgrims made their offerings in good faith, but
where there were pilgrims, there was money, and where there was
money, soon there were highway robbers. Basingwerk Abbey in

North Wales, for example, was established specifically to protect the pilgrims who were coming to St. Winefride's Holy Well. The monks accepted the responsibility for protecting the pilgrims and caring for the well—and also took custodianship of the pilgrims' alms. In a very short time, Basingwerk was one of the wealthier abbeys in that section of Britain.

Such a scenario was repeated all over Christendom. Where there were shrines, there were pilgrims; where there were pilgrims, there was money—and the church ready to step in and take charge. Canterbury was, and still is, the wealthiest pilgrimage site in the British Isles. Indulgences, the system of buying forgiveness to gain entrance into Heaven, were also common in the Middle Ages. Naturally, indulgences were granted to pilgrims—for a fee. St. David's, in southwest Wales, still reminds its visitors that Pope Callistus II in the sixteenth century decreed that in terms of indulgences two pilgrimage visits to St. David's were the equivalent to one pilgrimage to Rome, and *three* to St. David's, to one pilgrimage to the Holy Land.

In reading Chaucer's *Canterbury Tales*, that marvelous and lively description of human nature and life in the Middle Ages, one quickly realizes that most of those pilgrims were not truly on a search for that which is holy. Perhaps the Clerk was, and the Knight, the Parson, and the Plowman, but the other characters surely had entirely different motives in mind. For example, the Wife of Bath was definitely looking for an amorous escapade, and the Merchant was on the run from his creditors. Others had their own unique motives. A few were simply along for a good time. Chaucer's portrayal of life in the late Middle Ages and of pilgrimage in particular was accurate: there were among the pilgrims those who searched for the Holy, but by and large, by the fifteenth century the pilgrimage experience had gotten out of hand. This kind of rampant corruption in the church inevitably ushered in the Reformation.

With the Reformation and the Age of Reason, society and Christian theology changed drastically. Instead of the hierarchical ultimate authority of the Church in Rome, denominations with varying organization, administration, and theologies developed. In the countries that became predominantly Protestant (for example, Germany, Scandinavia, and Great Britain), pilgrimage almost ceased. In countries that remained Catholic, however (for example, Italy, France, and Spain), visits to the Holy Land, Rome, Compostela, and other traditional pilgrimage sites continued. As reforms within the Roman Catholic Church took effect and the Renaissance and the Scientific Movement unfolded, intellectualism and rational thinking began to dominate human thought. Literacy began to replace easy credulity; new social structures and new ideologies emerged. The modern period had begun, and the great Age of Pilgrimage was over.

Pilgrimage Today

THE GREAT AGE OF PILGRIMAGE may have ended with the Reformation, but human curiosity about the world and an interest in travel, plus the never-ending search for the inner self and a connection to God, certainly did not. Those who could afford it traveled extensively during the eighteenth and nineteenth centuries. In Great Britain, a huge upsurge of fascination with antiquities furthered extensive field work in archaeology, which discovered and uncovered many Celtic and pre-Celtic sites and sparked new interest in Britain and Ireland's Celtic heritage. The same period spurred the renovation of hundreds of ancient buildings, particularly churches. Two world wars in the twentieth century slowed travel down, but by mid-century there was a marked increase in travel to faraway places. The development of commercial air transportation and the general rise in income for people in the West made possible visits to parts of the world formerly only dreamed about.

In most cases today we seek to visit holy places in the company of other seekers of the Holy, traveling together across vast distances on jet airplanes and in luxury coaches. The great pilgrimage shrines throughout Britain and Ireland, many of them with Celtic roots, report numbers of visitors at an all-time high, and those numbers continue to increase. New visitor centers and museums in the Celtic lands are opening yearly. Now almost any place in the world is accessible to anyone who can afford a plane ticket, and the tourist industry is booming. Travel of all kind is actively promoted, and most areas are quick to capitalize on the economic benefits of an influx of visitors, be they curiosity seekers, students, tourists, or pilgrims.

The Search for Wholeness

Describing pilgrimage traditions in the past is far easier than discussing the emerging pilgrimage traditions of today. And yet, in the last decade or so, interest in spirituality has increased and the attraction of pilgrimage is at a very high level. Just as pilgrimage in the Celtic period reflected the authentic spirituality of its day (evangelistic and mission-oriented), and the Middle Ages its day (hagiocentric), contemporary pilgrimage reflects today's spirituality, which tends to be more holistic. During the Celtic period the church had not yet reached its universal influence, and pilgrims tended to travel in very small groups or as individuals; in the Middle Ages, the church dominated people's lives, and pilgrimage was almost without exception church-related. Today's holistic pilgrimage (and "holistic" as a word derives from "wholeness") may not be church-related at all but rather related to a widespread disillusionment with the institutional church. Pilgrimage today is likely to be undertaken as a way of assuaging spiritual hunger—a hunger that for many people may no longer be fed by the church.

Pervasive spiritual hunger that longs for healing and wholeness transcends many of the barriers that separate and divide us as humans, and the sharing of commonalities within the pilgrimage experience thus can be deeply bonding. There seems to be a general movement away from dualistic thinking, which sets arbitrary boundaries between physical and spiritual, between body and soul, and between many other opposites. Holistic theology moves away from dualistic thinking and sees all creation as one integrated and interrelated whole. A holistic pilgrimage, therefore, will combine all aspects of our humanity, including intellectual, spiritual, and psychological aspects, as well as healthy physical exercise.

Today's spiritual hunger causes people to feel alienated or excluded, and certainly deeply wounded—hence the longing for any experience that leads to healing, reconciliation, and wholeness, as modern pilgrimage certainly seems to. People are seeking to deepen their spiritual lives by connecting with their own history and are fascinated with exploring their genealogical roots. Many are taking a fresh look at traditions we associate with Celtic spirituality, which is leading to greatly increased interest in poetry and mysticism and in ecumenical outreach. There is energy in the women's movement and a commitment to ecological concerns. All these contribute to the search for spiritual wholeness and are a part of pilgrimage today.

Canterbury and Knock

A good example of the holistic character of present-day pilgrimage is seen in the widespread appeal of Canterbury in southeast England and Knock in western Ireland. While Canterbury is not a Celtic site in and of itself, nevertheless it dates from the Celtic period, and because of its long history, any discussion of pilgrimage in Britain, whether medieval or modern, must include it. Canterbury was established by St. Augustine in 597, making it among the oldest Christian foundations in Britain; only the Celtic foundations in North Wales and southwest Scotland are older. Canterbury has been a major pilgrimage center for centuries and for many people is a part of their spiritual inheritance.

The present cathedral is surely one of the most magnificent medieval buildings to be found anywhere, and its more than a millennium of unbroken worship to God assures its being as important a spiritual destination today as it was during the Middle Ages. After the murder of Thomas Becket in 1172, it became a pilgrimage shrine of international importance, and it was pilgrimage to Becket's shrine that in the 1380s inspired Chaucer to write his famous *Canterbury Tales*. Even though Henry VIII destroyed Becket's shrine (and pocketed the wealth) in 1538, Canterbury continued to be the burial place of kings and archbishops. In the people's eyes, Canterbury has never ceased to be of enormous ecclesiastical and spiritual significance.

There is an ancient and well-documented (and well-trodden) "Pilgrims' Way" over the North Downs in the south of England that leads from Winchester to Canterbury. Along the way are any number of pubs, bed-and-breakfasts, guest houses, and tea shops called by such names as the "Pilgrims' Rest," the "Pilgrim's Hotel," the "Pilgrim's Pint," and so forth. It is not unusual for church groups or individuals to walk all or part of this historic track as a personal pilgrimage to Canterbury. Shirley du Boulay's book, *Pilgrimage to Canterbury*[19] gives an account of her walking the entire length (130 miles) in 1993. Ms. du Boulay reflects deeply from many different perspectives on her pilgrimage experience, mile after mile, and expresses her great feeling of peace when she finally arrives at the cathedral, her spiritual as well as her physical destination. Her journey was in every way a holistic pilgrimage.

It is unlikely that Canterbury will cease to be a major tourist attraction at any time in the near future, and it is equally unlikely that the Cathedral Dean and Chapter, well aware of Canterbury's history and spirituality, will ever allow it to cease to be a place of prayer and worship, a pilgrimage center for seekers of the Holy.

A similar statement might be made for Knock in western Ireland, although as a pilgrimage shrine, Knock is barely more than a hundred years old. Like Canterbury, Knock is not an original Celtic site per se, but for the Irish people with their Celtic heritage, their more than a century of unbroken tradition of pilgrimage to Knock is far too important to be overlooked.

In 1879 the tiny poverty-stricken village of Cnoc (the Gaelic word for "hill") in County Mayo was relatively unknown. Its population, only a few hundred people, was mostly humble farmers and their families, all of whom had suffered terribly in the recent famine years. On the evening of August 21, in weather thick with rain and fog, a small group of fifteen villagers—both adults and children—saw the unforgettable vision of the Virgin Mary, with St. Joseph on her right and St. John the Evangelist on her left. As news of the apparition spread, people came in droves, and miracles of healing began to be reported. The Roman Catholic Church set up a commission to inquire into the authenticity of the vision, but no rational and satisfactory explanation was ever found, and the fame of Cnoc (now anglicized to Knock) spread. Organized pilgrimages were established, and pilgrims came from literally all over the world. By 1964, St. Peter's Basilica had been built and Pope Paul VI said Mass there; by 1980, Knock had its own airport.

Knock has more than two million visitors each year. Pilgrims come seeking healing and reconciliation, and the Center has responded to the influx by building an enormous complex in this tiny once unheard-of village in County Mayo. Besides the original church, there is the Apparition Chapel, the Blessed Sacrament Chapel where the Reserved Sacrament is always exposed, the huge basilica built for the pope's visit in celebrating Knock's one hundredth anniversary, and the Chapel of Reconciliation. Within the latter is provision for as many as sixty priests to hear private confessions simultaneously, as well as a counseling center. The shrine is dedicated to healing in all aspects—physical, spiritual, psychological—and priests, religious, and counselors are always available simply to be present, to listen, or to help pilgrims who are struggling with their faith. Although the Center is Roman Catholic, any and all are invited to come here on pilgrimage, and they will find acceptance and welcome. As at Canterbury, those who come seeking the Holy will surely find it.

Pennant Melangell

Both Canterbury and Knock are pilgrimage sites known all over the world, but something exciting for today's pilgrims in Britain is the number of relatively unknown ancient sites, many of them dating from the Celtic period, that are increasingly becoming available. Such places have only recently been opened and perhaps only recently been discovered by those beyond the immediate area. Because these sites tend to be smaller and certainly are less known, and because frequently they are located in out-of-the-way places and therefore less accessible, they retain their original rich aura of sanctity and historical authenticity. Visiting such places can be a deeply meaningful spiritual experience—because a place is less known does not necessarily mean it is any less holy.

One very old pilgrimage center in mid-Wales that has reopened in recent years as a place of healing is Pennant Melangell, near Llangynog. It is not a place one is likely to happen upon by accident. Located at the end of a long narrow valley surrounded by steep hills, it is a place of great serenity. The present medieval church lies above a much older Celtic foundation within an ancient circular churchyard.

St. Melangell was a virgin and hermit who had fled from an unwanted marriage in Ireland. She had been living as a solitary in the valley for fifteen years, when, according to the story, the local prince sought her favors. Rather than taking her by force—as so often was the case—he recognized her humility and accepted her vocation as a handmaid of the Lord. He granted to her the entire valley and protection for all who came there, because she had saved beneath her skirts the life of a small hare fleeing from his hunters. Since then Melangell has been considered the patron saint of hares, perhaps the only instance of a wild animal having its own patron saint.

In the 1980s, Pennant Melangell was all but deserted; only a few people from the nearby village of Llangynog walked or drove up the isolated valley to exercise their dogs or perhaps hold an occasional worship service. The church building was in serious disrepair, and a decision had to be made: should the church be torn down and Melangell's shrine (or what was left of it) be taken to the National Museum of Wales, or should funding be sought to repair and restore this ancient historic and holy place? Thanks to enormous dedication and effort on the part of a few far-sighted people, funding was sought and found, and by 1992 the shrine had been reconstructed, and the church was reopened for regular prayer and worship. Today it is an important center for prayer and counseling, and a place for those facing serious or terminal illness, particularly cancer, to come for times of quiet and prayerful healing—for a temporary respite from the pain of daily life. In 1998 the newly built center was dedicated, a place where small pilgrimage groups can meet and have quiet time together. The church and shrine are once again open at all times, and there is a regular daily round of worship.[20]

Lough Derg

By way of contrast, across the sea in Ireland, some of the ancient pilgrimages have never lost their popularity and their traditions have never died out. The "pattern" (a kind of formula for visiting a pilgrimage site) at Patrick's Purgatory on Lough Derg in County Donegal, Ireland, which dates back to at least the twelfth century, is still as popular as ever and has changed little since the Middle Ages. The origin of the importance of this particular island in the middle of Lough Derg, not far from the Ulster boundary, lies in a tale about St. Patrick. Patrick is said to have been shown by Christ himself a cave (or dark pit) on the island, where, if believers spent twenty-four hours, they could be purged of all sins for the rest of their lives. The appeal of such a shortcut to salvation hardly needs amplification. The cave quickly became known as "Patrick's Purgatory."

The first documented account of the Lough Derg pilgrimage, and the one that brought it international reputation, came from the pen of an English Cistercian monk known as Henry of Saltney in about 1184. He has left us a long and graphic description of the experience in Patrick's Purgatory, and some have suggested that this may have been an inspiration for some of Giotto's paintings and perhaps also for Dante's *Inferno*. In subsequent centuries, the cave was sealed up, reopened, lost, refound, and finally closed permanently. The buildings on the island were completely destroyed in 1632 by a Protestant reformer; not long after, following an ecclesiastical power shift, they were built again. Since the late seventeenth century, the buildings have been maintained and added to. In spite of any and all disruptions, thousands of people continue to make the pilgrimage, attempting to validate or disprove for themselves the visions and hallucinations of others—no doubt hoping the Patrick legend may indeed be true.

The medieval pilgrimage to Station Island, as it is sometimes called, was never suppressed, although there were certainly attempts to do so. Today more than twenty-five thousand pilgrims participate in it each year. The traditional Lough Derg experience is three days with little food and less sleep. Participants stay up the whole first night and consume only black tea and dry bread; the obligatory prayer routine includes nearly two thousand Our Fathers, Hail Marys, and Creeds, in addition to attendance at Mass and other services. The outdoor rounds, or stations, are always performed barefoot, regardless of the weather.

Lough Derg is not a place for tourists, or indeed for any kind of visitor. One goes to Lough Derg as a pilgrim or not at all. The regimen sounds so demanding that we might be tempted to wonder whether it is on its way out—but not so, not at all. All ages of male and female youth and adults participate in the ancient pattern, and most seem to come away feeling energized and renewed in their physical as well as their spiritual lives, ready to resume their daily

life and work. During the summer months there are sometimes even
waiting lists for participants. The popularity of Lough Derg continues; it speaks to our own age just as it did to previous generations.

The Pilgrims' Way to Penrhys

It is not just pilgrimage centers that have reopened; in some cases,
the actual pilgrim trackways have been researched, reclaimed, and
reopened to walkers. One such example again comes from Wales.
In about 1993, almost by happenstance, a local historian was asked
if the medieval pilgrims' way from Llantarnam Abbey near
Cwmbran across the mountains into the Rhondda Valley to the
Marian shrine at Penrhys could be retraced. The answer was that
undoubtedly it could, and the project was undertaken by a local
interest group deeply committed to ecumenism. By identifying
other minor shrines in the area (which medieval pilgrims would
have been likely to visit), by studying local traditions and early
records of travelers, by examining field names and land boundaries,
by locating possible medieval bridges and fording places, and above
all by walking the land themselves, the team came up with a carefully researched and reasonably plausible route to the holy well and
medieval shrine of Our Lady of Penrhys.

Dr. Maddy Gray, of the University of Wales at Cardiff, pointed
out that uncovering the route and studying the archaeology of the
ancient path was only one aspect of the project. Equally important
was making available a route that could be walked by modern-day
pilgrims on a spiritual as well as a literal journey—a true pilgrimage. Dr. Gray told me that the conversations within the group while
walking together had brought greatly increased ecumenical understanding among the members and real healing in relationships. We
have here, then, an example of how the sharing of the journey
together is every bit as important a part of pilgrimage as is the
arrival at the site and whatever liturgies or patterns may be performed there. In 1995 the first formally organized Ecumenical
Pilgrimage from Llantarnam to Penrhys took place and has since
become an annual affair.[21]

Pilgrims' Way 1997

The year 1997 was an important year for pilgrimage, particularly in Britain and Ireland, where pilgrims were consciously drawing together traditions from both past and present. Fourteen hundred years before, in 597, two important events occurred: St. Columba died in his monastery on Iona, and St. Augustine arrived in what is now Canterbury, bringing the Roman understanding of the Catholic faith to England. The anniversary year was celebrated by a number of different pilgrimages, collectively called "The Pilgrims' Way." Walkers, cyclists, sailors, automotists, and any combination thereof followed in the steps of St. Augustine from Rome across the European mainland to Britain and Ireland. There pilgrims pursued a number of different routes, wending their ways across to Ireland or to Britain and journeying northward to Iona in Scotland, or traveling to Columba's homeland of Derry in Ireland. Thousands of people from different areas of different countries took part in this ecumenical venture. The intention was to take one more dedicated step toward ecumenical healing and to honor more fully the huge contributions of the Celtic Christians and that of Augustine of Canterbury. "Pilgrims' Way 1997" was not only an acknowledgment of an anniversary, it was a celebration of the experience of pilgrimage itself. People who participated unanimously agreed that they grew in their faith and were strengthened in their spiritual journeys: they were in touch with the Holy.

The Sacred Land Project

Britain and Ireland are both increasingly aware of their rich history and have large commitments to preserving their heritage. Countless thousands of citizens in each country are supporting these efforts. Both countries are also aware of how the spread of urbanization and secularism is eroding their priceless artifacts and treasures. No one denies the importance of tourism as an economic stimulant, but at the same time there is general recognition of the potential destruction of sacred sites resulting from overvisiting. How to balance this dichotomy is a major challenge facing both countries.

The Sacred Land Project, established in the United Kingdom as a millennium project (1997–2003), is one such response to this challenge. Its mission statement describes its aim as specifically to do the following:

> … reopen ancient pilgrimage routes, create new pilgrimage paths, assist in restoring old shrines and sacred sites and develop sacred gardens where humanity and nature can create an environment of spiritual significance…. [The Sacred Land Project] is designed to make us aware that everywhere is potentially sacred, and therefore to encourage us to walk gently, for we tread on sacred ground. Rooted in practical ecology, it also aspires to put a sense of the sacred back into our everyday lives…. It involves all major religions and conservation groups in the UK.[22]

Whether the Sacred Land Project and the many organizations like it have emerged in response to the resurgence of interest in pilgrimage today or whether interest in pilgrimage has grown because of their efforts is rather like the question of the chicken and the egg. What ultimately matters is not which came first but the realization that interest in sacred space, in journeying together, in reclaiming our heritage, and above all in seeking healing and reconciliation through fellowship and the shared journey are all parts of the spirituality of our own day. We can go together to Ireland, where the traditions of pilgrimage have continued essentially unbroken, be they local shrines or national ones; or we can go to Britain, where that which was once broken and destroyed is being resurrected. And we will still find the same thing: people searching for that which is holy. Together as one human family we can see the angels.

Secular Pilgrims

There is an additional and perhaps unexpected aspect of pilgrimage today that is observed by Simon Coleman and John Elsner in their *Pilgrimage Past and Present in the World Religions*:

A pilgrimage is not just a journey; it also involves the confrontation of travelers with rituals, holy objects and sacred architecture... moreover, pilgrimage is as much about returning home with the souvenirs and narratives of the pilgrim's adventure.[23]

[One] goal for the [modern] secular pilgrim is the museum. Many museums (at least in the Anglo-Saxon world, for instance the British Museum) are traditionally designed as if they were Greek temples, imbued with a classical rather than Christian sanctity, a holiness vested in the distant past. Like the relics in the treasury of a medieval cathedral, objects in a museum are enclosed within a series of frames which add to their sanctity. The glass museum case is a kind of reliquary.[24]

All the well-known pilgrimage sites today have comfortable, up-to-date visitor centers, usually offering some kind of museum or audiovisual exhibition about the site. Additionally they have a gift shop, rest rooms, and a coffee shop or cafeteria. Furthermore, as managers are quick to point out, it is income from the shops and restaurants, supplementing the admission fee (if there is one), that enables these pilgrimage sites to be adequately maintained and to remain open. Donations to support sacred places that were given by pilgrims of yesterday are now provided through the purchase of souvenirs (today's relics?) in the gift or coffee shop. The manager of the Cathedral Shop at one of the British cathedrals told me almost apologetically that the cathedral needs the income from the shop simply to make ends meet for its daily operation; thus the sale of books, tapes and CDs, note cards, jewelry, and other items is essential. Further, it is now recognized that people spend more time in the shops buying books and souvenirs or having a snack in the coffee shop than they do actually visiting the sites they have ostensibly come to see.

Given such facts, one must pause to rethink exactly why so many people "go on pilgrimage" today: where are they going and what do they expect to find? At major pilgrimage sites, strongly promoted by local and national agencies and tourist boards, the line between tourist and pilgrim becomes increasingly blurred. Perhaps it is fair to say that many, if not most, people approach the cathedral or shrine (or whatever holy place they may be visiting) as pilgrims, do their best to experience the richness of the place, pray together, and allow themselves to be touched by the spiritual ambience and to be open to the Holy. Then they switch hats to become *secular* pilgrims (that is, tourists) when they enter the shop and begin the purchase of postcards, gifts, and mementos. This scenario is repeated at each holy site visited, and thus typically people move back and forth between the two roles.

If we acknowledge that pilgrimage today, while still a search for the Holy, reflects the age in which we live, then the frequenting of museum and shrine shops is understandable and even to be expected. The purchases we make—postcards and souvenirs and such—are surely today's "pilgrim emblems." The consumer orientation of our modern age makes purchases relating to our pilgrimage journeys inevitable.

The Call of Pilgrimage Today

Countless Christian sacred places are reasserting themselves as places of life-giving peace, places that radiate a healing presence and a great sense of welcome to all. People come to ancient holy places for times of silence and prayer, for opportunities to draw closer to God. People are going on pilgrimage again, walking, cycling, and riding together, visiting ancient holy places, but seeing them in a new light, and finding in the pilgrimage experience renewed spiritual strength and nourishment. Worship at holy sites varies widely, ranging from a liturgical Renewal of Baptism Vows and Eucharist to free-form healing services, candlelight hymn sings, prayer vigils, liturgical dance, intercessions of all kinds, and many other creative expressions of prayer. What seems to be most significant is the sheer number of people, regardless of denominational or credal persuasion, who are participating in pilgrimages, visiting both ancient and modern holy places. Pilgrimage seems to speak to our generation with a magnetic voice.

Many people are taking a new look at the Communion of Saints, both as a teaching of the church and as an experience that informs our daily lives and gives them more meaning. Increasingly we recognize that we are not alone, that those who have gone before us as well as all who live on earth today are interconnected. Nor can we consider ourselves independent from those who in years to come will follow us. Accepting the concept of one human family that rejoices in diversity and embraces inclusivity is an important step toward wholeness and freedom.

Thus pilgrimage is once more assuming great importance for the people of God. Men and women who would never have expected to become twentieth-century pilgrims have found themselves drawn to ancient pilgrim places and have found in them not some esoteric devotional luxury, but a clarity and a vision that are necessary for truly human life and growth in holiness. People who do not consider themselves regular walkers or hikers are finding themselves walking ancient pilgrim pathways, "praying with their legs," as the saying goes. The pilgrim instinct is deep in the human heart, and the kind of pilgrimage we undertake, the kind of search for the Holy we engage in, reflects our own understanding of God and the world we live in.

But the specific kind of travel that we call "pilgrimage" remains travel with a particular focus: to seek that which is holy. We seek the Holy in order to grow more holy ourselves. This undergirding motive is the ultimate distinction between a pilgrimage and a tour, and the resultant growth in holiness is surely joy.

So, a pilgrimage is an outward journey reflecting an inward journey, a spiritual exercise that helps us to reach out toward God and deepens our relationship with God. Today's holistic pilgrimage reflecting a holistic theology will contain all the elements of a holistic life—prayers of praise, thanksgiving, penitence, and intercession; intellectual and emotional stimulation; spiritual growth and a strong sense of the importance of relationships—but above all, joy: joy in being alive, alive in the same sense that Irenaeus meant when he wrote, "The glory of God is the human person fully alive," or Teresa of Avila, when she said, "Joy is the flag that flies when the King is in residence." Any spiritual exercise has a better chance of bearing fruit in our lives if we are removed from our normal everyday responsibilities and distractions and can get away, and in this sense, pilgrimage today is more popular than ever. Soulfarers are on the go.

When T. S. Eliot wrote *Four Quartets,* he addressed himself specifically to visitors to ancient holy places and making contact with the Communion of Saints:

If you came this way,
Taking any route, starting from anywhere,
At any time or at any season,
It would always be the same: you would have to put off
Sense and notion. You are not here to verify,
Instruct yourself, or inform curiosity
Or to carry report. You are here to kneel
Where prayer has been valid. And prayer is more
Than an order of words, the conscious occupation
Of the praying mind, or the sound of voice praying.
And what the dead had no speech for, when living,
They can tell you, being dead: the communication
Of the dead is tongued with fire beyond the language of
    the living.[25]

Part Two

Calanais

IONA • KILMARTIN

SCOTLAND

• Lindisfarne

•WHITHORN

Lough Derg

•MAUGHOLD

•CROAGH PATRICK
• Knock

ISLE OF MAN

KELLS • •Newgrange
KILDARE •

• ST WINEFRIDE'S WELL
• Pennant Melangell
•LLŶN PENNISULA

•THE BURREN

Bardsey
Island •

IRELAND

WALES

Walsingham •

• TOBAR NA MULT
•DINGLE PENINSULA

ENGLAND

Skellig Michael •

• NEVERN
Ramsey Island • •ST. DAVID'S

• PATRISIO

• Penrhys

Canterbury •

MAJOR PILGRIMAGE SITES MENTIONED IN THE TEXT

A Pilgrimage Journal

WITHOUT SOME DESCRIPTION, the invitation to "come and see" would have little meaning for fellow soulfarers who might like to visit some of the sacred holy places in the Celtic world. The ones described in the pages that follow are only to be "teasers," to introduce people to the riches of our Celtic heritage and to encourage people to visit such sites—and the thousands of others—on their own. All these sites can be located on the accompanying map.

Scores of organized pilgrimage programs to the Celtic countries are offered each season. Many of them are listed in the quarterly newsletter published by Anamchairde Network, Inc. Information can be obtained from

Anamchairde Network, Inc.
2374 Madison Road
Cincinnati, OH 45208
513-321-6781 (ph); 513-321-6758 (fax)
e-mail: MacAoidh@eos.net

For those who may wish to explore some of these holy places themselves, relevant addresses, contacts, and map references are included in the Appendix.

Additional information, including certain maps, may be obtained free of charge from the major Tourist Information Centers, whose addresses are also listed in the Appendix.

Some pilgrimage sites in

Ireland

The Unfinished Cross at Kells

Market Cross at Kells

St. Columba's Oratory, Kells

Unless otherwise noted, all photos by Cintra Pemberton.

Kells

THE SMALL TOWN OF KELLS, population about 3500, is deeply proud of its history and in recent years has made concerted effort to preserve its ancient monuments, particularly its ecclesiastical foundations. These include what is left of the Columban monastery, four fine high crosses, a round tower, and a ninth-century stone oratory known as Colmcille's (Columba's) house. Part of the town's appreciation of its own past has been the return to its original Irish name, Ceanannus Mór, which was corrupted by the Anglo-Normans into "Kells." It is now certain that this Ceanannus has a prehistoric past, having begun as a *dún* settlement or early fort. Its location where three ancient trackways intersect assured its continued existence. These same three roads still cut through Kells today as paved highways: the N3, the N52, and the secondary highway R163.

Scholars disagree about the date of the original establishment of Kells. Some think it was founded by monks from Iona fleeing the Viking raids in the early ninth century, two hundred years after Colmcille's death. Others present a convincing case for acknowledging the long-standing tradition (not without some factual basis) that Colmcille himself founded it in the middle of the sixth century, in the same period as his undisputed foundations at Durrow and Derry. Either way, what cannot be argued is that modern Ceanannus grew out of a typical Celtic monastic foundation.

Throughout the Middle Ages and continuing to today, the layout of the town is distinctly related to its early monastic foundation. The settlement was located at the top of a hill, surrounded by a circular enclosure, a typical Celtic feature. The remains of the circular enclosure can still be seen in the outline of the city streets, especially when viewed from the air or looked at on a map. The present Church of Ireland St. Columba's Church, with its magnificent carved high crosses and its round tower, undisputedly built on top of very early foundations, is clearly situated within that ancient enclosure.

Early sources refer to the monastery at Kells as "the splendor of Ireland," and by the tenth century, Kells had replaced Iona as the head of all the Columban foundations in Ireland. By this time, Kells monastery was famous for its school of stone carving (the high crosses still bear witness to this), for its artists in metal working (such as the Kells Crozier, with splendid bronze and silver ornamental work that came from the ninth through eleventh centuries), and for its scriptorium, which produced the *Cathach* (or Psalter) of Columba and probably completed the magnificent Book of Kells which was begun on Iona.

The Cathach, dated to the late sixth or earth seventh century, may well have been executed by Columba himself. Incomplete as a psalter and badly damaged, it nevertheless has beautifully illuminated capital letters introducing each psalm and is one of the oldest surviving examples of Irish manuscript. It is currently in the care of the Royal Irish Academy in Dublin.

Until January 1997, the great Market Cross of Kells stood at the near-center of the town, presenting a striking witness to the Christian message in the marketplace. The Market Cross is not as tall as many of the other high crosses in Ireland, but its carvings are of an extremely high caliber. At the center on one face is the Crucifixion, with two Roman soldiers at the foot of the cross, one of whom is piercing the side of Christ with a lance. Carvings on the upright panels of the cross are nearly all biblical scenes, including Adam and Eve in the Garden, Abraham's Sacrifice of Isaac from the Old Testament, and the Arrest of Christ. It was probably built in the middle of the ninth century and may originally have been a boundary marker indicating the outermost edge of the monastic city. The cross has had a disturbed history and over its eleven centuries of life has sustained many insults and injuries. Besides its damaged surfaces and missing cap, it was allegedly used as a gallows during the riots and uprisings of the eighteenth century. Finally, in 1996 it was struck by a bus turning at the busy crossroads. Ireland's Office of Public Works then removed the cross from its vulnerable position and took it off to safety, where it is being cleaned and repaired for re-erection, but at this point no one quite seems to know where that will be. Practically speaking, the huge cross in the center of town at an extremely busy crossroads was very much in the way. For many people to whom it was an important witness to the Christian faith, though, its presence will be sorely missed if it is not returned to its original place.

Some years ago the Reverend William Ritchie, Rector of the Anglican St. Columba's Church of Ireland in Kells put together a pilgrims' walk for the people of his parish, using the magnificent historic features of Kells as a meditative teaching technique. He has shared this same walk with my pilgrims each time we have visited Kells, and with his permission, I have included some excerpts from his meditations and offer here his basic outline.

The walk begins at the spot where the Market Cross used to stand. People gather wherever they can around the sides of parked automobiles, straining to hear over the noise of traffic. Although the cross is not there anymore, the pilgrimage walk still begins in the marketplace where cross the crowded ways of life in Kells.

As Canon Ritchie begins the pilgrimage walk, we pray especially for the town of Kells and all urban areas, for the homeless and hungry, for the hurried and harried, and for all the problems afflicting our inner cities. *Lord, have mercy…*

The walk then moves up the hill, passes the church, and continues outside the ancient monastic boundary to Colmcille's House. It would be lovely to think that Colmcille's House had indeed been a house of St. Colmcille himself, but archaeology says flatly not so; the building simply is not old enough. It is, however, according to most scholars today, very likely the oldest *damhlaig* or stone house in Ireland, and it was probably erected by the monks fleeing from Iona in 809 C.E. or thereabouts, perhaps built to serve as an oratory or residence. Another suggestion is that the fleeing monks may have built it as a tomb-shrine to house St. Colmcille's relics. Still another possibility is that it might have been a scriptorium, a place for the copying of manuscripts, but being entirely of stone with only two small apertures for light, it would have been very dark and damp (as it still is) and a difficult place for such fine work. A small hole in the stone ceiling opens onto an upper level, or attic, which today is reached by a long ladder. Those who squeeze through that tiny hole find themselves looking at a row of three very small chambers, not one of which is tall enough to stand up in. One hypothesis is that this might have been a sleeping area, but archaeologist Peter Harbison suggests it was more likely built for pragmatic and structural reasons: it prevented the roof from collapsing.[26]

A strong local tradition suggests that an underground passageway once connected Colmcille's House and the church some distance away within the enclosure, but if so, it has been filled in and there is no trace of it now. It is fun to speculate, though: did the residents of either the monastery or the stone house have secret assignations by night that required a hidden passageway? Or was it just to go from building to building with protection from the rain? Who knows?

Like the Market Cross, Colmcille's House has had its share of woes. At some point the ground was removed from the foundations of the south and east walls and the original doorway in the west wall was blocked up. We enter now through a new door in the south wall at what would have been at basement level, about five or six feet below the original floor. At some later time, a fireplace was built into the west wall. By the nineteenth century, the building was in such poor state that it was home for a poverty-stricken family who, so the story goes, eked out their living by stealing sheep. The building is now in the safe care of the Office of Public Works.

Before leaving Colmcille's House, the pilgrimage group prays together for all saints and pilgrims who follow in the footsteps of St. Colmcille. Prayers are said for those whose lives are in darkness, or poverty, or squalor, and for those whose lives have been forced into unwanted directions because of economic pressure. *Lord, have mercy...*

We next cross the street and walk through the gate into the churchyard, into the ancient monastic enclosure and over to the round tower. These round towers are not totally unique to Ireland—there is one at Peel on the Isle of Man and there are two in east Scotland—but they are a common feature of the landscape throughout Ireland. In addition to the sixty-five towers standing complete or nearly so, the rubble at twenty-five other sites indicates the existence of a tower in days past. The Irish name for these towers is *cloigtheach*, meaning "bell house," and that is probably why they originally were built, so the monks could sound their four-sided cast bronze or iron bells from the top and call the people to prayer. There are several of these Celtic monks' bells to be seen in the National Museum in Dublin, one of which supposedly belonged to St. Patrick.

The round tower at Kells is missing its original conical top, but the five windows at the top of the tower, looking out at the five main roadways into Kells, are still there, as well as several small windows lower down that were inserted to provide light. The towers are usually about one hundred feet high, with six or seven stories inside connected either by steps or ladders. Because in times of attack the monks used to hide themselves as well as the monastery valuables inside these towers, the doorways were usually twelve to fifteen feet off the ground and accessible only by a ladder. Such a ladder could be pulled up when all the monks were safely inside. At Kells the ground has been built up on the side of the tower where the doorway is so that the door way is not quite as high as it was originally, but it is still out of reach for most people.

On one of my pilgrimage visits to Kells a few years ago, while we were standing outside the tower and looking at it, an athletic young Swiss gentleman clad in black motorcycle leathers vaulted himself up to the doorway and disappeared inside. After a few minutes the vicar called to him, "What do you see?" His tousled blond head appeared in a window shortly after, and he called down, "Nosseeng boot peejon sheet." We asked no further questions.

When we pilgrims gather for prayer around the base of the round tower, we remember all those whose work is in construction. Prayers are offered for all those in the service industries who protect us in so many ways, for all who reach for the sky in order to achieve new vision, for experimenters and inventors, and for those who can look out in all directions and thus bring insight and vision to others. *Lord, have mercy…*

The next stop is the South Cross, known also as the Cross of Patrick and Columba, or, alternatively, the Cross of Kells. This is a splendid monument, the least damaged of all the Kells crosses and filled with wonderfully ornate carvings on all four sides. An inscription on the east side of the cross reads PATRICII ET COLUMBAE CRUX, which is why it is called the Cross of Patrick and Columba. This cross is eleven feet high and probably dates to the ninth century. The carvings, nearly all illustrations taken from Scripture and strongly reminiscent of the drawings in the Book of Kells, are quite wonderful to behold. Among the depictions are Daniel in the Lions' Den, Abraham's Sacrifice of Isaac, David with his harp, Paul and Antony in the Desert, the Crucifixion, and Christ in Majesty surrounded by the symbols of the Four Evangelists. Tucked in all the otherwise unoccupied spaces are abstract designs and angels. It is a mind-boggling piece of sculpture that one can pray in front of for a long time. Presumably this is why the great high crosses were erected in the first place: to serve as places of prayer and instruction. Around this cross we pray for all sculptors, artists, and musicians, for all who create beauty, and for all who share and appreciate beauty. *Lord, have mercy…*

Of the other crosses at Kells, perhaps the most unusual one is the East or Unfinished Cross outside the south wall of the church. It is immediately obvious where the sculptor intended to carve the different panels, but only the Crucifixion scene in the center of the east face is fairly complete. Here Christ on the Cross is depicted standing fully erect with his arms outstretched, and his hands are unusually large. This fairly common feature of the Irish crosses is often interpreted as the hands of Christ being large with blessing. It is intriguing to study this cross carefully simply because it *is* incomplete. Prayers here are for ourselves, for all of us, too, are incomplete; we pray for the strength and courage and grace to grow daily more and more into the image and likeness of God. *Lord, have mercy…*

Then, inside the church, we see the great Book of Kells. The original is in Trinity College Library in Dublin, but the Anglican church in Kells has not only a fine exhibit on it but also an excellent facsimile edition. In some ways, seeing this facsimile is even more interesting and rewarding than seeing the actual book. Though viewing the original book at Trinity College does take one's breath away, visitors can see only whichever page happens to be open that day. The book is encased in extremely thick protective glass in a room with very dim light, and visitors are part of a hurried crush of other people in a steadily moving line. Here at the Kells visitors can turn all the pages one by one and see the brilliant designs, all the incredibly minute creations—birds, butterflies, dogs, cats, mice, serpents, leaves, vines, and flowers and a bewildering assortment of wiggles, squiggles, and interlace. Here can be seen the softly muted colors, the beautiful Irish majuscule script—in short, the majestic sweep of the whole book.

The magnificent Book of Kells is surely Ireland's greatest artistic treasure. Its splendidly decorated pages represent not only the high point of Celtic artistic achievement, but also some of the finest artwork ever executed by humans. The endless variety of spirals, whorls, symbols, foliage, animals, and humans continues to fascinate artists; for those of us who may not be artists, simply admiring the beauty of each page and looking at the intricacies in the designs can occupy us for hours. When I first saw the Book of Kells at Trinity College I was impressed with the extensive exhibits relating to the book. Various panels explain the religious symbolism, the kinds of instruments that were used, and where the dyes and pigments came from. Huge backlit panels show individual pages enlarged many times so that the incredible detail in the artwork can be appreciated. The makers of the Book of Kells were not without their own humor; on one page in particular I was delighted to find two mice tugging at the sacred communion Host, while a watchful cat hovers nearby.

Kells does not seem to have been a popular pilgrimage site, either in the Celtic period (if the foundation indeed was made during the sixth century), or during the Middle Ages. If St. Colmcille's relics were brought there in the ninth century, though, it would be most unusual for those relics not to have attracted hundreds of pilgrims. We simply do not know.

Today we went to Kells, and I admit that I was looking forward to it very much. There is fascinating history at Kells, much of it connected with the Celtic period. Did Columba—or Colmcille as they call him in Ireland—really found the monastery here? Was the great Book of Kells actually put together here? Were there really monastic treasures stored or hidden in the great bell tower? We'll probably never know, but for me the spirit of Columba is certainly there.

Most of the rest of the group was either in the little bookshop "stimulating the economy" or in the church looking at the splendid facsimile of the Book of Kells. The Rector had taken it out of its case so that people could see the different pages, but I was more interested in being outside in the churchyard and looking at the stone crosses, the Unfinished Cross in particular. That one seems very like my own life.

I have tried to put Christ and the Cross at the center of my being for many years now, but for certain I'm no finished product yet. Parts of the Unfinished Cross are beautifully carved, and I will readily admit that parts of my life have been wonderfully shaped and are satisfying—I suppose beautiful, too—but so many other parts of my life seem to be totally blank, like parts of that cross—waiting waiting waiting. To have to wait is something very difficult for me. When I want something, I tend to want it right now. (Lord, give me patience, but I want it right now...) Much has been written about "delay of gratification" and how important it is, but I recognize within myself much more restlessness and impatience than willingness to wait. Perhaps that's partly why the Unfinished Cross speaks to me so eloquently.

The Unfinished Cross stands in the churchyard in a grassy place among other graves and tombstones, but in no way does it feel like a tomb or death-stone. It feels more like a life-stone. I stood there and looked at it for a long time. Those huge hands and outstretched arms of Christ on the cross feel like an invitation, an invitation to love and to stretch and to grow. The hands remind me of the crucifix in our chapel at home, where Christ's hands there are also outstretched and overly large. They are invitation, too—invitation and blessing. I think part of the message in those hands is Christ's reassurance and acceptance of us in love, exactly as we are each day—but inviting us to be open to the person we will one day become.

I suppose it's fair to say that all of us are unfinished. Even the Crucifixion, in one sense, is unfinished, in that Christ's suffering has not ended. The church is unfinished, or at least I hope it is. Surely the Body of Christ has more growing to do, not so much in numbers as in attitude. Surely the church needs to be more embracing and including of all God's children. Perhaps even the earth itself is unfinished, for surely it is constantly evolving.

It's wonderful to stand in front of that Unfinished Cross and think about God as the Great Sculptor; I know it is God who, in spite of my impatience, is carving away at me, day in and day out, chipping away here, chipping away there, working toward something more beautiful than the Me I am today. I can trust and follow a God whose love for me is so great that I need never fear standing still. God's love is always there, ready to help me to grow and change.

I want always to be that way—constantly evolving. I want to continue to grow, to be more patient in waiting, and there is much more I'd like to do with my life in order to become more Christlike. If I could ask God to carve one of my own unfinished areas in a specific way, like the blank panels on the cross, I'd like it to be of the Feeding the Five Thousand. Not a day goes by, not ever, that I do not walk along the streets near home and see the suffering of hunger and homelessness there—and I feel terribly helpless. My very feelings of helplessness and impotence are surely part of my recognizing my unfinished state. "Feed my sheep," Christ says. There is so much to be done by and for us all. May I learn how to do more. And may I never forget those empty panels on that cross. As the hymn says, Take my life and let it be... consecrated Lord to thee...

Kildare

KILDARE IS A TYPICAL medium-sized Irish town, all a-hustle and bustle, like dozens of other Irish market towns. Yet Kildare is definitely unique, having a very long history linked with the name of Brigid. St. Brigid's statue is at the center of the town, and just a little behind her, at the top of a hill, is St. Brigid's Cathedral. Behind that, St. Brigid's round tower looks down over all.

St. Brigid's Cathedral, belonging to the Church of Ireland (Anglican), was originally built in the twelfth century, on the site of

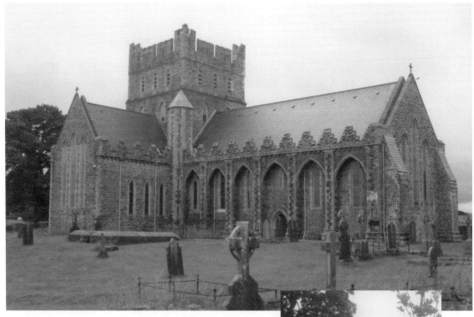

St. Brigid's Cathedral, Kildare

St. Brigid's Celtic Cross, Kildare

St. Brigid's Holy Well, Kildare

a much earlier monastic foundation. Like most other Norman cathedrals, St. Brigid's was added to and altered over the centuries, but today it remains very much as it was at the close of the fourteenth century. Its severe gray stone tower topped with battlements and crenellations dominates the town by its superior location. High walls surround the cathedral close; entrance is gained through iron gates that are locked at the end of each day. Within the close is a blessed sense of quietness, and scattered about are the usual aging limestone grave markers. Everything is neat and well tended. During the day visitors are free to wander around the cathedral grounds as well as to enter the cathedral itself.

In the close, northwest of the cathedral building, are the remains of Brigid's Fire House, where Brigid and her sisters are said to have at all times tended a living flame symbolizing the never-ending light of Christ. Today the ancient Fire House is simply three low stone walls marking a rectangular open space in the ground, the fire having been intentionally extinguished during the Reformation, and, equally intentionally, never relit on cathedral property.

A few feet away stands the tall round tower, probably from the tenth century, which is almost the only one today that is open to the public and climbable. The view of Kildare from the top is spectacular, and the town's original circular enclosure dating from the Celtic period is quite evident. Not far from the south door of the cathedral is an unadorned, much-weathered Celtic cross, which may date from the tenth century but is more likely from the late thirteenth century. Its top part is missing, most likely broken off during the Cromwellian era. A great deal of history thus lies within the cathedral close walls.

From its beginnings as a sixth-century Celtic monastic foundation through the Middle Ages when church and cathedral dominated all aspects of people's lives, St. Brigid's Cathedral stood at the heart of life in Kildare. This is not so today. The throb of daily life now is in the market square and surrounding areas, outside the cathedral precincts.

After a long period of depression during the seventeenth and eighteenth centuries, Kildare began again to grow in size and prominence early in this century with the opening of the Irish

National Stud, where some of the finest racehorses in the world are bred, and the adjacent Japanese Gardens. At that time a gray limestone statue of Brigid in a style connoting Victorian piety was erected in the market square. Brigid's posture is unassuming, her eyes are downcast, and her hands are folded in prayer. The statue is positioned at the busiest crossroads in Kildare, in the shadow of the cathedral, and not far from one side is a pub puckishly called "The Vatican." Brigid is depicted as standing in the midst of Christ's people, not in a defiant or arrogant way, not "making a statement," not even causing any particular attention. She seems quite content to represent the past and remain oblivious to the present.

St. Brigid's Roman Catholic Church, only a few hundred yards away, radiates an architectural and ecclesiastical joy. Originally built in 1833 when the anti-Catholic laws in Ireland were still in force, it was enlarged and rebuilt in 1975 incorporating some of the new architectural ideas following Vatican II. The altar is in the center of the church surrounded by seating on three sides, and the shape of the Brigid's Cross is a prominent architectural feature throughout, and is the shape of the altar itself. In the Blessed Sacrament Chapel is a modern stained glass window portraying a modern Brigid, a woman for today. The whole church is wonderfully spacious, airy, light-and above all, welcoming. The theme of welcome is proclaimed on the main doors where the handles are a pair of bronze hands extended outward. Visitors cannot even open the door to get into the church without taking hold of one of those welcoming hands.

Brigid

Not many documentable facts about St. Brigid of Kildare are reliable; a few scholars doubt she even existed at all. Most, though, accept the premise of a historical Brigid even while acknowledging that the little we do know is heavily overlaid with imaginative medieval hagiographies and legends. Scholars also admit real confusion between the historical Brigid and the pagan goddess Brig, who was associated with the Celtic festival of Imbolc, the time when lambs were born and ewes began to lactate.

Brigid is said to have been born near Kildare about 453 C.E., just a few years before the death of Patrick, of a slave woman and a pagan chieftain named Dubhtach. Some say Brigid was baptized by Patrick himself. It is generally acknowledged that she was an unusually bright child and from a very early age given to acts of generosity and charity. She entered the monastic life before she was twenty, and soon she had a following of other young women.

Brigid's great monastic foundation was at Kildare: *Cill Dara* in Irish, meaning the "Church of the Oak Tree." It can safely be assumed that her abbey, if that is the right word, was typical of the Celtic monasteries of the period; that is, it was a circular settlement consisting of a small church surrounded by simple wattle-and-daub huts. In time the monastery became a double monastery housing both women and men, with Brigid as head of both. Cogitosus, who wrote the *Life of Saint Brigid* during the seventh century and apparently was a monk in this double monastery, has given us a description of what must have been an extraordinary church:

> The bodies of that glorious pair, the Bishop Conláeth and this holy virgin Brigid, lie right and left of the ornamented altar, placed in shrines decorated with a variegation of gold silver, gems and precious stones, with gold and silver crowns hanging above them...

> And so, in one great basilica, a large number of people... offers prayers with a single spirit to the almighty Lord.[27]

Cogitosus's description, even allowing generously for exaggeration, is impressive, and the idea of a large number of people offering prayers with a single spirit is surely a goal of the church today.

The statue of Brigid in Kildare town, depicting Brigid in an attitude of subservient reticence, presents a sharp contrast to what we know of the real Brigid. The historic woman was a dynamic, energetic, and unflagging leader of the church. Brigid knew her worth, she exercised communal guidance, she respected the dignity of every human being, and she was known throughout Ireland for her witness to the mission and ministry of Jesus Christ. She was a woman who today serves as a role model for all women.

The cult of Brigid was extremely widespread; in Ireland she ranks with Patrick and Columba as one of the three greatest of the Irish saints. Her name is variously spelled as Brigit, Bridget, or Bride (and in Wales she is Ffraid), and church dedications to Brigid using any one of these names are widespread. There are at least nineteen in England and as many in Wales. St. Bride's Bay off the Pembrokeshire coast of Wales emphasizes the strong Irish-Welsh connection in the spread of Christianity. There are even a few Brigid churches on the European mainland, in Scandinavia, France, Belgium, and Portugal.

Brigidine Sisters

For my pilgrimage groups, the visit to Kildare is greatly enhanced by our time spent with the Roman Catholic Sisters of the Restoration of the Ancient Order of Brigid. Established in 1807 in Ireland, they now have foundations all over the world. A small group of sisters who returned to Kildare in 1992 have developed a unique ministry. Continuing to look to Brigid as mentor and guide, as well as for inspiration, they recognize that she is an important symbol for women, as relevant today as she was in the sixth century. The sisters in Kildare, along with their friends in the association Cáirde Bhride, work toward the full equality of women and men in the church and in society today and have a strong commitment to promote peace, justice, and reconciliation. They greatly value their Celtic heritage and open their house to people who wish to learn more about Celtic spirituality and who share their ideals. They offer spiritual direction and counseling, lead small discussion groups, and offer generous hospitality to visiting pilgrims. Says Sister Mary, "We want to be a center where all may experience community so that the spirit of Brigid may find appropriate expression in our time." Sister Mary is a woman of dedication and energy; she is following a vision of ecumenical unity and is quick to offer herself as a guide to the world of Brigid. When we visit the Brigidine Sisters in Kildare, we are welcomed as pilgrims. We pray together in their little oratory, we are served tea with jam and scones, and as we leave, we are each given a little hand-woven Brigid's Cross. Thus we are offered Irish hospitality at its best.

My favorite part of Kildare is neither the cathedral nor the Roman Catholic church nor the town itself, but rather St. Brigid's holy well. The Brigidine sisters tend the well area carefully; the grass is mowed regularly, a number of young trees have been planted recently, and garden flowers bloom all along the stream. It's just like a little park, a much-loved park.

Just before I crossed the bridge to enter it, I read a small sign saying

Welcome to the Well.
Wells are sacred places
where people gather to pray, to reflect, to find peace.
Please respect this sacred place.

While I stood there reading the sign and thinking about sacred places, a bird began to chitter at me, and I gradually became aware of the brooksong as well as the birdsong. That certainly put me in the right frame of mind. I dropped some coins in the donation box and said a prayer for all pilgrims and for healing of our unhappy divisions within the church. I wasn't in a hurry and walked quite slowly, taking time to notice a young oak tree that had been planted as recently as 1995.

When I saw two bicycles leaning against the fence, I was selfishly dismayed not to have the place all to myself, since I had come specifically to take pictures. However, I saw that my fellow visitors were two young girls, perhaps eleven or twelve. They were sitting quietly on the step, as well-behaved as anyone could hope. I also saw they had a small towel, so they had dipped in the water of the well. They noticed my camera and asked me if I wanted them to leave. I was so astonished at their thoughtfulness, I didn't know how to answer. While I hesitated, they hopped up and said, "We'll sit over there," meaning a secluded bench behind some bushes where they would not interfere with my picture taking. I cannot think of anything that could have impressed me more deeply with the holiness of that place and with the very "infectiousness" of holiness itself. What a privilege to meet those youngsters, who knew what a holy place they had in their midst, and who so obviously appreciated it. They did not stay much longer, but soon waved a cheery goodbye to me and took off on their bicycles.

Before beginning to take pictures, I sat down beside the water, took off my glasses, and washed my face three times, in the Name of the Trinity, as I always do at a holy well. I was so grateful for the silence and solitude that I put my camera aside and looked, really looked, at the flowers and trees all around, especially at the young oak tree that had been planted by Thomas Berry. I realized I was surrounded by investments in the future. The two young girls were like the young oak tree, spiritually planted in an area filled with peace and love. May they grow strong in their faith even as the oak tree grows.

As I took the time to look about, I realized there were a number of newly planted trees, all with sturdy branches pointing to God's sky. It reminded me of ministry and my own involvement in ministry. I can try to witness to the love of God, I can plant ideas, I can offer encouragement, share insights, and work at building relationships, but the real results of my ministry will be like those trees. The real fruit will not come until long after my own lifetime. But rooted and grounded in love and pointing to the sky, like the young trees, the maturation will come.

I thought about the different pilgrim groups I have brought to this holy place in the past. We always come with Sister Mary or Sister Rita or both of them (they are siblings as well as religious sisters), plus a few of their friends, and we pray together for all kinds of healing and reconciliation—those wonderful Catholics always so welcoming to us non-Catholics. Surely that's what the church's ministry is all about—reaching out in love and hospitality and eating and praying together. Typically we end the time doing a simple circle dance around the upper well. The circle moving together is symbolic of the church moving as one, and at least at those times, we are that church, all growing and maturing together. Praise God.

The Dingle Peninsula

IT WOULD BE HARD to find another place in Ireland more richly endowed with both history and scenery—to say nothing of gracious, hospitable people—than the Dingle Peninsula. Corca Dhuibhne, as it is called in Irish, has been inhabited by humans since very early times. Shell middens testify to residents during the Mesolithic Period (6000 B.C.E.), and countless standing stones, dolmens, tombs and graves date back to the Neolithic Period (5000–4000 B.C.E.).

Thus, the Dingle is an archaeologist's paradise—or headache, as the case may be, given the superabundance of artifacts and the impossibility of studying them all. The official archaeological reference guide to the Dingle section of County Kerry alone is an enormous fat tome, far too heavy to carry in a backpack for a day's outing. Simply looking at a map of the national monuments in state care is daunting, and such a map does not even show the literally hundreds of other ancient sites not under the protection of the Office of Public Works.

Teampull Manchán

My pilgrimage groups typically begin a day on the Peninsula at Teampull Manchán, meaning the "church (or oratory) of the little monk." Our first stop is a farmyard, and we trudge along a *bohereen* (a very narrow farm track) to a gate in the fuchsia hedgerow and climb a gently rising green hill to the oratory. Sitting on the ledge just outside the ruined oratory, we can rest and reflect in peaceful quiet before beginning our morning prayers together. Afterwards we can wander around with only sheep and each other for company and see, besides the oratory itself, several cross-inscribed stones. One in particular is marked with *ogham*, an early form of writing unique to the Irish. The whole oratory region is on a reasonably level "shelf" on the slope, roughly circular in shape. Surrounding this flattish area are the vestiges of a stone wall, enclosing an area

Coast of the Dingle Peninsula

Kilcolman, Dingle Peninsula

Kilmalkedar Church, Dingle Peninsula

just large enough to have enabled the resident saint to till the soil and raise a few crops.

When the weather is clear, miles away on our right we can see the rocky points of Skellig Michael emerging from the sea. Straight ahead of us is the shimmer of the sea in Dingle Harbor, and in the sky way off to our left is the dominating peak of Mount Brandon. Thus spread before us is a breathtaking panorama, essentially unchanged since the small settlement was first inhabited, however many centuries ago. It is interesting to note that had the Celtic period oratory been situated even a few feet lower on the hill, the Skellig rocks would have been impossible to see. St. Manchán must have selected this exact site so that it could serve as a visual link between two extremely important pilgrimages sites: Skellig Michael in one direction and Mount Brandon in the other. Many of the characteristics of Celtic spirituality seem to converge on this one point: respect for the beauty of God's world, the love of solitude in isolated settings, and dedication to pilgrimage.

Skellig Michael

Nowhere is the mystique of the islands more prevalent than on Skellig Michael, about nine miles offshore. This dramatic rock outcrop rising straight above the waves of the Atlantic has lured men and women from very early times. To this day, its siren call remains loud and clear, but the site is still difficult to get to. Weather, waves and tides might keep the would-be visitor waiting for days, or even weeks, before a crossing can be made safely.

Tradition tells us that Skellig Michael was founded as a Celtic monastery in the sixth century by a monk named St. Finan, but there is no recorded history relating to his monastery until 823, when the death of some monks is mentioned. Few scholars, however, question the existence of a settlement on Skellig Michael from a much earlier date. Monks continued to live on the inhospitable rocky island in small beehive-shaped huts some 550 feet above the sea until the twelfth or thirteenth century.[28]

Those wanting to visit Skellig Michael must take a boat from the end of the Iveragh Peninsula, south of the Dingle Peninsula, and hope for good weather. The crossing, often extremely rough, takes a little more than three hours, and landing on the island—there is no quay as such—requires a certain athletic agility. Then follows a steep climb upwards of more than four hundred stone steps, partly laid and partly hewn from the bedrock, built by those monks so many centuries ago. There are no handrails, and at times the drop-off on one side or the other is extreme. Those who have difficulty with heights or any kind of vertigo should never attempt this climb.

Entering the monastic area is like stepping back a thousand years. The actual beehive cells of those ancient monks, the tiny oratory, a hermit hut some distance away, the cemetery, and the garden plot are still there, maintained by the Office of Public Works in as near as possible their original state. Sensitive and careful preservation has made this amazing place one of the most unique of its kind anywhere in the ancient world. Archaeologists, historians, and naturalists, as well as laypeople, continue to be fascinated with this remote island. In recent years, in order to protect this fragile environment, visitors have been limited to a strict daily quota.

The whole area exudes an ambiance of prayer and holiness—at least when the weather is gentle. However, when Atlantic gales whip the sea into crashing waves that pound against the rock, sending spray hundreds of feet into the air, and when gale- or hurricane-force winds howl and rage around this totally unprotected spot, we might perhaps feel more surrounded by the devil than by God. A visit only makes us appreciate more than ever the tremendous faith our monastic forbears must have had to inhabit such a place.

Much has been written about Skellig Michael and its companion island, the Little Skellig. Because of the difficulty of accessibility, a fine visitor center has been built on the mainland. Here one can catch the flavor of the Skelligs through an excellent audiovisual presentation, see models of the monastic settlement, study the indigenous bird life, experience the richness of the sea, and learn about the hard but dedicated lives led by Skellig's lighthouse keepers for more than a hundred years. A recent book by Geoffrey Moorhouse, *Sun Dancing*,[29] combines historical fiction about the island, incorporating all the accepted legends and traditions with historical facts. It is interesting, informative, and accurate, and for those who cannot make it to either the island or the visitor center, the book provides a fine substitute.

Kilcolman

A pilgrimage to the Dingle Peninsula would be incomplete without a visit to Maumanorig, where a chunky boulder is found in the middle of a circular enclosure. Inscribed on this so firmly embedded boulder is a four-equal-armed cross made of arcs, undoubtedly by use of a compass. On the left edge of the stone and continuing across the top is an inscription in ogham that reads ANM COLMAN AILITHIR ([pray for] the soul of Colmán the pilgrim). This enclosure may have been a major starting point for pilgrims landing in nearby Ventry Harbor, who perhaps had crossed over from Skellig Michael and who were beginning a pilgrimage to the top of Mount Brandon. The presence of this cross of arcs at Kilcolman and at numerous other places along the Pilgrims' (or Saints') Road leads archaeologist Peter Harbison to believe it was a kind of logo marking the pilgrimage route.

Today Kilcolman is an isolated island in the middle of a hay field, surrounded by an ancient low stone wall, its location no doubt causing considerable inconvenience to the farmer who must plow around it. We who visit must cross the farmer's field, clamber over the stone wall, and wend our way through a maze of gorse bushes to find the stone. Once there, though, we find the clarity of the incised cross itself, often magnificently lit by the midday summer sun, is permanently etched into our memory. The sea twinkles on the horizon not so very far away, and it is easy to picture scores of pilgrims, leaning on their trusty staffs, trudging up to Kilcolman, where they could look forward to a hot meal and lodging before heading on toward Mount Brandon. Once at Kilcolman, they certainly would have prayed not only for the soul of Colmán the Pilgrim, but for all pilgrims. Today we do the same.

Gallarus Oratory

From Kilcolman the pilgrims would have continued several miles—at least a day's walk—crossing a low pass between two higher hills and following a route in a long sweeping curve along the slopes of Leataoibh Meanach. About a quarter mile off the Saints' Road is Gallarus Oratory, one of the most perfectly preserved buildings of this type from the early Middle Ages. It is tempting to assign it to the sixth or seventh century, but most experts agree it is more likely from the ninth or tenth century. So perfectly constructed is it, carefully corbelled from a rectangular base into an upturned boat shape, without any use of mortar whatsoever, that its age is of less interest than its graceful structure and architecture. While its basic design is not unique (there are a number of examples of similar "Gallarus type" oratories on the Dingle), all except Gallarus have collapsed inward and are in ruins, as is the one at St. Manchán. Gallarus, however, is perfectly preserved; after twelve hundred years, it is still waterproof and windproof, truly an architectural masterpiece.

One year when my pilgrims got there in late evening, at dusk, we met a local resident who had come to the oratory simply to be still at the end of his day, perhaps to think some things over or to pray or just to rest. It did not take more than a moment or two to realize that for him this was truly a holy place, and when we invited him to join us in our evening prayers, he gladly and reverently did so. We all went into the oratory and looked out the doorway toward the sun setting over the Atlantic, sending orange sparks along the surface of the water. After reading a poem by Seamus Heaney about Gallarus Oratory and saying a few prayers, quite spontaneously we began to sing a familiar evening hymn. The sound of our voices in that ancient sacred space, men and women creating harmony together, made a song of holiness few of us will ever forget.

Kilmalkedar Church

Kilmalkedar, too, is along the Saints' Road, not far from Gallarus, and undoubtedly is one of the most important ecclesiastical sites on the peninsula. The dedication is to St. Maolcethair ("Malkedar" in English), who died in 636. The present church, mid-twelfth century, is Irish Romanesque and is most likely built on top of

Maolcethair's earlier foundation. The design of the church is unmistakably Irish. Following construction patterns from an earlier period, the stone finials at the gables imitate the wooden cross beams of roof supports, and the projecting sides, called *antae,* also recall building techniques in wood.

There is evidence to suggest that Kilmalkedar was a center of Christianity and scholarship; the very size of the church reinforces and validates this. Inside the church are several stones of interest, including an "alphabet stone," which in all likelihood was used as a teaching device. The letters on it are Roman, in a style thought to be from the seventh century. In the east wall of the chancel is an opening called "the eye of the needle," and local tradition still says that if one can squeeze through it, one's wish will come true.

Most scholars agree that Kilmalkedar was originally a pagan religious site. In addition to the vestigial wish-making practice, until fairly recent times, on Easter Sunday local people made nine circuits of the churchyard, going around sunwise (clockwise) and throwing white pebbles on a particular grave. Local historian Steve MacDonogh suggests that the several standing stones in the immediate area, which have had holes bored through them, are pagan in origin and symbolize regeneration. Most likely these were used in rituals involving healing. The holed stone in the Kilmalkedar churchyard, however, may have been converted into a sundial. It is quite reasonable to assume that a significant pagan religious site such as this would have been taken over and Christianized by saints like St. Maolcethair, and its importance continued.

The name "Brandon" dominates the area. Mount Brandon itself looms large; Brandon Creek flows from the side of the mountain to the sea; there is also a Brandon Head and a Brandon Bay. Just across the lane from Kilmalkedar church is a medieval building known as Brendan's House. Tempting as it thus might be to attribute so many local place names to Brendan the Navigator, it seems unlikely that St. Brendan himself ever set foot on the Dingle, in spite of the tales told in the *Navigatio.* In the reorganization of the church during the twelfth century, and perhaps even as early as the ninth century, it is more probable that the well known St. Brendan replaced the little known St. Maolcethair, who subsequently faded into oblivion. Only local tradition has kept the name of Maolcethair alive. This was a typical pattern throughout all the Celtic lands during the twelfth and thirteenth centuries. It was important that churches be named after "authorized" saints, and local dedications to local holy men and women were overwritten by apostles and martyrs more familiar—and more pronounceable—to the Normans.

The Saints' Road

On the Ordnance Survey map of the Dingle Peninsula, a line drawn straight from the top of Mount Eagle (the second highest point on the peninsula) to Mount Brandon (the highest point) will pass almost exactly through Kilcolman, St. Manchán's, Gallarus, and Kilmalkedar. Further, except for some allowance for the natural contours of the land, the Saints' Road comes close to being along this same line. Scholars stress the importance of sight lines for the pilgrims; to be able to see their goal from time to time must have been a major source of encouragement for weary travelers.

If travelers came by sea on a maritime pilgrimage, Mount Eagle would have been a landmark to help them find their landing spot. After beginning the land portion of their pilgrimage, they would then have tried to keep their eyes on Brandon itself, cloud cover permitting. The folding of the land prevents the ability to see very far along the Saints Road at any one point, but at certain points it would not have been difficult to locate the road climbing up the next rise, hopefully dotted with other pilgrims that much further along the way.

Additionally, the western end of the peninsula is literally peppered with *clocháin* (beehive huts), an estimated six hundred of them. Many are on the coast near the foot of Mount Eagle, more are at the southwest end of the Saints' Road, and even more are on the slopes and at the base of Mount Brandon, not far from where the road begins its ascent to the top. Given the frequency with which the sea is too rough for a crossing to Skellig Michael or the clouds too thick to risk climbing Mount Brandon, it stands to reason that these beehive huts were temporary residences for pilgrims, headed in either direction, who might have had to wait weeks for clement weather. The western end of the Dingle Peninsula, with the Saints' Road linking the landing areas near Mount Eagle and the climb to the top of Mount Brandon, is thus indelibly linked to Celtic pilgrimage.

This morning I was poring over the map of the Dingle Peninsula, wondering how to spend a free day. The weather was definitely uninviting—one of those wet drippy days—more gray than light, with what one might call a very heavy mist, or thick fog, or light rain—take your pick. I finally decided that, weather or not, I wanted to take a walk and find a stone circle that was off the beaten track so I could have some time there by myself. I had seen a little red dot on my Ordnance Survey map: • STONE CIRCLE, *and thought that might be a possibility, so I decided to try to find it. I bundled up warmly in my rain gear and waterproof boots and took off.*

It took me a while to find the right place even to park the car. Although I was following my map very closely, still I had to ask the help of a farmer who happened along on his tractor. He spoke with such an Irish accent that I had trouble understanding him, but he pointed vaguely off in the distance, and I gathered the circle was somewhere over in that direction. My spirits sank a bit, for all I could see was rolling mist and more fog, but I took the farmer at his word and headed off. Needless to say, I was surprised when I actually found the circle. Perhaps some kind of instinct led me to it—I don't know.

Once at the circle itself, I realized it was not out of the ordinary in any way: just a ring of medium sized stones, perhaps three to four feet high, with only one considerably taller—perhaps six or seven feet—in the center. The mist was swirling in an eerie kind of way, and I remember thinking it looked like a typical set for a spooky movie. Had I given my imagination a free rein, I easily could have pictured a werewolf or a science fiction monster emerging out of the fog and entering the mysterious circle.

I had wanted to sit with my back to one of the uprights and pray, to feel the energy in the stone, to ponder, to meditate, to whatever, but it was too wet to sit on the ground. Certainly there was no view to enjoy. So I stood and wondered why on earth I had sought out this place. To this day I have no idea why I wanted to see that particular stone circle, and why I wanted it so badly that I had walked over a mile across lumpy wet moorland, avoiding as best I could cow pats, small streamlets, boggy places, gorse, and heather; and why I also had to climb over a securely locked aluminum farm gate and scramble over several stone walls to get there. Why? What was it that called to me? I still do not know—but I remember the experience as clearly as though it were yesterday.

Eventually I noticed that the central stone was leaning over and provided a small dry and protected spot. There was enough space there for me to sit down, which I did. I was not conscious of time, and I have come to realize that I was not conscious of particular place, either. I would be hard pressed to find that stone circle again. But as I sat hunched with my knees against my chest in the protected over-lean of the stone, I entered a kind of reverie that put me in touch with my inner self and with God. I think I may even have dozed off, coming back to reality rested and refreshed. I want to say those ancient stones "spoke" to me, reassured me, comforted me, in a way that transcends conscious awareness. I know I was in touch with an energy that I will always call God. It was a numinous experience, more mysterious than material, and for me it was one more threshold event that recognized the presence of the God I know and love in the long-ago pre-Christian world.

Before leaving, I made the sign of the cross on each of the stones—there were seventeen of them—and I wondered as I did so if that was what my ancestors had done when they were spreading Christianity to a pagan land. I walked slowly through the fog back in the direction where I thought I had left the car, and I knew that the journey was a mini pilgrimage. My outer journey, with its uncertain direction and stumbling footsteps reflected my equally uncertain and stumbling inner journey. Even so I knew I was in touch with the Holy.

Tobar na Mult

TOBAR NA MULT, a holy well near Ardfert in County Kerry, is a very special place. My finding it was an example of the Holy Spirit's leadership, because it is not listed in any book or guide that is in the mainstream of publication. I found it strictly as a tiny red dot on the Ordnance Survey Map. A friend and I were in County Kerry in the spring of 1995 searching for this well, simply because it was in the vicinity of Ardfert Cathedral. We drove up and down a number of extremely narrow country lanes (*bohereens*) before we finally saw a faded hand-painted sign on a farm gate indicating where it was. We got out of the car and went up to the farmhouse nearest the gate to inquire if we could have permission to visit the well.

Thus Jeremiah and Kathleen Clark entered my life. Both elderly, they had been born and raised in this section of Kerry, and they had returned there after Jeremiah's many years of teaching English literature in a high school in London. The well is an important part of their life and heritage, and Jeremiah, leaning heavily on his cane and walking slowly across the fields, was delighted to walk us down to it. So on a gray misty day we crossed the green pasture speckled with grazing sheep, went through a farm gate, crossed another pasture, through another gate, and then we were in the yard around the well.

I caught my breath in excitement: the well itself was a roughly circular pool, at least ten or twelve feet in diameter, edged with a rim of flat stones. The water was typically dark, with green algae thriving on the ring of stones, and the water's surface reflected the gray-bottomed clouds above. The well had no hood or protection overhead—it was too big for that—but there were narrow and steep steps leading down into the water. Nearby was a small building about the size of a single car garage, which I realized was a pilgrims' chapel. A few feet away stood a stone altar with three carved figures on the front face, positioned so Mass could be celebrated with the priest facing the well and the chapel. Behind the stone altar was a rectangular, grass-covered mound rather resembling a grave, and surrounding the whole area was an enclosure of blooming shrubs

*The altar with carved heads
at Tobar na Mult near Ardfert,
County Kerry*

The holy well, Tobar na Mult

and bushes, many of which had prayer rags tied to their branches. I felt a deep joy in simply being there.

Since that time, I have regularly brought my pilgrim groups to visit this place. As we get off our bus, we begin a brief worship service with a hymn; then we walk across the field, read some passages from Scripture, say a few prayers, and sing more hymns. We have Eucharist together at the well, Catholics and non-Catholics alike, and we take the opportunity to share our reflections and observations with one another as we stand in a circle around the water. Then, one by one, we wash our faces in the holy well's water, three times, in the name of the Trinity.

Tobar na Mult is not listed in the usual guide books, and information on it is scarce. The *North Kerry Archaeological Survey* assigns to it only a few lines plus a sentence or two about legends associated with the well. Tobar na Mult is just one among literally thousands of obscure wells scattered throughout Ireland, each with its own story and its own local interest. This particular well is of no greater significance than any of the others. But for those who over the centuries have been there and prayed there and celebrated Eucharist there, Tobar na Mult is a personal place, and in its being personal, it becomes Holy.

Some experts estimate that there are nearly three thousand holy wells in Ireland, and the religious practices associated with them most likely have their origins in pre-Christian Celtic celebrations. Many of the "patterns" used at the wells during the last several hundred years are probably Christianized versions of pagan practices. Rarely did holy wells attract pilgrims from far afield; people came from probably no more than a day's walk away. And the visits to the wells were not solely for religious reasons. Sometimes they were occasions for social festivities also—so much so that at one point local church authorities sought to ban visits to the holy wells in an attempt to abolish the "superstitions and idolatry" and the "drunkenness and debauchery" associated with them.

The religious patterns, or rounds, usually consisted of recitations of the rosary and repeated circling of the well, with the pilgrims perhaps on their knees performing acts of penance. A longing for healing was a major motivating factor in such visits to the wells, with the waters being bathed in, drunk, or carried home. Specific wells were reputed to offer cures for eye problems, headaches, toothaches, backaches, and injuries and ailments of various kinds. Modern scientific analysis has in many cases shown that the mineral content of certain wells does indeed contain medicinal qualities and may assist in the healing of certain sicknesses. Typically the one seeking healing would leave behind at the well, tied to a tree or a bush, a small rag torn from his or her garment, symbolizing the leaving behind of the ailment. Modern pilgrims may still leave a prayer rag, a coin or a medal, or other offering as an act of intercession or thanksgiving.

With its stone slab altar and three carved figures, Tobar na Mult is somewhat different from other holy wells. Some experts say this slab was once part of a medieval tomb originally in Ardfert cathedral, only a few miles away, and that the carved figures are "weepers" at the grave of the person buried. Local tradition, however, will have none of such scholarly explanations. The altar slab "has always been there" and is thought to have magical powers. The story is told of one of Cromwell's soldiers using an ox cart to remove the slab from the altar at the well, but at a certain point not too distant, the ox pulling the cart came to a halt and refused to go any farther. The soldier decided to leave the completion of his task until the next morning, but mysteriously, during the night, the slab returned of its own accord to its rightful place on the altar at the well, where it remains to this day.

In Celtic mythology the head was considered to be most sacred, and the fact that each of the three heads in the altar at Tobar na Mult is etched deeply with a cross strongly implies the Christianization of a pagan tradition. Pilgrims made the usual rounds at the well, then knelt before the heads, tracing the cross over each of the three in turn, then made the sign of the cross on themselves as well. Following that, pilgrims immersed themselves fully in the well. Such total immersion was possible only at certain wells where the water was deep enough to permit it, and Tobar na Mult was one such place—hence the steps going down into it.

There is also a grave at Tobar na Mult, said to be the grave of St. Ita, the foster mother of St. Brendan. St. Ita is most often associated with the monastery she is said to have founded at Killeedy near Limerick, and her connection with Tobar na Mult is not clear, but that is a detail not cared about much. Locals assert that the well sprang up at the prayer of St. Ita, and subsequently she baptized St. Brendan in its waters. At the time of his baptism, three wethers (castrated rams) appeared, hence the name assigned to the well: the Well of the Wethers.

I am always of two minds with regard to holy wells. Much of my academic background is that of trained historian, so factual authenticity is important to me, but at the same time, I have a rich imagination and love legends and stories, so the mystical association with wells is also important. I will always go out of my way to visit a holy well, and I am intrigued by the different ambiance—almost "personality"—of each one. I faithfully pray at each one, but still, I remain of two minds...

However, there is certainly something special about Tobar na Mult, and one time when I was there, in spite of the well's acknowledged local importance, I forgot all about being a historian. On this particular visit, the well was a gaping hole of emptiness—no water at all. It was actually dry. My mind wandered embarrassingly often during the Eucharist, for that emptiness haunted me. How does one live when the well goes dry? Just having the water temporarily turned off in our houses often causes untold inconvenience, but suppose the source of water is gone? Many of the reflective thoughts we shared that time had to do with emptiness and dryness.

After our worship service, I went slowly down the stone steps into the emptiness. There was a little dampness in the bottom, but real water—not a drop. What I saw instead were scores of coins that had been tossed into the well by previous pilgrims. There were pennies and tuppences and all the others up to pound coins. I gathered up all I could (and by this time one or two others were in the well and helping), and we gave them all to the parish priest. I did not count it, but I guessed it came to perhaps twenty-five pounds (Irish)—about thirty-seven dollars. Later I wondered if it had been right to take the money from the well. The people who had thrown the money in—who knows how long ago—had they intended their offerings to go to the parish? It is unlikely they thought any money would ever be recovered; after all, one does not expect to find a well dry.

In addition to the coins, we found one or two religious medals, tarnished and blackened almost beyond recognition. These moved me even more than the money, for these were visible tokens of someone's prayers at the site at some time in the past. Prayers for what? for healing at this healing well? for a petition of some kind? for thanksgiving, perhaps for the birth of a child? or for a son returned home safely from war? All the coins and medals were eloquent testimony to me of the faith of the people in a God who cares for all creation, a God who hears prayers through the living waters.

I did not get back to Tobar na Mult for another year, but when I did, the well was filled again. The round surface of the water was unruffled and serene… and I smiled at it. I stood on the pilgrim steps leading down into the well and handed a small dish of water to each of the pilgrims in turn, inviting them to wash their faces three times, in the name of the Trinity. Then we had Eucharist together, and we continued that fellowship later in the O'Connors' home, meeting a number of their Irish friends and enjoying a magnificent high tea with all kinds of tasty homemade goodies. Thanksgiving for abundant Irish hospitality—again.

On still another occasion, I was especially moved by the service of worship called "A Pilgrimage Walk." As soon as we read that prayer about "knit together in one communion and fellowship," I knew all I cared about was being in touch with the Holy. There was something mystical about the way we walked across the pasture down the slope to the well. Perhaps it was because we were going so slowly, but I felt waves of tension drop away as we walked together. When we stopped we sang hymns, one of which had the line "yet all are one in thee, for all are thine." We did not sound polished like our choirs in church, but we sang under God's heaven with an unselfconscious enthusiasm that indeed marked us as one.

When we got to the well, I thought the water looked like a great mirror bringing the sky down to earth, or like the eye of God reflecting the image of God that is each one of us. I remembered how the well had been dry once before, but it definitely was not today. We stood in a circle and shared with one another what the Communion of Saints meant to us, and all I could say was "This is It." We were Americans and Canadians and Irish, and we were Catholics and Methodists and Episcopalians and a Presbyterian and a Baptist and some of us were even unchurched, but we were all one body, together singing and praying and washing our faces in that holy well.

When my turn came, I didn't just wash my face—I took off my shoes and washed my feet also. I thought about Peter who was reluctant to have Jesus wash his feet, and then when Jesus insists, says, "Lord, not my feet only but also my hands and my head!" (John 13:8–9). A little later, in this same passage, Jesus says, "If I, your Lord and Teacher, have washed your feet, you also ought to wash one another's feet" (John 13:14). As I washed my hands and face and feet in Tobar na Mult, I wondered if perhaps all of us should have been washing one other's feet as well.

The water was so cool and refreshing that it seemed to fill my entire body with new life in a kind of spiritual rebirth. I thought of another place where Jesus says "Very truly, I tell you, no one can enter the kingdom of God without being born of water and Spirit" (John 3:5). At that moment there was no sign of the historian in me—I was all pilgrim and penitent, focused on the sacramental mystery of water and the Spirit hovering over the face of the water in creation. And I knew I was at that moment being born of water and Spirit.

The rest of our group was milling around in a comfortable togetherness. Some were going into the prayer chapel, or stooping in front of the stone altar tracing the deeply grooved crosses worn into the heads. I saw someone kneeling at the grave, praying with rosary beads, and someone else sitting on the ground writing in what I guessed was a journal. Still other people were talking quietly, asking questions, getting to know one another, generally enjoying a truly holy and happy time. What was all around me was the Communion of Saints, very much alive and well.

The Burren

MY FIRST IMPRESSION of the Burren definitely was not a positive one. All I could see in every direction were flattish slabs of gray stone, punctuated here and there by a patch of scraggly bushes, a lonely green pasture in a hollow, an occasional farmhouse. It looked pretty dreary to me, and the sky matched. I was essentially in a world of gray, and I came close to returning to Galway without exploring further. However, my curiosity—reluctant as it was—got the better of me, and I made a long and careful visit to the Burren Center in Kilfenora. I came away with a different set of eyes.

Why would anyone want to make a pilgrimage to the Burren? What is its lure? These forty square miles of barren, hilly, rocky, and infertile land in County Clare lie south of Galway Bay and comprise an area filled with hundreds of ruins, from Mesolithic to medieval times. This is an area unmatched anywhere else in the world not only for its history and its archaeological treasures, but also for its unique ecosystem and its botanical diversity. It is a haunting and hallowed place.

I begin pilgrimages in Kilfenora where, besides the Burren Center, is located the medieval cathedral (Kilfenora is the only diocese in Ireland to have as its bishop the Pope himself!) with several very fine high crosses in the churchyard. The cathedral is dedicated to St. Fachtnan, a sixth-century saint who is said to have founded a Celtic monastery here but about whom we know almost nothing. It is likely that the present building dates from the end of the twelfth century, and although it is still used for regular worship by the Church of Ireland (Anglican), little remains to show the casual visitor Kilfenora's early ecclesiastical significance. Where it becomes most apparent, however, is in aerial photographs, which clearly show the outline of the original, typically Celtic circular enclosure.

The cathedral is not remarkable in its architecture, being plain and relatively unadorned. Some people even describe its west front with its squat stepped gable as downright ugly. The great east window, however, beautifully proportioned with interesting carved capitals atop the supporting shafts of the great Romanesque arch,

A wedge tomb on the Burren

*The Kilfenora High Cross,
the Burren*

Limestone slabs on the Burren, County Clare

has a simple redeeming beauty that can be readily appreciated. Two grave slab effigies of bishops stand at either side of the arch, but since they are propped upright rather than reclining over a grave and date from a different period, clearly these are not their original positions.

The high crosses in the churchyard are impressive. Six of them survive, at least in part, with a seventh having been removed some time ago by a covetous bishop to his cathedral at Killaloe. Two of the six are fairly complete; the Doorty Cross near the west front of the cathedral is perhaps the most intriguing. The east face of this cross is as distinct as it is, no doubt, because it lay face down in the graveyard for several centuries, raised only as recently as 1951. This east face depicts three bishops, one at the top wearing an unusual mitre, and two immediately below carrying different style crosiers. Below these three bishops is a winged, presumably mythical, beast devouring what looks like human skulls.

Scholars cannot agree as to interpretation of this carving. One identifies the topmost bishop as being Christ himself, abbot of the world, directing his church leaders on earth (the two bishops immediately below) to destroy the devil by crushing him beneath their feet. Another identifies the top bishop as (perhaps) St. Fachtnan, founder of the monastery, with Saints Paul and Antony below using their respective crosiers to stab the beast beneath them. Still a third interpretation assumes the top bishop to be St. Peter, with his hand pointing downward (in blessing?) to one of the two bishops immediately below him. The bishop receiving this blessing is holding a crosier of the Romano/Irish style while the other holds that of a Celtic abbot. The suggestion is that Peter, the Bishop of Rome (the Pope), is giving his blessing to the Roman (European) church rather than to the more ancient Irish or Celtic monastic church.[30]

Traveling a bit eastward we find Kilnaboy, one of dozens of tiny medieval but now roofless churches in the Burren area. This one is unique in that it has an unusual cross in its west gable, made of original building stones pulled slightly outward to form a double-armed Byzantine-style cross in high relief. Scholars do not know the source of this; certainly such a cross is not typical in Ireland. Did some crusader return to his native land and build it because of some experience he had had in the Holy Land?

Also at Kilnaboy, above the south doorway, is a *sheela-na-gig,* that intriguing carving of a female figure exposing and exaggerating her genitalia. No one is completely sure of the origin or purpose of the *sheela-na-gigs,* found in a number of different places throughout Britain and mainland Europe, but particularly associated with Ireland. Until fairly recent times they were considered obscene, and only those with "dirty minds" displayed interest in them. Nevertheless, fascination with these unique carvings is quite understandable, and in recent decades they have become the focus of much scholarly research.

They seem to have begun to emerge during the twelfth century. While some scholars see the *sheela-na-gigs* as female fertility figures, others declare them medieval teaching devices against the sinful lusts of the flesh. Contemporary interest seems to focus on them as showing the importance of female sexuality in a positive and creative way, particularly by honoring the birth canal, the doorway to life through which all of us come. *Sheela-na-gigs* are to be found in many different kinds of locations—over doorways or above windows, at the corners of castles, within or at the tops of arches, even built into town walls. The *sheela-na-gig* above the south doorway at Kilnaboy is badly weathered, but she still watches over all those who enter the evocative roofless ruin.

In spite of my inauspicious introduction, I have come to recognize that the Burren is endlessly fascinating. This is a unique area where through the glacial action of the last Ice Age, some 15,000–13,000 years ago, the land surface was eroded away. The remaining exposed layer of limestone is still acted on by rain in much the same way that caves are; that is, water falling on the limestone creates a chemical reaction, and the resulting acid erodes the stone slabs into ever-deepening channels. Indeed, below the Burren surface are miles and miles of limestone caves, largely unexplored.

From a distance, the limestone pavements on the surface (called "clints") seem to be smooth, but as one walks across the great irregularly shaped slabs, stepping carefully across the deep clefts (called "grykes") between them, one realizes how potentially treacherous such walking can be. The slabs (clints) are uneven and bumpy, varying from the size and shape of a small human foot to

huge stone platforms, and on their surface are depressions and con-
volutions ready to cause a twisted ankle or jar a knee or hip. It is
all too easy to miss a footing and step into a gryke, some of which
are several feet deep. Careful walking is of the utmost importance,
yet only by such walking can one truly appreciate the uniqueness
of the Burren.

Assuming one can set aside the concentration needed for walking across the pavements and stop for a moment to examine things
growing inside the grykes, one discovers an amazing assortment of
plants and wildlife. Botanists and plant lovers are endlessly astonished at the diversity of flora and seemingly contradictory ecosystems. Species of warm Mediterranean plants (southern) are found
growing alongside arctic-alpine (northern) plants; similarly, lime-
loving plants are thriving side by side with lime-hating plants. It
seems that seeds of Alpine plants were deposited in the grykes millennia ago by the retreating ice sheets, so that growing here now are
such plants as hart's tongue fern, maidenhair fern, mountain avens,
and the rare blue gentian, not found anywhere else in Ireland or
Britain, but only in faraway Switzerland. Because of the depth of
the grykes, many different kinds of plants flourish, protected from
the restless winds blowing in from the nearby Atlantic. Dwelling
happily in this protected space are countless species of snails,
moths and butterflies, and various insects. Also at home in the
Burren are rabbits, hares, foxes, stoats, pine martens, mice, and
bats, along with cattle, sheep, and goats—and thousands of birds.

Every tourist board publication on Ireland and every shop that
sells postcards of western Ireland always has pictures of the
Poulnabrone dolmen, one of the most popular and often visited
sites in western Ireland. Although we drive past it, my pilgrim
groups do not stop there. We go on somewhat farther, park the bus,
and walk up a lane into the Burren itself to visit a wedge tomb and
a nearby holy well. Other visitors seldom come here, and only
those who study a large-scale map will find it. Thus, well off the
beaten track, we can appreciate more fully the mysterious atmosphere, even the loneliness, of the inner Burren.

The tiny holy well that we visit first is simply a small circular
opening in the limestone clint, no more than six or eight inches

across. To get to the water, one must kneel or squat and reach down ten or twelve inches. We stop and pray here, but what is far more important than words is the chance to hear the sound of silence and to feel the wind, the *ruach* of God, against our faces, and to breathe the freshness of the open air. Most people dip their hands in the water and quietly make the sign of the cross on their foreheads, and many people leave a small offering behind. Pilgrims who have been there before us have left behind an eclectic collection of offerings—coins, holy medals, shells, prayer cards, bits and pieces of various things—and once I even saw a bright red Virgin Airlines toothbrush. This well has a reputation for curing toothache, so perhaps the toothbrush was in some way related to that. One can only wonder what kinds of thoughts and prayers might lie behind the assorted gifts.

From the well we scramble onward toward a nearby wedge tomb, walking carefully across the clints and grykes and climbing steadily up a pathless but gentle incline as we go. The particular wedge tomb we seek, dated to about 2000 B.C.E., has never been excavated; what with thousands of such artifacts all over Ireland, there is no way all of them could be. That, however, adds to its appeal. It is a typical tomb of its type (there are more than 130 of them in the Burren), isolated, dramatically situated on a hillside. When the weather is clear, a breathtaking view of limestone hills and valleys stretches for miles in one direction, broken only here and there by scrubby green outcrops of hazel; far off in another direction are the glistening waters of Galway Bay.

Approaching the tomb, we enter an unexpected grassy section, reasonably level, which in the spring and summer is carpeted with abundant wildflowers. Walking across this area in early June, one cannot avoid stepping on wild orchids, mountain avens, blue gentians, cranesbill geraniums, buttercups, Queen Anne's lace, and dozens of other blooming plants. Their fragrance is in every breath; bees and butterflies are busy at their job of pollination. At the interpretive center we learned that the making of perfumes from local flowers is an important small industry for the Burren.

The tomb itself is evocative, with a huge slab about ten feet long by three or four feet wide forming a steeply sloping roof. Like others of its type, it is aligned on an east-west axis, with the higher edge opening to the west, tapering and sloping backward to the narrower east. It is supported by upright slabs graduated from two to four feet high. Though it is completely open and exposed today, when this kind of tomb was built, it was covered with loose stones and soil, which formed an extensive mound or cairn. Where we are, we can just make out the extent of what must have been the edge. Because it is now uncovered, we can climb up onto the roof-like slab or crawl into the open space below it and wonder what kinds of rituals must have accompanied the unknown number of burials that took place here four thousand years ago—and perhaps watch the sun set in the same way our forbears did.

I didn't care much for Kilfenora cathedral. I was interested in its long history, of course—who wouldn't be?—but I thought of the rich Roman Catholic tradition in Ireland, and this historic place seems to me rightfully to belong to the Catholic people. It was a cathedral in Ireland long before the Reformation, and I didn't want it to be attended by only a handful of people each week. I wanted it to belong to all the people. I wanted to see Catholics and Anglicans and Protestants and people who may not be anything in particular (in terms of church) worshiping together in this ancient, holy place. The divisiveness we Christians have to live with doesn't make any sense to me at all. God is God of all, not just of a few. No wonder so many of us are disillusioned with the institutional church. We build walls, literally as well as figuratively, and the walls lock people out and lock God in.

I was thinking particularly about this when we had morning prayers in the ruins of Kilnaboy church this morning. There was something about the Byzantine cross from the Middle Ages, the pagan sheela-na-gig over the door, the contemporary graves with their faded plastic flowers, the roofless church, and the glorious day all together that impressed me deeply. We had two Scripture readings:

Have we not all one father? Has not one God created us?
Why then are we faithless to one another, profaning the
covenant of our ancestors? (Malachi 2:10)

Now that faith has come, we are no longer subject to a disci-
plinarian, for in Christ Jesus you are all children of God
through faith. As many of you as were baptized into Christ
have clothed yourselves with Christ. There is no longer Jew
or Greek, there is no longer slave or free, there is no longer
male and female; for all of you are one in Christ Jesus.
(Galatians 3:25–28)

*Both those passages reminded me how interrelated and intercon-
nected we all are. Everybody prayed aloud for a particular personal
concern. I prayed for the various church commissions who interview
people for possible ordination to the ordained ministry. Those who are
approved will in all likelihood be ordained into the same universal
Christian church that this ruin at one time was a part of—a rich tradition and heritage indeed. My prayer, of course, was for the renewal
and revitalization of the entire church.*

*During our silent period I looked up at the blue, blue sky without a
sign of a cloud. I was conscious of the smell of the grass that we had
crushed as we walked in and also the fragrance of the bright yellow
wildflowers—I don't know their names. From where I was standing, the
sky was a perfect rectangle, because we were inside the ruin and the
standing walls had us inside an open box. I thought, as many have
thought before me, do we do right building buildings and putting God
inside such a "box"? By enclosing God inside our churches, even though
they may be protection from the weather and beautiful beyond description, have we thus boxed God out of our daily lives? I continue to wonder how we can maintain our churches, which of course we need, but at
the same time find ways in our cramped city lives of worshiping God
beneath the blue sky, too. How? We cannot continue to keep the God of
our church liturgies separate from the God of the open sky. While I was
thinking, a bird suddenly flew down, landed on the gable, and began to
sing with us as we rejoiced together in the praise of God.*

When we spent the afternoon walking on the Burren, it all came together. What an amazing area of incredible diversity! If totally different plants and ecosystems can live productively together, why can't we humans? Why should our differences divide us rather than enrich us? On the Burren I realized that it isn't God's ways that are mysterious and inscrutable; it's our ways that are. It was the bird in the ruins at Kilnaboy that gave me the answer: people song and bird song and fragrant flowers were there united in one glorious hymn of praise. Together we had sung a magnificent Te Deum.

Croagh Patrick

MORE THAN ONE PERSON has pointed out that certain mountains have an irresistible call to men and women, a call to come and climb. Croagh (pronounced "crow") Patrick is one such mountain. There are mountains much higher than "The Reek," as it is sometimes called, but few mountains have more history or are held in greater affection by men and women all over the world. Rarely does a day go by, in any weather or in any season, that climbers are not working their way to the top.

Croagh Patrick rises 2510 feet (765m), in the northwest of County Mayo (Ireland), a solitary quartzite cone dominating the landscape for miles around, typically with its head hidden in the clouds. On a clear day, however, the view from the summit is spectacular, a full 360 degrees, with breathtaking views of the ever-changing colors of the sea in one direction, tumbled hills with heather-covered slopes in another, and smoky blue mountains on every horizon. Scattered about on the lower slopes of the mountain are countless remains of pre-history—cromlechs, burial chambers, cup-and-ring markings, standing stones, and such. Máire MacNeill, in her book *The Festival of Lughnasa* (Oxford, 1962), presents a convincing case for the mountain's importance in prehistoric celebrations of the Celtic god Lugh. Thus, by the time tradition says St. Patrick climbed the mountain to fast for forty days and forty nights, the mountain was already a holy place.

Pilgrims climbing Croagh Patrick on Reek Sunday
Photo by Peter Harbison (used with permission)

Chapel atop Croagh Patrick

The path up Croagh Patrick, County Mayo

I was alone the day I climbed Croagh Patrick. I had heard and read about the holy mountain, seen countless pictures of it, and I was curious as to why it had such an attraction. Thus I made my plans to climb it myself. I stopped in a small shop in an obscure village in County Mayo to get an apple, some buns, and a bottle of water for a picnic lunch to carry with me, and I mentioned to the lady at the counter where I was headed. I'll never forget the inner glow she radiated when she nodded her head and said, "Yes, I've climbed Croagh Patrick. Three times." There was something deeply inward about her smile, as though the experience had been for her a profound and obviously unforgettable one. "Drive toward Westport," she said, "and you'll see it all the way. It will call to you."

She was right. As I drove across the Owenwee valley, the mountain loomed against the sky on my left, and even from so many miles away, I could see the wavy white scar that marked the path up. That path did indeed call to me. I had wondered why this particular mountain had caught the spiritual attention of so many, when there are so many other mountains throughout Ireland. However, there is something about the way Croagh Patrick stands so totally alone, a perfect cone lacking companion heights on either side, that does set it apart. I had no trouble finding the car park, and after filling my backpack with jacket, raincoat, and lunch, I set off.

The path went almost straight up the mountain, a wide white gash the entire length, and I knew there would be no trouble finding the way and no chance of getting lost or turned around. I saw no trees or shrubs; the only apparent vegetation was low gorse and heather in great patches around exposed sections of tumbled scree. The very bareness of the mountain presented a sense of nakedness and vulnerability, an unashamed exposure to all the elements. Surely that was part of its spiritual appeal.

Following the route up was easy; climbing the mountain was something else again. I vaguely remembered having read in Alannah Hopkin's book on Patrick[31] that the climb takes two and a half to three hours. I started at 10:30 and reached the top at noon, but I was not able to do it without frequent rest stops, even in as good physical condition as I was. The climb is positively relentless, a merciless ascent without respite. And the walkway itself is far from smooth; it is rocky, uneven, and covered with loose stones. It was like walking over rubble, and many times I was absolutely convinced some enormous stone and gravel truck had dumped ton after ton of loose rock along the way. That, however, was an absurd thought. I was walking on the stony bones of the mountain itself, as Christian pilgrims have done for more than fifteen hundred years, and as Druids and others did probably a thousand years or more before that.

A sign at the bottom of the path at the edge of the car park, near a statue of St. Patrick, reminds climbers that the walk is a holy one, a path of prayer, penitence, and penance and that the journey should be undertaken in that kind of an attitude. I found that easy. The walk was so challenging for me that I found it easy to pray— to offer thanks to God for the joy of moving my body in such a way, for the beauty of the day, for the glorious views of Clew Bay spreading a sea-blue mantle around the green islands sprinkled far below me, and for the cooling breeze that became close to a gale as I neared the top. It was easy, too, to pray for all those for whom life is painful and difficult, for those who find each day strenuous and relentless, for those whose handicaps, whether physical, intellectual, spiritual, or emotional, prevent them from participating in such an experience as I was having. As my heart pumped harder and harder through the exertion of the climb, I prayed for people with heart conditions and other physical ailments. I certainly prayed for myself—a lot. I thought of the many, many ways in which I fall short of my commitment as a religious, and perhaps the difficult and strenuous walk was indeed a penance. It was certainly humbling.

The walk was very like the Christian journey—totally demanding, totally absorbing, requiring total commitment for authenticity. On Croagh Patrick, "the straight and narrow" easily translates into the "twisting and difficult underfoot," the kind of commitment that requires undivided attention to careful walking. When I wanted to admire the beauty of the day, look at the panorama below me, or consider the looming mountain above me, I had to stop. There was no walking without total concentration on where I was putting each foot. I thought about that in relation to all of life—how urgent it is for all of us to stop from time to time to rest and reflect, to catch our breath and to ponder our individual life pilgrimage. Perhaps most important of all, I contemplated how essential it is to look about at the beauty of our fragile world and to cherish our tiny place in it.

After I had been walking for more than an hour, I could see that by far the most difficult part was yet ahead of me. So when I reached the saddle, or Leacht Benain as it is called, I stopped to eat and rest. The wind was increasing, and I had to put on my warm jacket, in spite of my perspiration from the climb. Much to my surprise (and relief) there was a comfort station there, complete with flush toilets. Then I did the "rounds," as they are called, circling the enormous cairn seven times slowly and prayerfully, reciting the required number of Our Fathers, Hail Marys, and Creed, and adding a rock of my own to the huge pile already there. I was acutely conscious of walking round and round on an extremely well-trodden path, a reminder to me of the countless pilgrims who had been there before me. I rejoiced in being one of the ten thousand times ten thousand.

People ahead of me on the ascent to the cone were surely climbing upward at about forty-five degrees, straight up the tumbled rocks as though climbing a steep set of stairs—except that there were neither handrails nor any secure stair treads, only the loose scree underfoot. From where I was, the climbers above me were silhouetted against the sky and looked like tiny insects crawling up a steep slope. It took me another hour and a half, plus a number of short rest stops, to reach the cone itself. In one section, the going was so steep I was almost on all fours, going nearly straight up. I wondered any number of times whether I would have undertaken the climb had I known what it was like—but I know I would have.

Despite the physical difficulties, there was something deeply spiritual about the climb. On the way up I overtook only two people. I had the walk essentially to myself until I got higher and began to meet people coming down. The descending people were wonderfully encouraging all the way. "Keep at it—you'll make it," said one bewhiskered man many years my senior. And somewhat later, a young couple said, "You're almost there, maybe ten more minutes."

I did make it, finally, and as I looked around, I was astonished to see a full-sized church on the very top. Another bank of comfort stations with flush toilets indicated that obviously many thousands climb to the top regularly. Certainly I was grateful for the convenience and comfort, but I could not help but wonder how on earth those buildings were built in the first place. There were more cairns and more prayer stations, and I learned later that archaeologists have found the remains of a stone rampart encircling the summit, and within it about thirty circular stone huts. Many of these date back to the third to fourth century B.C.E.—long before Patrick or any other Christians came. These barely discernible remains of an Iron Age community on top of Croagh Patrick must have come from a settlement very like the one atop Yr Eifl in North Wales, where there are similar but well-preserved remains of a contemporary community at Tre'r Ceiri.

At the top of Croagh Patrick I sat at the edge of the mountain and looked down over Clew Bay. The tide had been coming in as I climbed, and at each resting point as I ascended, I realized that the shades of blue, green, and aquamarine in the water were constantly shifting. The funny dome-shaped islands in the bay, called drumlins, were a brilliant green, lined at their edges with the reddish brown rock of their seaside cliffs. They looked like green warts in the blue water. I finished my lunch and simply absorbed the beauty of the place and pondered the incredible appeal of such an arduous journey.

After a full two hours at the top, which I spent in quiet prayer (including a short nap on a bed of rocks), I started back down. I was decidedly uneasy about the descent; my knees and ankles would have a tough time of it. Lines from Psalm 18 rang in my ears and gave me courage:

It is God who girds me about with strength and makes my
way secure.
He makes me sure-footed like a deer and lets me stand firm
on the heights.
You lengthen my stride beneath me and my ankles do not
give way.
(*Book of Common Prayer,* Psalm 18:33–34, 37)

I did not, however, pray consciously as I went back down. I was too intent on being careful where I placed each foot. Going down was every bit as demanding as going up—in some ways even more so.

Some way down I met a woman at the side of the path weeping and white with pain. She had slipped on a loose rock and apparently had broken her ankle. I offered what little assistance I could, but I was assured that the rescue service had been notified and professional help was on the way, so I continued my descent. I met dozens of people on their way up—very much a steady stream of them—and I was glad to speak to them the same kind of encouragement that had been given to me on my way up.

Then I saw a man well below me wearing a fluorescent green jacket and carrying an enormous backpack, but walking very fast, steadily overtaking other walkers. I knew he had to be one of the rescuers. A little further along I met two other extremely fit and sturdy-looking young men who were also on their way, heavily loaded with rescue equipment, including a stretcher. They had stopped briefly for breath, and I exchanged a few words with them, learning that a branch of the Order of Malta had been founded specifically to assist with accidents on Croagh Patrick. A typical day for them might mean four or five trips up the Reek, and in the high pilgrimage season, often there would be even more, every trip being a loving offering to rescue us from our own hurt.

My particular hurt at that moment involved my knees, my ankles, and my feet, and they all cried out to me "Enough!" As the statue of St. Patrick gradually came into view, they seemed increasingly insistent. Near the bottom of the mountain I sat down on a sun-baked rock at the edge of a small stream, took off my shoes, and bathed my aching feet, which by this time were entirely too large for my shoes. The coolness of the water was refreshing, and as I soaked my feet, gradually the aching subsided and I had time to think. I pondered how soft and out of condition I am, even though I had thought I was in pretty good shape. Perhaps the purpose of such undertakings is to assess just how fit we really are. Traditionally that is what asceticism is all about: stopping and taking stock of our own spiritual fitness. Such thinking and stock-taking was with me for many weeks after.

Who climbed Croagh Patrick first? It is certain that it was not Patrick. In the *Book of Armagh*, housed in the library of Trinity College, Dublin, is a memoir of St. Patrick written by Tírechán about 670, recording the first known reference to Croagh Patrick. Tírechán was the first to promote the association of Patrick with the mountain, but he was no doubt writing and responding to long-standing tradition, even as he was offering a "sales pitch" to promote his own Diocese of Armagh. He wrote his memoir two hundred years after Patrick's death, so we cannot know for certain that Patrick ever even visited Croagh Patrick, much less climbed it and spent forty days and forty nights there. R. P. C. Hanson, one of the most highly respected of the Patrician scholars of this century, thinks such a visit is highly unlikely, and D. A. Binchy, another of the great Patrician scholars, agrees.[32] So much of Patrick's story is intermingled with fantasy and imagination that untangling fact from fiction is totally impossible.

I also considered the tradition of climbing *barefoot*: at what point had that begun? I am still appalled at the idea of walking over those loose rocks with their terribly sharp edges without shoes. In times past, when shoes were not as common as they are now and to go barefoot was fairly normal, perhaps then it might have made sense, but today? It seems that pilgrimage in Ireland has tradition-ally included an attitude of penance and mortification, encouraging acts of voluntary asceticism. This may stem from Ireland's Celtic heritage, for bodily mortification, often extremely harsh, was an important aspect of monastic practice during the Celtic period. It is true there is certain amount of scriptural basis for subduing one's body, for St. Paul says, "I do not run aimlessly, nor do I box as though beating the air; but I punish my body and enslave it" (1 Corinthians 9:26–27a). What ultimately matters, of course, is whether the practice draws penitents into more fullness of life and therefore closer to God and to one another. Surely that must be the goal of all such religious practices.

By the ninth century, printed literature contained many refer-ences to penitential pilgrimages and fasting, and by the fifteenth century, indulgences were granted to those who undertook them. During the Middle Ages the practice began of starting the Croagh

Patrick climb in the dark with the intent of reaching the summit by sunrise. Mass then would be celebrated as the sun rose. Not long after that, pilgrims began to make the climb barefooted, following the example of Moses on Mount Horeb when he saw the burning bush and heard God's voice: "Come no closer! Remove the sandals from your feet, for the place on which you are standing is holy ground" (Exodus 3:5). Although this practice is today strongly discouraged by ecclesiastical, civil, and medical authorities, an occasional penitent still makes the climb without shoes, for Croagh Patrick is indeed the holy mountain of Ireland.

There are countless historcial references to a small chapel, Teampall Phádraig, on the top of the mountain, and recent archaeological investigations (1994) do show the foundations an ancient oratory, radiocarbon-dated to between the fifth and ninth centuries—possibly the oldest stone Christian building found in Ireland. No doubt this very early building was in use for several centuries. By the thirteenth century, however, the tiny chapel had been replaced by a larger and more substantial one, and we find the Archbishops of Tuam and Armagh in fierce argument as to which diocese was entitled to the revenue from it. This newer church continued in use until the present modern building was erected in 1904.

Considering the harsh repression of Roman Catholicism and the penal laws of the seventeenth and eighteenth centuries, the fact that the practice of pilgrimage and the celebration of Mass atop the mountain continued in an unbroken tradition is astonishing, a real tribute to the religious faith of the Irish people. By the end of the nineteenth century, when political repression of Catholics had begun to diminish, concerted efforts on the part of the Catholic leadership led to the building of a new chapel on top of Croagh Patrick.

Appeals for funds were sent out nationally, and construction began in 1904. As much of the building as possible was done at the bottom of the mountain, with finished parts and other construction materials, including iron girders, sand, and cement, laboriously hauled up the mountain by donkeys, pack horses, and human workers—many of them volunteers. The new church was dedicated on Sunday, July 30, with ten thousand pilgrims at the top of the mountain and more than thirty priests, bishops, and archbishops in attendance. Archbishop John Healy of Tuam celebrated Mass on August 14, 1904, on the top of the Reek. In the rain and cloud he addressed the thousands of pilgrims saying:

> Think of this mountain as the symbol of Ireland's enduring faith and of the constancy and success with which the Irish people faced the storms of persecution during many woeful centuries. It is therefore the fitting type of Irish faith and Ireland's nationhood which nothing has ever shaken and with God's blessing, nothing can ever destroy.[33]

Rarely does a day go by that someone is not climbing Croagh Patrick on a pilgrimage, whether penitential or not. Each year on the last Sunday in July, about thirty thousand pilgrims come from all over Ireland to participate in the annual pilgrimage climb on Reek Sunday. Some still follow the medieval pattern of beginning the climb in the dark of midnight and walking the three-hour ascent with simply a lamp or candle and without shoes, but most people begin after daybreak and wear normal hiking clothes. An article in *The Independent* in 1989 describes the climb on Reek Sunday that year:

> [It is] an extraordinary, almost medieval sight. Above you, the line stretches along the brow of Ireland's Holy Mountain till it disappears in the thickening cloud. Below you, hundreds more are on their way up or down. The young are in everything from multi-coloured anoraks and trainers to satin jackets and high heels; the old in tweed jackets, like characters from *The Irish RM* [a popular Irish novel].[34]

It is unlikely that pilgrims will ever stop climbing Croagh Patrick, certainly not in our day. The mountain is holy and undoubtedly has been for countless centuries, long before the coming of Christianity, and it would be a holy mountain even if there never had been a Patrick. Croagh Patrick is sacred space, and surely it epitomizes Father Noel Dermot O'Donoghue's statement, "Sacred space is where we see the angels."[35] Whether Patrick ever climbed the Reek and actually saw the angels from the top, we will never know, and such is entirely beside the point. We can be certain that as long as people go on pilgrimage, seeking that which is holy, there will always be those who will climb Ireland's holy mountain.

Some pilgrimage
sites in
Scotland

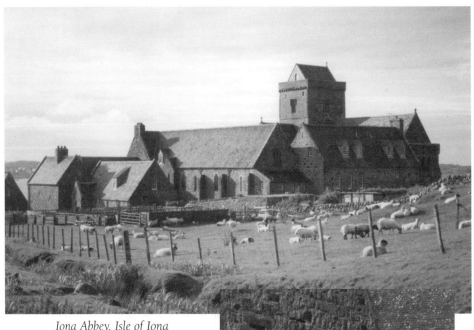

Iona Abbey, Isle of Iona

*St. Martin's Cross,
Isle of Iona*

*St. John's Cross and St. Columba's Oratory,
Isle of Iona*

Iona

IONA, THAT MAGICAL ISLAND off the west coast of Scotland, is no doubt one of the best known of all the Celtic sites. A monk from Ireland by the name of Columba (whose name in Irish is Colmcille, the same Colmcille as in Kells) founded a Christian monastery on Iona in 563 C.E. Because Columba had a biographer by the name of Adomnán, who wrote only a century after Columba's death, we have unusually reliable information about the life and ministry of Columba and his monastery.

Columba was not, however, the first missionary to the area we now know as Scotland. Archaeological excavations have proved beyond question that the Christian settlement at Whithorn is at least a century older, but because of the happy accident of history's giving us Adomnán's writings, we know more about Columba than any other of the Celtic saints. Had the founder of Whithorn (be it Ninian or someone else), or had the missionary (or missionaries?) who evangelized the Picts in northern and eastern parts of Scotland had reliable biographers, Columba might not stand out in the sharp relief he does.

Undoubtedly Columba was a remarkable man. Born of royal lineage in Ireland and trained for the priesthood there, he set sail in 563 from somewhere near Derry on the northern coast of Ireland and settled on the small island we now know as Iona. Much has been written about this voyage: whether it was an intentional missionary endeavor or a journey of exile we shall never know. But reach Iona he did, and soon after his arrival Columba made contact with the local secular ruler on the mainland, probably at Dunadd, who granted him possession of the island. From there he evangelized the nearby islands and parts of the mainland, and ruins of his monastic foundations remain to this day.

A great deal has been written about Columba and Iona. The man and the island have been thoroughly studied and analyzed by historians, theologians, archaeologists, geologists, anthropologists, and many other -ologists, and their writings range from elementary material for school children to extremely sophisticated researches. For anyone who wants to visit the island, for whatever reason, there is no shortage of information about it.

When I went to Iona for the first time in 1990, I had no idea what to expect. I was privileged to stay with a personal friend in her home on the island for a week, and it was there, sitting cozily in front of a peat fire, I read Adomnán's biography of Columba. Soon after that I began to pore over the *Carmina Gaedelica,* that amazing collection of Scottish prayers, poems, and incantations collected by Alexander Carmichael in the nineteenth century.

Getting to Iona for that initial visit was not easy. I traveled by public transport, coordinating trains, ferries, bus, and—above all— weather. By the time I got to Glasgow, rain was pouring down and a ferocious wind was blowing, but I optimistically boarded the train for Oban, where I would need to take a ferry, hopeful that the weather would not prevent me from making the crossing.

Without question, that train ride from Glasgow to Oban is one of the most scenic rail rides anywhere in the world. It is advertised as such, and with good reason. Because of the streaming rain, I did not see any splendid vistas through the Scottish Highlands, but I saw some beautiful mist and cloud effects, and soaring across Loch Lomond, one of the most breathtaking rainbows imaginable. All along the route, countless waterfalls plunged off the mountain-sides, looking like raveled white strings.

Oban was shrouded in thick fog, but I crossed on the huge ferry over to Craignure without difficulty. There I boarded the bus that would drive me thirty-five miles across the island of Mull to the tiny village of Fionnphort (which is pronounced *finny foot!*), and from there I would take a second ferry across to Iona. That bus ride had a magic quality to it, for as we drove westward, the skies began to clear, and by the time we arrived in Fionnphort, Iona was spread out in welcome across the water before me, looking so perfect it resembled a stage set. The sky was a bright blue without a cloud in sight. As the tiny ferry chugged over to Iona, I looked out at the shimmering water of Iona Sound and the rosy cliffs of the island of Mull, and it was hard to remember fog-bound Oban and rain-drenched Glasgow.

Iona is a rugged island with no trails beyond the village and immediate farm area, only sheep tracks; over several visits, I think I have explored most of them. I always thrill to the various climbs up the steep hills through the scrubby heather, catching glorious views of the sea in all directions. When there is clear weather and shining sun, the water glistens brilliantly, reflecting greens, purples, deep blues, and aquamarines, and the sea surface is sprinkled with white wisps from breaking waves. When the weather is less pleasant, fog can descend in a disorienting way, the wind can cut through like a knife, and the sea can become a raging tumult. On the west edge of the island is a "spouting cave," which waves enter when the sea is wild. They send plumes of water high into the air with sounds like the boom of a cannon shot.

My first visit was in April, when the spring wildflowers were just beginning, carpeting the ground with violets and pale yellow primroses. Huge patches of wild yellow iris were sending up their green bayonets, and tiny fiddleheads of early ferns were unfolding. Later, as summer comes, there is a glorious procession of other wildflowers: sea thrift, cowslips, foxgloves, ragged robin, campion, Queen Anne's lace, and acres and acres of blooming heather. And sheep, omnipresent sheep, are everywhere on the island. Columba's monastery had had sheep, too, and surely sheep are as much a part of Iona as Columba himself is.

Iona's northern and eastern beaches are reminiscent of Florida with their pure white—even blinding—sands and transparent aquamarine water, but totally unlike Florida are the rocky cliffs that encircle the bays. The bays to the south of the island are not sandy, but instead consist of round and oval polished rocks, many of them marble, that look like enormous eggs. They are very smooth and come in an astonishing variety of sizes, colors, and patterns. Walking across such a beach is like walking on rolling balls—an unusual sensation, to say the least.

The medieval monastic buildings of Iona Abbey went to ruin after the Reformation, and not until 1899 did the Eighth Duke of

Argyll make a gift that in time became the Iona Cathedral Trust. The abbey choir and nave were rebuilt in the years before 1910, and in 1938 the Iona Community was founded by the Reverend George F. MacLeod. He came from a long line of ministers in the Church of Scotland, and after the Great Depression he was driven by two motives: he wanted to offer meaningful work to underprivileged youth in depressed Glasgow, and he wanted to spark a renewal within the church by providing physical and meaningful work for a spiritual purpose. Thus was the Iona Community founded, not monastic in the traditional sense, but an intentional community of prayer and service for young people and men and women in the twentieth century.

From the time of its founding, the Iona Community has had a tremendous emphasis on community and on prayer and a strong focus on outreach and social justice. Today only a core group of community members lives on the island; others live in inner-city locations on the mainland, particularly in Glasgow. The members of the community on the island today, especially during the summer months, contribute mightily to providing for the needs of the hoards of tourists and pilgrims who visit Iona daily. The abbey itself is run as a study and conference center, and guests come to participate in specific programs on specific dates. Prayer, however, remains central, and daily worship of morning and evening prayers is open to all.

During the Middle Ages, when the original abbey was flourishing, a Benedictine community for women was also founded. Their complex was located several hundred yards away from that of the men, and although it was never as large as the men's, it was built on the same basic pattern of monastic church, cloister, and domestic buildings. This Nuns' Church is one of the most evocative ruins on the island today, and it is sad that almost no records of its life and work have survived. The church today is roofless, as are the domestic buildings, but the cloister is a beautifully kept meditation garden where anyone can go to find both beauty and peace.

Also situated on Iona is Bishop's House (Anglican), founded during the nineteenth century and at one time owned by the Anglican Society of St. John the Evangelist (Cowley). In recent years it has been run by the Scottish Episcopal Church (Diocese of

Argyll and the Isles) and serves as a house of rest and retreat. Bishop's House offers the daily office plus Eucharist, and visitors to the island are always welcome to share in worship.

Probably the best-known Celtic features on Iona are the great standing crosses. People seeing any of these high crosses for the first time invariably are taken aback at how huge they are; on Iona the St. Martin's cross and the St. John's cross, both dating from the eighth century, are nearly fifteen feet high. The superior quality of the workmanship and intricate sculpture bear testimony to the prestige and wealth of Iona in that period. Scholars believe that many of the other high crosses on nearby islands in the Hebrides and even on the mainland were executed by Ionan sculptors. Many other splendid carvings—more crosses, sculpture, grave slabs, and such—from the Celtic, medieval, and modern periods are now housed in the abbey museum, a building which once served as the monastic infirmary.

St. Columba's influence is strongly felt on the island, and to climb up the mound a few feet away from the abbey to Columba's cell or to pray in his tiny oratory attached to the abbey church has great spiritual impact. A small group of stones on Iona, roughly circular in shape, are the foundations of a "beehive cell" or hermit hut. Part of a pilgrimage to Iona ideally includes a visit to that ancient place of prayer. It is not easy to find, for it is hidden back in the cliffs behind Iona's mountain Dun Í, but once there, sitting quietly in that 1500-year-old stone ring with an unbroken view out to the Atlantic, one can see why those early Celtic hermits chose it for a place of refuge.

Not far from Iona is the Isle of Staffa, an amazing piece of land made of hexagonal columns formed by volcanic lava flow eons ago. Viewed from Iona, because of its tall parallel black basalt columns, the island rather resembles a huge automobile air filter sitting on the top of the ocean. Staffa is owned by the National Trust for Scotland and has no human habitation, but it is home to thousands of sea birds. Also located on Staffa are a number of sea caves. It seems that when the composer Mendelssohn visited Staffa, he was much impressed by the sound of the sea in one cave in particular, Fingal's Cave, and thus he composed his famous "Fingal's Cave Overture."

*Today we went on a Pilgrimage Walk around the island with Philip.
I was well prepared with my raincoat and picnic lunch in my backpack, my camera in my pocket, and my binoculars around my neck.
I had to laugh at myself; what would Columba have thought of such
impedimenta?*

*We went first to the Nuns' Church and prayed there especially for
women—women and minorities and underprivileged. For me, it was
an easy place to pray in. I liked the green grass and the pink stone. I
liked the well-tended garden in the remains of the old cloister. I liked
the tufts of something or other growing between the stones in the walls,
and I liked the way the birds swooped around above us. Truly it was a
warm and pleasant place and a good place to begin a Pilgrimage Walk.*

*From the Nuns' Church, we trudged along a rocky road between
pastures filled with sheep, passing one or two barking collies who
seemed to think we might either be members of their flocks needing to
be herded or Unknown Threats to be chased away—I wasn't quite sure
which. It wasn't hard walking, and I hummed hymns to myself the
whole way, feeling very close to God. I'm glad we were walking in near
silence so we had time to reflect.*

*We passed the Hill of the Angels, where, so the story goes, Columba
had gone one night to be alone and to pray, but one of his brothers
sneaked out to spy on him. Needless to say, this did not sit well with
Columba. I spent the next few minutes thinking about the privacy of
prayer; Jesus tells us:*

> Whenever you pray, go into your room and shut the door
> and pray to your Father who is in secret; and your Father
> who sees in secret will reward you. (Matthew 6:6)

*That is a particularly meaningful concept for me, because much of
the time I do not want to share my prayer experiences with anyone.
Much of the time I don't even have words to express what I feel, even if
I did want to share it. Prayer is—well, just private. Part of me wanted*

to climb the Hill of the Angels and explore this idea further, but the group was moving on, so I moved with it.

As we walked along, I reflected back to my first visit to Iona so many years ago. It had been the time of year when the ewes were dropping their lambs, and each morning while I was there, I began the day in the pasture with a quick count to see how many new members of the flock had been added during the night. One day I happened upon a ewe for whom the birth process was just beginning and thus had the unforgettable experience of watching a wet white lamb come into the world right at my very feet. The ewe did not seem to mind; if she was frightened at my presence she gave no indication of it. Within minutes the little lamb was struggling to get to his feet and was soon nursing; Mama meanwhile was grazing again, munching bits of grass alternately with consuming the products of birth. Surely birth is always a miracle. Later I went to Evening Prayers at the abbey and then walked back to my host's home under a night brilliant with stars. The birth of the lamb was uppermost in my mind; much in our religious imagery about the Good Shepherd and sheep and lambs took on a new dimension for me that evening. For the remainder of the week I watched the sheep with renewed interest. The shepherds did indeed know their flocks, and their flocks knew them. I will always, I think, associate sheep and lambing with Iona.

When our pilgrimage group with Philip got to the Bay at the Back of the Ocean, where Columba is supposed to have landed and buried his boat (symbolic of his having "burned his bridges" I wonder?), we went down to the water's edge to pray. Getting down there wasn't easy because the smooth and rounded stones kept slipping and rolling underfoot. That, too, gave me pause: can I say that a well-rounded spiritual life may mean some hard walking? That's a play on words, of course, but still… I wonder.

At the water's edge Philip told us of an old Iona tradition. We were to select one of the stones—any one that seemed to "call" to us—to hold it, to pray, and especially to think about all the burdens that we tend to carry with us throughout the day. We had walked more than an hour by that time to get there, and a number of people had even turned back as the going got rougher. All of us were tired and exhilarated at the same time. I, having set aside my loaded backpack before descending the hill to the beach, did feel a little less burdened—or at least I thought I did—but I had no trouble identifying with those for whom the way was too difficult. Nor did I have trouble recalling all the baggage I carry within myself all the time. Philip told us to take the stone we had chosen, and when we were ready, to throw it as far away into the ocean as we could, letting the stone carry all our worries and woes into the bosom of the sea. There was a holy solemnity as each of us did this. I confess that I threw more than one rock.

The weather had been warm and sunny, but gradually it was growing cloudy and cooler, and the wind was picking up, too. We walked back to the grassy area called the Machair and had our lunch sitting on top of a small knoll. I was astonished when Philip pointed out that we were looking down on the Iona golf course, where once a year there is a golf tournament—the Iona Open. What a wonderful place to play golf! One of the holes was down in a declivity, and a scratchily painted sign pointed down to it, so the golfers could see more or less where to aim their balls.

After lunch the sun disappeared, the wind picked up considerably, and we needed our warm jackets (at last I was glad I had lugged so much with me in my backpack!). Then the weather became wild, and when Philip mentioned the "wildness of God," I knew immediately what he meant. From where we were we could see the sea, and where formerly there had been gentle wavelets washing in, now there was real surf. We could hear the boom of the waves pounding against the cliffs even above the wind. All the majesty of God was laid out before our eyes, in the wind, the waves, the sea, the waving grass, and the blowing sand, with the trusting sheep continuing their grazing totally unconcerned. I was a little afraid on top of that small hill in such a high wind, I admit, and I was not sorry when we headed back to shelter.

But I had to think about that, too. Yesterday we had visited the hermit's cell on the side of Dun Í, and now I was imagining myself there again. How much shelter would a beehive hut give me in such a strong wind? Would I have had a small fire for warmth and for light? Would I have had a warm wrap to bundle up in? Would there have been enough food to sustain me so that I need not go out into the raging elements to gather? Food indeed—food for thought. When I talk about Celtic Christianity and imitating the Celtic monks, am I being selective? How can I be a modern Celtic monk with my L. L. Bean Gor-Tex jacket and my warm waterproof boots? Furthermore, I know that a tasty gourmet meal is waiting for me at our hotel. How then am I imitating one of the Celtic saints who lived in such dedicated austerity? What, then, is Celtic Christianity to me? What has so captured the imagination of countless people today?

And then there is the wildness of God. With the wildness of the elements raging around me, I find it easy to think about the wildness of God: God in wild passion for creation, God laughing with delight at the raging of the sea and the turbulence of the wind... God in love with creation. If God is in love with all creation, then God is in love with me. This was my thought as we walked back to the calm and security of our hotel: God in love with creation; God in love with me. God in love with creation; God in love with me.

Kilmartin

I STUMBLED ACROSS the riches of the Kilmartin Valley quite by accident; a passing comment in a book about Columba referred to a place called Dunadd, stating that such was where Columba had anointed one of the kings of Dalriada. Dunadd, the book said, was the secular capital of that part of Scotland as surely as Iona was the ecclesiastical capital, and there is little doubt that Columba had more than casual contact with the secular rulers of his day. I was determined to see this place.

Dunadd, about eighty miles northwest of Glasgow, is a lumpy rock rising above the River Add. It takes its name from the Scottish dún Add, meaning the hillfort situated above the River Add. The river's multiple serpentine bends loop inward from Loch Crinan to form an enormous flat peat bog, the Mòine Mhór. Also flowing through the Mòine Mhór is the Kilmartin Burn, and the relatively isolated hump Dunadd is thus in a position to control the entire Y-shaped valley. Excavations have shown the valley to have been occupied as early as 3000 B.C.E., and Dunadd itself from about 600 B.C.E.

Temple Wood stone circle, Kilmartin Valley

*Cup and ring marks at Achnabreck,
Kilmartin Valley*

*Three standing stones in the Nether Largie
South group, Kilmartin Valley*

The rock of Dunadd is ideal for defense, not only because of its isolation from other elevations in the area, but also because there is a deep cleft between two rock promontories on the east face of the rock and sheer cliffs on the other sides. Thus one can only access the fort itself by ascending a steep path between the two rock cliffs, and such a narrow defile could easily be defended. Each time I have climbed Dunadd and walked through the defenses, I am reminded of the high likelihood that St. Columba himself walked this same path 1400 years ago. In fact, tradition holds that Columba consecrated the kings of Dalriada here on the famous Coronation Stone, or Stone of Destiny, originally at Dunadd but later removed to Scone.

Steep as it is, the climb up Dunadd is worth the effort, for the view up the valley on a clear day is quite spectacular. Even when the weather is cloudy, still visible on Dunadd itself is the outline of a wild boar carved into the bedrock, which scholars date to the sixth or seventh century C.E., and a distinct foot-shaped depression that most scholars seem to think formed part of the coronation ritual of the early kings of Dalriada. When I climbed Dunadd the first time, the weather was too hazy for much of a view, but I was able to put my foot in that footprint as untold thousands have undoubtedly done before me, and I could trace with my finger the outline of the boar.

Earlier I referred to "the riches of the Kilmartin Valley"; Dunadd is not the only one. Nor is it the oldest, although it is the only one that can claim a clear connection with Columba. Stretching northward up the valley from Dunadd toward Kilmartin village lies the "Linear Cemetery," consisting of seven burial cairns in a roughly straight line about three miles long. The oldest of these is the Nether Largie South cairn, which is dated as far back as the fourth millenium B.C.E. Excavations have demonstrated that it served several generations of inhabitants who used different burial practices over the years. The cairn was built with four internal compartments totaling about twenty feet in length, with stone slabs on the sides as uprights and flat stone slabs above as a kind of ceiling. The whole area was then covered over with loose stones and dirt to form the typical rounded mound, or cairn, probably with an open area or "court" at the entrance. One description says Nether Largie

South is built "like a house of cards," but the huffing and puffing of winds and storms for three thousand years have not been able to blow it down. Since this cairn today is open at both ends, visitors can see from one end through to the other, but in order to wriggle through the compartments, a person would have to be very tiny indeed.

All the cairns in the Kilmartin Valley have been excavated to some extent, and scholars tell us that they were used and reused and built and rebuilt over many centuries. Nearly all were clearly burial sites, as human remains, some cremated and some inhumed, were found—along with pieces of pottery, jewelry, weapons, and other artifacts. Sadly, most have been "robbed," meaning that some of their artifacts, as well as stones, were removed at some point and put to other uses, whether into homes or museums or stone walls or barns or whatever.

The stone circle at Temple Wood lies just beside a paved road and is thus readily accessible. Thoroughly excavated several times, it has apparently been reassembled more than once. One of the uprights is covered with a double spiral. The carving is unique in that half of the spiral is on one face of the squarish rock and the other half is around the corner on the adjacent face. Trees were planted around the area some time during the early nineteenth century, making the area shady and inviting, unlike most of the other artifacts that are in totally exposed areas. Temple Wood is hardly as visually impressive as Stonehenge, and it has obviously been "prettied up," but still, it is an evocative site.

Scattered about the whole Kilmartin area are exposed areas of bedrock that have been carved with cup-and-ring marks, spirals, and other designs. These markings are so prevalent that they are obviously an important, even if not understood, part of the total ritual landscape. The best known of these are at Achnabreck, not far from Dunadd, although some can also be seen near the Nether Largie South cairn. At Achnabreck, several fairly broad expanses of exposed rock faces are literally covered with these mysterious designs, and no one yet has been able to decipher them. Historic Scotland has recently built a car park and opened a graded walkway to the site, making this extraordinary place easily accessible to those who do not mind a short uphill walk on a graveled pathway. But what do these hundreds of amazing spirals with what seems like radii—or perhaps gutters—pointing in different directions mean? When were they carved, and for what purpose? We simply do not know. What we do know is that they have been there, either under grass or exposed to all the elements, for countless centuries.

Even more fascinating, to me at least, are the dozens of standing stones. Isolated single stones, and occasionally pairs, can be found in all the Celtic countries, but many at Kilmartin are in groups and distinct rows. At Nether Largie, for example, seven stones form a specific pattern, rather like an X. The centermost stone is more than nine feet high and is nearly covered on one face with cup and cup-and-ring marks, very like the ones found at Achnabreck. Not far away, the Ballymeanoch stones form another linear arrangement consisting of two rows, four in one row and two in a parallel one, and three of these stones are covered with cup marks. Still farther down the valley is another group of standing stones arranged in groups of three, two, and three. We can only guess at the amount of human labor required to erect these huge monoliths.

At the northern end of the valley is Kilmartin church, the third or possibly fourth building to be constructed on this site. There is little doubt as to its originally having been a Celtic foundation, most likely a Celtic monastery, possibly founded by Columba. A reasonable conclusion is that this may have been the church serving the people of Dunadd and the rest of the Kilmartin valley in the early Christian centuries. Its dedication to St. Martin (*kill martin* meaning "church of Martin") is significant, since it is known that dedications to Martin were common in this area. The present Kilmartin church building, however, dates only from 1835. In the churchyard are about twenty-five West Highland grave slabs, some with intriguing early medieval carvings. Inside the church, and in the care of Historic Scotland, are some very fine Celtic crosses from the same school of carving as those found on Iona.

It is easy to understand why the entire valley is one of the most prolific archaeological sites in all Scotland. Fascination with the area continues because even the most expert of the experts, after years of excavations and research, still do not know exactly why the multiple standing stones are aligned the way they are, why the stone circles are positioned where they are, what the mysterious cup-and-ring marks mean, or when the burial cairns were first built. Perhaps most significant of all, no one knows why this particular valley, appropriately referred to as a "ritual landscape," was selected by our forbears as such an obviously sacred space. What we do know is that some of the ancient constructions date back to five thousand years ago—even earlier than the Pyramids—and that the valley's population and importance began to decline sometime around the tenth century when peat bogs began to cover the area. Peat is an unusually good preservative, and a high percentage of artifacts uncovered in recent decades have come from peat bogs. More artifacts, therefore, will likely come to light as more of Mòine Mhór is drained and put to the plow.

The recently founded Kilmartin Trust, which runs Kilmartin House, has done much to bring attention to this remarkable place. In the visitor center in Kilmartin village, besides the inevitable shop and café, is an audiovisual presentation and a very fine museum dedicated to the area. The riches of the Kilmartin Valley are plentiful indeed.

So why bring a Christian Celtic pilgrimage to this place? Other than the connection of Columba with Dunadd and the carved stones in Kilmartin church, what is here that would justify a Christian Celtic pilgrimage (although perhaps Dunadd and the little church are enough)? Nearly all the sites are long pre-Christian, and most are even pre-Celtic. Yet, if a pilgrimage is a journey undertaken in search of that which is holy, then surely such is justification enough to visit this exceptional valley. That it has been an area of religious observance, a place sacred to our forbears, can hardly be questioned. When we limit our own understanding of God to Christian doctrine and the worship of God to Christian practice, we limit our appreciation of such holy sites. It may be another century before all the mysteries of Kilmartin are understood—if then—but mystery and numen are certainly abundantly present for those who are sensitive to such things and consciously seeking the Holy for their own lives.

The Communion of Saints is a doctrine very dear to my heart. I won-
der if it stems from my deep feelings of insecurity, my need to feel that
I belong, that I belong to my family, to my sisters in the convent, and
to my friends. It reminds me that I do not exist just for today but that I
am one with all those who have gone before as well as with those who
will follow. I'm glad the American Book of Common Prayer *has a spe-*
cial day to celebrate the Saints of the Old Testament, because when I
was in the Holy Land it was very significant for me to realize that
Moses and Abraham and Rachel and Leah and Isaiah are my also
brothers and sisters.

But here at Kilmartin, I found myself equally moved to realize that
the unknown inhabitants of this amazing valley from thousands and
thousands of years ago are also my brothers and sisters. It's humbling
to think along those lines. I am just one grain of sand on the ocean's
shore, and God's love is so limitless that every grain of sand on every
shore is dear to God's heart. I wonder if the writers of Matthew and
Luke who tell us that every sparrow matters and even the hairs of our
head are all counted (Matthew 10:29–30; Luke 12:7) were aware of the
ten thousand times ten thousand humans who have gone before us and
who were still precious in God's sight—to say nothing of the millions
of people alive on the planet today and those who will be born tomor-
row. Trying to grasp this extent of God's love and concern for all crea-
tures is indeed too much for us to comprehend.

I began to think along these lines when I had my foot in the foot-
print on top of Dunadd. The sun was out and the day was amazingly
clear—I could see for miles. I was overcome with the realization that
more people than could ever be counted had lived in this very valley.
While I was pondering such thoughts, a young family arrived at the
top, husband, wife, and two children aged perhaps six and four, a boy
and a girl. Naturally they wanted to put a foot in the footprint, just as
I had, so I moved away a bit and sat down by myself. To my amaze-
ment, I heard the father ask the children, "How many people do you
think have done that?" The younger child looked up at her daddy and
thought for a minute, pointed at me, and said, "Well, that lady did. I
saw her." After a warm smile, the father then went on to explain to the
two children that this place was older than anyone could figure, and
that so many people had been to the top of Dunadd and looked down

on that looping river that no one could ever count them. "More than a million?" asked the little boy. "More than a million million," said their daddy. I was touched at the gentleness and simplicity of this family and their sense of history, and I was pleased to think that they are my brothers and sisters, too—also members of the Communion of Saints, regardless of what their religious beliefs might be, or regardless of even whether they had any religious beliefs.

On another occasion when I was at Kilmartin, I was looking at the ancient carved spirals on one of the uprights at Temple Wood Circle. The spirals are quite prominent once you see them, but unless you know which is the right stone, they can be hard to find. I was just pointing them out to an elderly couple who were interested when a whole troop of bike riders came by, maybe fifteen or twenty of them in their brightly colored riding attire, and they did not seem to find much of particular interest in the circle. As best I could tell, only one or two of them even glanced at the interpretive panels, while the rest were busy with their cameras taking pictures of one another. One young man climbed up on one of the uprights—quite a feat, since they are not flat on top—to have his picture taken. He called out something to his friends in a language I did not understand. They did not stay long but soon moved off to presumably more impressive sites.

A little later that same day I was at the Ballymeanoch standing stones, sitting amidst the sheep and waiting for the sun to come out from behind a small cloud cover so I could take a photograph, when a young man, perhaps college age, walked up to the tallest of the stones and without any self-consciousness or hesitation, threw his arms around it and laid his ear against the stone. I couldn't take my eyes off him. What was he hearing? Was he hearing the stones sing (Luke 19:40)? Whatever it was, it occupied him a very long time (the sun came out and went in again, and I could not move!). He went to each of the four stones in the line, one by one, and then wandered off toward the other two a little distance away. Each time he did exactly the same thing. Utterly oblivious of me or the sheep or anything else, as far as I could tell, he put his arms around each stone and his ear to its surface— and listened. His was an attitude of total reverence. Happily for me a little later the sun came out again and I could take my pictures, but I kept thinking about the family atop Dunadd, the roisterous cyclists, *and the young man, all so different, with such individual approaches to the holy sites and valuing them in such different ways.*

As I look back, I think I was as taken with the contemporary as I was with the ancient human presence. Yet, all the people I have met at the various sites are still part of the same Communion of Saints. Much as I may wish it otherwise, I cannot pick and choose my brothers and sisters, any more than a grain of sand can choose its own beach. Surely, somehow, all of us fit together in God's scheme of things.

Whithorn

THAT WHITHORN IS THE FIRST recorded Christian settlement in Scotland can no longer be disputed; that this settlement was established by a saint named Ninian is highly debatable. Ninian, a shadowy and elusive figure at best, continues to intrigue students and historians alike, and no one yet has offered a sufficiently convincing explanation that is generally accepted as to who he was or where he came from. However, the establishment of a fifth-century Christian foundation at Whithorn is now an unarguable fact.

A friend of mine who also leads pilgrimages once said to me, "Why do you go to Whithorn? Everyone I have talked to says there is nothing much there." In a certain sense that is true; there are no alluring Celtic ruins to roam in, no high crosses to stand before in awe, nothing of overwhelming grandeur. That does not mean, though, that there is nothing there. Recent archaeology has given us some exciting finds. When the Whithorn Dig was begun in 1984, no one was quite sure what would be uncovered, but by 1990 it was clearly established that Whithorn had been a Christian settlement from very early times. Some scholars speculate (but without hard evidence) that it may have been Whithorn to which Tertullian referred when he wrote in the third century that there were Christian settlements in Britain beyond the boundaries of the Roman Empire.

In the museum at Whithorn is a large collection of early Christian stones. Detailed analysis of the inscriptions, including

Looking out from St. Ninian's Cave, Physgill, Whithorn

studying the shape of the carved letters as well as the content of the message, is an essential aspect of historical research, for these stones are authentic historical documents for their period. By far the most important of the Whithorn stones is the Latinus Stone. In 1992 the Honorable Charles Thomas, one of Britain's most eminent archaeologists, after exhaustive research and years of comparative studies, suggested that the Latinus Stone was not a memorial stone on a tomb, as had formerly been thought, but instead was a place marker denoting the presence of a church. The details of Professor Thomas's argument are not necessary here, but suffice it to say his thesis has now been widely accepted and has altered the direction of Whithorn and Ninianic studies.[36]

Accepting the presence of a mid-fifth century Christian monastery at Whithorn, which predates even Patrick's foundations in Ireland, still does not shed much light on St. Ninian himself. The Venerable Bede, writing in the eighth century, remains our earliest literary source for Ninian. Bede asserts that Ninian, a "most holy man" had studied in Rome, thereby implying Ninian's total theological orthodoxy. Bede also tells us that this Ninian (or Nynia) built a Candida Casa, or White House, of stone, something most unusual for the Britons. Bede does not tell us how he got this information, but most scholars tend to think he may have learned it from his friend Bishop Pechthelm of Whithorn, who was passing on to Bede a strong local tradition that Ninian was the founder of Whithorn.

Only two other early literary sources of information about Ninian exist. One is a poem, also from the eighth-century monastery at Whithorn, the "Miracula Nynie Episcopoi" (The Miracles of Bishop Ninian), which, even while drawing on the same local tradition as did Pechthelm, tells us more about life in the monastery of that time than it does about the historical Ninian. The other source, from the twelfth century, is Ailred of Rievaux's prose *Life of Ninian*. This latter, more hagiographical than historical, is the source for most of the Ninian stories set forth today as authentic.

"Will the real Ninian, then, please stand up and identify himself?" There is no doubt that there was an apostle to the Pictish peoples during the fifth century, but we do not know exactly who that apostle might have been. That there was a real Ninian is also without doubt, but exactly when he lived we do not know. There is too strong a tradition connecting Ninian with Whithorn, however, to disregard it; and there are too many place names and too strong a Ninian cult in the later medieval period to erase him from history as fantasy. Nevertheless, it seems unlikely that we will ever be able to answer all of our questions about him.

And what about Candida Casa, the "shining white hut," as some have translated it—was it for real? Archaeology has given us a reliable answer to that: yes, Candida Casa was for real. As the Whithorn Dig continued into the nineties, it gradually became possible to trace the outline of a circular Celtic monastery. There were any number of Christian graves. Many other artifacts, such as fragments of glass, pieces of pottery, and shards of amphorae implied a lively trade with the Mediterranean world and a wealthy and sophisticated society. Most exciting was the discovery of a pile of builders' rubble consisting of stones of gray lime and coated with a thick skin of calcium carbonate. Any building made from such stones would indeed have been a shining white hut, especially when wet. And, not long after that discovery, the foundation wall of a small building constructed of those same stones was found beneath the western end of the medieval cathedral. Most scholars today, therefore, are satisfied that there was indeed a Candida Casa and that the remains of it can still be seen at Whithorn.

Whithorn itself is situated in a hollow, about two miles inland from the sea. Although it was an ecclesiastical settlement, there is little doubt that a secular establishment, a commercial seaport from which trading could take place, must have been nearby. We can assume that the Isle of Whithorn with its fine protected harbor, three miles further down the peninsula, was such a port. Plans are being considered at present to excavate the far end of the Isle of Whithorn promontory where what looks like the remains of a coastal promontory fort barely can be discerned. Such forts were common during the Celtic period and can be found elsewhere in Scotland, in Wales, on the Isle of Man, and in Ireland. Evidence suggests that this promontory fort on the Isle of Whithorn stood in the same secular relationship to the monastery at Whithorn as Dunadd did to Iona, but until systematic excavation can take place, this is only speculation.

Today I went to St. Ninian's Cave near Physgill. I'd climbed many holy mountains, visited many ancient churches, prowled around dozens (probably hundreds) of venerable ruins, and been to more holy wells than I can now count, but Ninian's Cave at Whithorn was my first holy cave, and it did not take long to capture my imagination and spark my interest. I could tell that it is a popular place with local people, but I don't think it is very well known beyond Galloway.

The walk from the parking lot to the cave is about a mile and a half long, through some of the loveliest woods I have ever seen and following the course of a small stream. Birds were singing, the wind was rustling, the trees were furry with new growth, the bluebells were in full bloom, and the magic of all that sound and color in the dappled sunlight of the woods took my breath away. When I finally left the shady and musical spring woods, I stepped out into the bright sunlight of the beach, or shingle. The sea was calm and blue, shimmering with sunlight, and there, stretched out on the horizon, was the wavy profile of the Isle of Man. It had as strong a siren call to me as it ever had for any sailor or pilgrim, Celtic or otherwise.

The cave was a dark opening in the high cliffs ahead of me, not facing the sea as I had expected it to, but facing the shingle itself. In other words, I was walking right into its entrance. The walls of the cave were yellowish brown and not surprisingly marked in many places with graffiti, including some very old incised Celtic crosses.

I was not alone at the cave; others were there also, in particular a young adult couple who seemed more interested in each other than in anything else, and two young mothers with a bevy of children. The mothers were sitting together on the rocks, looking out to sea and talking together quietly while the children climbed on the rocks and played games known only to themselves.

After a bit, two men came to the cave, burly bearded men, who looked like they might be father and son. When they got to the cave, not far from where I was sitting, both took out cigars and lit them up. The smoke drifting downwind toward where I was sitting was offensive to me, so I moved away and sat closer to the water. The two men went into the cave and seemed to stay a long time; in the meantime the children and their mothers drifted back toward the path through the woods. The sound of their merry shouts and laughter grew dim as they walked away. The couple had gone long since, and after a while the two men left also. I was at the cave with only the great dome of the sky and the vastness of the sea for company.

I had been sitting for a long time, not praying, just woolgathering and staring out at the sea, but once all the others were gone, I got up and went back into the cave. I was taken aback by a strong smell of urine, and to my disgust, I saw two large wet patches against the back wall of the cave that I knew had not been there earlier. What was a holy place for me, and a place of recreation for the mothers and their children, was a latrine for the two men with their cigars.

Clouds had begun to obliterate the sun, a chilly breeze had sprung up, and suddenly I was very depressed. I tried to think of all the Scripture passages I could about caves. I could remember the Cave of Machpelah where Abraham had buried Sarah, and the cave where Joshua had hidden the five kings, and the cave where Saul had gone "to relieve himself" (just like the men with the cigars). I also thought of Lazarus in his cave, and I tried to picture Jesus calling Lazarus forth from Ninian's Cave. It just wouldn't work. Ninian's cave isn't big and cavernous like the caves in the Middle East; this is more like an enormous and deep cleft in the rocky cliffs. It would be nearly impossible to block the mouth of Ninian's cave with stones, so to use it as a place of burial would hardly be practical. This made me realize, of course, that "cave" must have brought to mind something very different for the Celtic peoples when they were first introduced to the Scriptures. My musing thus about all these caves was interesting, but it did not do much to lift my depression.

I could not forget Elijah. He had been depressed, too, when he went into his cave. "The word of the Lord came to Elijah saying, 'What are you doing here, Elijah?'" That's exactly what I felt like. What are you doing here, Cintra? Do you really need to travel 3500 miles across the Atlantic Ocean to deepen your own spirituality? Can you not find spiritual sustenance in your own country? I remembered only too well the Irish proverb:

To go to Rome, much effort, much pain;
the King whom you seek if you carry not with you,
little profit, little gain.

So why, then, was I here in Scotland?
I stood at the entrance to the cave in the fresh air and placed my hand against one of the ancient incised crosses and looked out at the shingle. Like Elijah, I listened for God's voice.

[God] said [to Elijah], "Go out and stand on the mountain before the LORD, for the LORD is about to pass by." Now there was a great wind, so strong that it was splitting mountains and breaking rocks in pieces before the LORD, but the LORD was not in the wind; and after the wind an earthquake, but the LORD was not in the earthquake; and after the earthquake a fire, but the LORD was not in the fire; and after the fire a sound of sheer silence. When Elijah heard it, he wrapped his face in his mantle and went out and stood at the entrance of the cave. Then there came a voice to him that said, "What are you doing here, Elijah?" (1 Kings 19:11–13)

The wind had picked up, and I could hear it well, but there was no earthquake and no fire—nor was there a still small voice or a sound of sheer silence. The only voice I could hear was the one asking me why I was here in Scotland.
It was getting cold now, with the evening coming on, and I huddled into my coat and bundled up as warmly as I could. As I walked slowly back to the car, across the rocky shingle and into the darkening woods, I thought about why I was in Scotland. I thought about the hundreds of

people who have shared a pilgrimage with me, and I thought about the many letters they have written to me telling me of their rich experiences while on those pilgrimages. I thought about all the wonderful people I have met, on both sides of the Atlantic, in connection with the pilgrimages, and I thought about all the gracious and loving hospitality I have received in so many places. I thought about all the incredibly rich experiences I have had in these Celtic countries, and my heart overflowed. By the time I got to the car, I was crying, and I knew why I was in Scotland.

Some pilgrimage
sites on

The Isle of Man

Praying in ancient Keeill, Maughold

*St. Maughold's Holy Well,
Maughold, Isle of Man*

*The fourteenth century preaching cross inside
Maughold Church*

Maughold

IF YOU'RE ON THE ISLE OF MAN on a very clear day, you can take the tram railway to the top of Snaefel mountain and have a grand view of all the Celtic lands encircling the Irish Sea. To the north, you can see the Mull of Galloway and Ninian's Whithorn; due east are the mountains of Cumbria, England's Lake District, which in Celtic times was part of Wales (Cumbria = Cymru = Wales). South are the mountains of Snowdonia in northwest Wales; and along the western horizon are the mountains of Ulster in northern Ireland. Similarly, if you are gazing at the horizon from any of these areas and the air is clear enough, the Isle of Man is just visible, a slim wavy profile beckoning across the blue sea. No wonder so many of the Celtic wanderers touched down here and the Vikings later used it as a base of operations.

Who was St. Maughold? As with so many of the Celtic saints, we don't really know, but tradition has it that Maughold (pronounced MACK-old) and Patrick did not get along at all. Some say Maughold even tried to murder Patrick, but we have no idea why. At any rate, Patrick banished Maughold to the sea in a coracle without rudder, oars, or sail, and in that wonderful way of the Celtic saints, Maughold trusted totally in the leading of God and managed to land safely on the Isle of Man. There he apparently repented of whatever it was that he had done in Ireland and founded a monastery, on the site that still bears his name. In due time Maughold became a bishop, and next to Patrick himself, Maughold is probably the most honored of the Manx saints.

We know that Mann was occupied by hunter-fishermen of the Middle Stone Age (Mesolithic), about 5000 to 3000 B.C.E., and archaeology gives evidence of human occupation through the succeeding periods. Dating from the New Stone Age (Neolithic period) we find standing stones, megaliths, cairns, and burial chambers scattered about the island. Much later, during the pre-Christian Celtic period, perhaps sometime in the second or first century B.C.E., an Iron Age promontory fort was built on the headland at what is now Maughold.

So, St. Maughold was not the first to occupy that particular promontory, and when he founded his monastery there in the fifth century, he was building on land that had been a sacred space for millennia. It is even possible that when St. Maughold first arrived (some say he was washed ashore just below the headland), a settled community was already living there in round houses, or raths. Perhaps it was those settlers who rescued him from his ordeal in the sea—and whom he subsequently converted to Christianity. It is said that a spring burst forth where he landed, promptly becoming St. Maughold's holy well and a place of Christian baptism. We don't know any of this, to be sure, but it is one possible way, perhaps even a plausible way, that things might have unfolded. Scholars do seem convinced, however, that St. Maughold is buried in the grounds of his own monastic foundation.

The Maughold site, regardless of its documentable history, is a palpably holy place. In the churchyard are the visible remains of three *keeills*, or small chapels; a fourth is marked only by a short granite pillar. A fifth *keeill* lies beneath the foundations of the porch of the church. More than 180 such *keeills* are scattered all over the Isle of Man, dating from perhaps the eighth to twelfth centuries, but it is likely that chapels of wattle and daub or even of sod predated the stone-faced remains that we see today. Typically a *keeill* has a rectangular shape, about ten feet wide by fifteen feet long, and sometimes the remains of an altar can be seen at the east end. At Maughold the three readily visible *keeills* are in various places within the modern cemetery, and there is a sense of continuity with these early Christians, with those who have been buried in more recent times, and with today's people, who still worship regularly in the parish church—sometimes even in the ancient *keeills* themselves.

But it is not only the *keeills* that remind us of the Isle of Man's early Christian past. Superb collections of carved Christian cross slabs are found at a number of places on the island. An especially fine group at Maughold is displayed in the cross house built in

1906. The oldest of these crosses, dated to about the seventh century, is a memorial to a Celtic bishop named Irneit, a successor to St. Maughold himself. At the top of the slab is a carved hexafoil pattern (sometimes called a "marigold") with the six perfect arcs forming the kind of "flower" children like to make when they first learn to use a compass. The inscription to Bishop Irneit surrounds this hexafoil, and below it are two more crosses of a simple Chi Rho form, with a Latin inscription reading, "I have made in Christ's name an image of the Cross of Christ." The style of the letters shows the connection of the early Manx Christian church with Ireland, Britain, and Gaul.

Irneit's Cross is only one of the twenty-five or so cross slabs at Maughold, but it seems to be the oldest. One of my favorites is another cross with two monks facing each other across the main shaft. This one is later, probably ninth century. A beautiful ringed Celtic cross fills the upper third of the slab, while the monks, most likely Paul and Antony from the Egyptian desert, sit on little cross-legged stools conversing with each other.

Branhui's cross slab, a little later than Irneit's, is broken and incomplete, but enough is left of the Celtic cross to indicate its beauty. The circle of the cross is in low relief, making the arms stand out clearly. What can be read in the inscription in the center says, in Roman lettering, "BRANHUI LED OFF WATER TO THIS PLACE." Traces of an eighth-century stone-lined conduit have been found at Maughold, so one might guess that Branhui was the engineer who laid it out. Branhui is a Welsh name, which is further indication of the travels and contacts between the Celtic monks from the different Celtic countries.

There are hundreds of carved crosses on the Isle of Man, not only at Maughold, but also at Kirk Andreas, Jurby, Kirk Michael, Braddan, Lonan, and Onchan—and still more in the Manx Museum. All of the crosses on the island are in the care of the Manx Museum and National Trust, although in the early part of the century the decision was made to keep the crosses in their original parishes. Most of the parish churches with crosses have either built cross houses, similar to the one at Maughold, or moved the crosses inside the churches to a display area.

Many of the later crosses, from the late tenth or early eleventh centuries, tell the Norse story of Sigurd. These carvings are wonderfully detailed, and all the aspects of the tale are depicted in the stone. Sigurd story crosses remain in a number of places. The one at Maughold shows Loki, crouching, throwing a stone to kill Otter, the Great Fisher, who holds a salmon in his mouth. Higher up on the cross is Grani, Sigurd's horse, carrying a heavy load of treasure on its back.

The present day Maughold church was built in the eleventh or twelfth century. Like so many churches in both Britain and Ireland, the original church was later enlarged by the Normans, with the most recent restorations taking place in 1860 and again in the early part of this century. The interior looks Victorian, but signs of the older architecture are unmistakable. There are two eleventh- or twelfth- century windows in the south wall and an Irish Romanesque arch with nail head over the west door. The window in the gable above the altar was apparently the original east window, but it was raised up into the gable when a new east window, a larger replica of its predecessor, was installed behind the altar in 1900.

Of greatest interest inside the church itself, however, is the parish preaching cross, which originally stood on the green outside the churchyard. Moved first into the churchyard in 1937 to a position across from the cross house, it now stands in the nave of the church for protection. The cross is dated to the fourteenth century and has carvings all around: on the east face is Christ on the cross; on the west, the Virgin and Child; on the south, the kneeling figure of a knight; and on the north, a shield displaying a rose with oak leaves. Some people speculate that the oak leaves might have some connection with Brigid of Kildare.

The most significant carving, however, is a shield on the neck of the cross that shows the Three Legs of Man, but going in reverse direction to present usage. No one seems to know why or when the change in direction occurred. The Three Legs found on the Sword of State in St. John's Church and those found on the cross at Maughold, from the twelfth and fourteenth centuries respectively, are the two earliest representations of the symbol that is now universally recognized as a "logo" for the Isle of Man.

Maughold Church is well cared for and obviously much loved. Perhaps the original Maughold was a scoundrel before he became a bishop, but the church he founded is an ancient, revered, and holy place, unquestionably established on a sure foundation. It continues as a regular parish church serving the people of the surrounding area, just as it has done for centuries.

Today I participated in a quiet day, a day of reflection, at Maughold. I wasn't sure how much exploring of the area I wanted to do, because the day was cloudy, cold, and blustery. Nevertheless I put on my warmest wool sweater over a thermal turtleneck and hoped for the best.

We began with a meditation in the church and were encouraged to think of silence as a doorway to our inner selves. What a wonderful thought! We were also told that silence is a gift, a gift from God, but it's also a gift that we must give each other. I'd never thought of it that way before. I can only be truly silent if you give that gift to me—and vice versa. That made me realize that silence isn't something that's imposed, meaning that nobody is allowed to talk to anybody, but rather something that is grace-filled and wonderful. So by intentionally not talking to you, I am giving that special gift to you, offering you the opportunity to enter that doorway into your inner self, and likewise, you give that same special gift to me. Since everybody was giving such a gift to each other all day long, it was truly a transcendent time, a time to really focus on God and to be overwhelmed by the closeness of God.

We had been given maps of the Maughold headland that showed paths and walks—how to get to St. Maughold's Well and the lighthouse and where the cliff walks were. So, with my map snapping in the wind, from the church I went first to the well, grateful the whole time to be alone and quiet (although the wind was so strong nobody would have been able to talk much anyway—another aspect of the gift). It was a little precipitous getting there, following a well-marked grassy track that wound around the headland and then descended steeply to where a clear spring emerged from the bosom of earth. The water then flowed softly across a small patch of smooth rock face before plunging down to the sea. Making a green halo around the opening were nodding ferns. I knelt down and washed my face in the water, three times, in the name of the Trinity, and then stood beside the well looking out at the sea while the air dried me. The wind and the waves were so loud that I could barely hear the gentle flow of water from the well, which made the water's song like the still small voice of God behind the roar of everyday life. A natural spring is hardly a burning bush, but I felt like I was standing on holy ground and wanted to take off my shoes.

After a short while I left the well and walked on alone, farther along the cliff path. At times the path was very near the edge, and I was grateful for the protecting fence—the wind was so strong I feared I might lose my balance and be blown off the cliffs several hundred feet into the sea below. The precariousness of my physical situation in some way seemed to match a certain precariousness in my spiritual life. Am I fearful of falling away from the church? Not falling away from God, surely, but away from so much in the church that in former years I have held dear. When I was younger I never questioned the male dominance or the hierarchy or authority or the clericalism in the church; now I question all these things. The majesty and transcendence of the liturgy still feeds me, but today I find myself with lots of questions. Too many people have shared aspects of their own faith journeys with me for me to be unaware how liturgy, so often the exclusive domain of the ordained clergy, can be a wall, a barrier, between the people and God. It's as though the clergy with all their defined roles come between people and God, rather than being a way to God. And yet, the beauty of the liturgy, when solemnly and reverently offered, is rich indeed. I am not clear about my own feelings, and I do not find it easy to talk about. The church today is one of the biggest mysteries in my life.

I wonder why I am so self-conscious about my spiritual life. I experience the presence of God so very strongly at times, yet not very often anymore in church, and usually I don't want to talk about it. Is it because I question too many things? Am I embarrassed about my faith (or perhaps my lack of it)? Do I somehow sense that what I feel is something no one else feels? Or is my deepest spiritual life something rather like parts of my body—best left private, undiscussed, and covered up?

If that is so, then how do we witness for our beliefs? How do we help one another along the spiritual journey? I know how nourished I often am by others' willingness to share parts of their spiritual lives with me, so why am I so reluctant to share mine with others? Then, on the other hand, perhaps it isn't self-consciousness or reluctance at all—maybe it's simply my inability to articulate something so deep and so profound.

Sitting on the bench above the lighthouse I tried to draw it all together. The wind was really strong, making the sea a foamy chaos, and I could hear the boom of the surf relentlessly attacking the rock faces below me. How could anyone not believe in God when surrounded by such awesome power and majesty? "You ride on the wings of the wind" says one of the Psalms, and somewhere else, "Your way was in the sea and your paths in the great waters, yet your footsteps were not seen." And in Genesis, the Spirit hovers over the face of the waters. I could feel that Spirit hovering over me, smoothing away the rough edges of my questions and becoming a liturgy of nature that was offering me new life. At this point I walked back to the church, where we were to have Eucharist in one of the ancient keeills. I did not see the footsteps of God, but for me on this quiet day, God's way to me was surely in the sea.

Some pilgrimage sites in Wales

St. David's Cathedral
Cadw: Welsh Historic Monuments. Crown Copyright.

St. David's

WHEN APPROACHING ST. DAVID'S from the south, you are abruptly confronted with the sea. Where there is a bend in the highway near the Newgale Sands, the view takes you by surprise, and someone with vision had the wisdom to build a pullout for parking, so you can stop and feast your eyes. Before you is the rich curve of St. Bride's Bay opening out onto the Atlantic. To the left are the towers of industrialized Milford Haven, where the *Sea Empress* oil spill took place a few years ago. To the right, beyond the tiny island of Green Scar, is larger Ramsey Island, home to an early Celtic foundation, and the jutting headland of St. David's. Curving up the heather-clad cliffs on both sides of the bay is the Pembrokeshire Coastal Path, a footpath that follows the coastline of southwest Wales for 186 miles.

A drive of another ten minutes or so takes you into St. David's, Britain's tiniest city, population three thousand. Upon arriving, visitors cannot see the cathedral in the town center as expected, but beyond the market cross they can spot the top of the square tower with its blue clock face. Scholars are not in agreement as to why the cathedral was built low down in the valley. Some say it was to keep it out of sight from the sea and to offer protection from marine marauders, such as Vikings. Others suggest that it was built in the valley simply to be near the water supply. For whatever reason, the cathedral stands in the Vallis Rosina on the bank of the Alun River, where St. David founded his monastery in the sixth century. Tradition holds that David himself is buried beneath today's building.

The present cathedral was originally constructed in the twelfth century, but it was enlarged and added to in later periods. Its crowning glory inside is the nave ceiling. One of the cathedral guides tells a delightful story of the American tourist who asked if the ceiling is a new one (the splendidly carved golden Irish oak does look fresh and new). The answer is a smiling, "Well, it's the newest we have. It was put up there in the sixteenth century."

The stone screen, or *pulpitum*, separating the nave from the chancel is most unusual in that it is asymmetrical, with three niches containing statues of saints above a stone altar on the north side and a statue of St. David and Bishop Henry Gower's tomb on the south. Another unusual feature in the cathedral is the tomb of Edmund Tudor, grandfather of Henry VIII, positioned most prominently (but most inconveniently) in the center of the passage between the choir and the chancel. It was the presence of this royal tomb, however, that saved the main cathedral from destruction during the Reformation. The reigning sovereign is a member of the St. David's Cathedral Chapter and has a permanent seat in the choir, a situation not found elsewhere in Britain.

Like all medieval cathedrals, St. David's is an architectural composite from several different centuries and is a storehouse of treasures and tales. Memorial alabaster and medieval stained glass are among the treasures, and the story of why the nave arches lean outward is one of the tales. They could lean for purely aesthetic reasons, an intentional symbol of arms stretched outward and upward in praise. They could lean for architectural strengthening to support the huge stone tower (the tower was at one time near collapse). They could also lean because of subsidence, an unfortunate result of the cathedral's being built on a marshy bank with the ground beneath soft and unstable. When the great architect Sir Gilbert Scott undertook his nineteenth-century restoration of the cathedral, dealing with the outward-leaning arches was one of his particular challenges. But ultimately, why the arches lean, no one really knows.

St. David's Cathedral radiates a special charm, with its purple-pink sandstone warm and welcoming. It is not so huge as to be overwhelming, and the atmosphere is nearly always quiet and reverent. Because St. David's is off the beaten track, it has nowhere near the vast numbers of visitors that other great cathedrals do, although it certainly has its share, particularly in high summer. Nevertheless, it is a cathedral that is easy to pray in, and it has an outstanding program of music. Departing from tradition a few years ago, the cathedral choir expanded to include young girls as well as boys, and the music has been greatly enriched as a result.

The entire St. David's area is quite remarkable, in many ways unique and with a gloriously numinous quality. Perhaps its mystique comes from its rich history, for although relatively insignificant today, St. David's was an outstanding maritime port for hundreds of years and a major pilgrimage site during the Middle Ages. Or perhaps it comes from the people who still live there, those who serve and worship in the cathedral as well as those whose life is centered in the town or the surrounding farm land. Perhaps its charm comes from a particular quality in the crisp air or the beauty of the Pembrokeshire cliffs and the magic of the sea. Probably all these things plus other intangible elements combine to make "Britain's tiniest city" astonishing. Whatever it is, St. David's has a undeniable essence that amounts almost to a siren call—people who have been there once tend to want to come back again and again. My pilgrimage groups stay in St. David's for almost a week, and still they are somewhat reluctant to move on. It is not at all unusual for pilgrims to return to St. David's later on their own for extended visits.

St. David is the patron saint of Wales, and because he neither left us autobiographical material as did St. Patrick nor had a near-contemporary biographer as did St. Columba, we have little reliable information about him. In an Irish Catalogue of the Saints, dating from the early eighth century, we find a reference to David as a bishop; his monastery is located at "Menevia" (today's St. David's). His feast day is stated as March 1, generally accepted as the date of his death in 589.

Only in 1090 did Rhygyfarch give us the first hagiography, and then it was written for political reasons, specifically to strengthen the plea for the Welsh church's independence from Canterbury (which, incidentally, did not finally take place until 1920). Although the writing was undoubtedly partly propaganda, most scholars agree that some of Rhygyfarch's details about David's early life are authentic. Dedications to David are found throughout South Wales and as far afield as Cornwall and Brittany. One strong tradition even holds that he founded Glastonbury. A number of medieval manuscripts name David as Glastonbury's patron.

David the Celtic monk was extremely ascetic in his practices and equally demanding of his fellow monks. Reputedly they even plowed their fields with yokes upon their own shoulders, refusing to use cattle or oxen. David is said to have prayed for long hours standing in the cold water of the sea; hence he is often called Dewi Ddyfrwr, or David the Waterman. David's monastery cared for the sick and indigent, all those who were in any way needy, and, of course, pilgrims. This severe way of living was not an easy existence, but it was not unusual in the Celtic period. When today's Christian Celtophiles look back longingly at the early Celtic church, it is all too easy to disregard these harsh and demanding lifestyles, so willingly adopted by the Celtic saints, not by necessity, but rather by conviction that such asceticism was pleasing to God. Few people are willing to follow such an example for today's living.

The traditional story of David's birth, his Christian mission, and his various church foundations—plus what we are told were his dying words—give us a picture of a very holy man. His mother, St. Non, is said to have been of royal descent and a niece of the great King Arthur, and David's birth was foretold by Merlin.

As the story goes, Sant went out riding one day, and seeing the beautiful young Non, he overcame and ravished her; thus was the young David conceived. Sant then abandoned Non and returned to his country of Ceredigion. When the time came for Non to give birth, she sought refuge from a terrible storm that was raging around her. When she lay down, suddenly she was concealed from prying eyes by the elements. Instead of the fury of tempest, she was bathed in a clear bright light, and all was quiet and calm. To this day, visitors can find the field where David was born and see the stone that Non reputedly grasped while in labor, which is said to bear the imprints of her fingers. At the edge of the field is St. Non's Well, still sending forth pure water from the womb of the earth.

This story, told long after the sixth century when David was actually born, has all the earmarks of a story designed to reinforce the Christian message. David was born of a human mother but without a father (who had conveniently disappeared); a great light shone above his place of birth, and the prophecies that he would be great, a leader among his people, came true. No great leap of imagination is needed to connect this with the Christmas story.

It seems that even when David was a young boy, his holiness and qualities of leadership manifested themselves. According to Rhygyfarch, he was educated at the best learning centers of the day, was ordained as a priest, and became an outstanding missionary bishop. The words David said on his deathbed are generally accepted as authentic and illustrate his own attitude to life:

Frodyr a chwiorydd byddwch lawen a chedwch eich ffydd a'ch cred, a gwnewch y pethau bychain a glywsoch ac a welsoch gennyf fi.

[Brothers and sisters, be cheerful and keep your faith and belief, and do the little things that you have heard and seen through me.][37]

Most of the many stories associated with David are probably apocryphal, but all probably contain a grain of authenticity. One of the best-known stories about him is his preaching against the Pelagian heresy at Llanbadarn Fawr, not far from today's Aberystwyth. According to tradition, David was a very powerful preacher. In order for his voice to be heard by all those around him, he needed to stand above the crowd. Calling on God's help, he placed his handkerchief on the ground and then stood upon it. Immediately the ground beneath him began to rise, and thus elevated, David could speak so that his message was received by all the people. A little church now stands on the spot that tradition holds was where this event took place. Atop a small hill, it is known as Llandewi Brefi, which translated from the Welsh means "Church of David the Short." David's eloquence was accepted as a genuine gift of the Holy Spirit, and he is typically represented standing on a small cloth with the dove of the Holy Spirit on his shoulder.

Other places of interest besides the cathedral in the St. David's area include a fine fourteenth-century preaching cross in the center of the village and several of the village buildings, which date from the Middle Ages. Porth y Twr, the bell tower, still guards the entrance to the cathedral precincts, and the original medieval town walls, while not exactly complete, are very much in evidence.

Next to the cathedral are the ruins of the fourteenth-century Bishop's Palace. My first impression of these was that they were just one more set of ruins in a country filled with ruins. However, learning more about the history of the building and its string of colorful bishops who lived and prayed and worked there (at least part of the time) has made these particular ruins among my favorites. One of many delightful stories is that of the bishop who was concerned about dowries for his five daughters. To meet this need, the bishop sold off the lead from the roof of his palace in order to give his daughters in marriage to other bishops. A charming story, but one problem exists: historically speaking, at the time the lead was stripped, none of the daughters had yet been born.

Construction of the original palace began in the same period as the cathedral, but in succeeding centuries, it was apparently not grand enough to serve episcopal needs, so it gradually became more and more elegant. During the episcopacy of Bishop Henry Gower (1328–1347), the building reached its final and most magnificent form, and the remains of Bishop Gower's palace are what we see today.

One guide describes the palace as having been "a medieval bed-and-breakfast," where the bishop could entertain the literally thousands of pilgrims who came to the shrine of St. David in the cathedral next door. In exchange for their accommodations and the bishop's hospitality, pilgrims were naturally expected to leave donations. One can assume that the size of the donation greatly influenced the quality of hospitality received. At any rate, the Bishop of St. David's grew to be very wealthy indeed.

The bishop's hospitality to his wealthy pilgrim guests must have been lavish. Impressive indeed are the remains of the kitchens and the great hall. The lodging spaces in the west range of the complex provided for the dozens of retainers brought by important visitors. The bishop had his own private chapel, or oratory, with lovely carved heads at each of the corbels supporting the roof. The plastered and painted walls of his private chambers were hung with ornate tapestries; his bedroom even had glazed and shuttered windows, plus a fireplace and a private *garderobe* (latrine). We may be certain that the bishop did not live in the simple manner of David, his patron saint and predecessor.

Episcopal opulence was lavished on the actual building as well. The entire roof line projects a series of wonderfully varied carvings of heads, human and beast, and the surrounding parapet is particularly unique in its use of colored stone in a purple-and-white checkerboard pattern. Behind this parapet is a walkway where the bishop could take his exercise without ever leaving the building. From it he enjoyed a view, to the east, of his cathedral and the bell tower beyond it. A little to the north of the cathedral he could see the collected houses of his archdeacons and retainers; in the south and west he could look over his extensive fields and gardens, including his fishpond and the Alun River leading to the sea. Far away along the horizon in the west stretched the line of rock outcrops, perhaps reminding him of the Celtic past. The dramatic outcrops of pre-Cambrian rock, Penberi and Carn Llidi, still dominate the skyline, and on top of them are abandoned Celtic hill forts and the pre-Christian burial chamber, Coetan Arthur. When the entire complex of the Bishop's Palace was at its height of glory and fully functional, whitewashed and gleaming, it must have been quite a sight indeed.

Not far from St. David's is a modern retreat house run by a group of Roman Catholic sisters, and in the adjoining field are the ruins of St. Non's chapel, where David is said to have been born. The chapel is in a truly beautiful location, near the edge of the cliffs with a breathtaking view of the sea. The ruins of the chapel itself cannot be accurately dated, but excavations have uncovered some stone-lined coffins that may in fact be early Christian cist graves. The incised stone standing in the corner of the ruin has been dated to the seventh to ninth century, but there is no firm evidence that this stone is in its original location. It is fairly certain, however, that there was a chapel here from a very early date. Because St. David's was such a tremendously important place in the Age of the Saints and in the Middle Ages, countless small chapels along the coast served the steady stream of pilgrims, many of whom approached from the sea.

Near the ruins but still on the retreat house grounds is St. Non's holy well, a place of healing since time immemorial. Even the

Reformation did not diminish its popularity, and it is still visited today by innumerable pilgrims. It is easily accessible, a fifteen or twenty minute walk from the center of St. David's, and a pleasant place at which to linger and pray. Today the well is covered by a small arched hood, built at a very early period, but most recently repaired and restored in 1951. A small ledge at the edge of the well allows pilgrims to stoop and dip their hands or feet in the water. Offerings of white pebbles or pins are still left in the well's bottom, silent testimony to the well's ongoing popularity.

Across the water from St. Non's lies Ramsey Island, separated from the St. David's headland by only about a mile of water. The tidal flow between the island and the mainland may run as fast as eight knots, and the tides themselves range between twenty and thirty feet; the fierce currents thus created are treated by the local boatmen with the highest respect. Consequently a crossing over to Ramsey is not always possible.

However, when the seas are not too rough, not only do the boats cross for day-only visits, but they also make a seven-mile circuit around the island itself, going out into the Atlantic to see the western side. The rocky cliffs of Ramsey are high and impressive, and there is only one safe landing place on the island. Recreational boats such as rubber dinghies can be used to explore the splendid coastal scenery and even venture into sea caves cut deep into the towering cliffs. Kayaks are frequently seen running the white water caused by the strong tide crossing a row of particularly treacherous rocks called the Bitches.

The island, now owned by the Royal Society for the Protection of Birds, is home to thousands of sea birds, hundreds of inquisitive Atlantic gray seals, many small mammals, and a herd of red deer. Interestingly, the much-loved puffin does not nest on Ramsey, but the normal bird population includes (besides the omnipresent seagull) kittiwakes, razorbills, oyster catchers, guillemots, shearwaters, fulmars, gannets, and even the relatively rare choughs. Lovers of the sea and bird and marine wildlife greatly value knowing that the area is preserved from any kind of depredation or future development.

The island's name, Ramsey, is Scandinavian—proof positive that the Vikings were in the area in the ninth and tenth centuries.

Whatever Celtic establishment(s) may have been on the island during the Age of the Saints likely were subsequently destroyed. The island features few archaeological remains, only the vague outlines of two Celtic hermitages and a holy well, long since capped and disused, and one small fragment of a carved stone, now on display in the National Museum of Wales in Cardiff.

Archaeology aside, however, local tradition assures us that during the Celtic period (sixth century), Ramsey was home to two hermits, Justinian, who came from Brittany, and Honorius. The story goes that Justinian arrived on the island and found Honorius already living there with his sister and her maid. This irritated Justinian, who insisted that there be no women on the island. Once that small problem was taken care of (the stories do not tell us how), Justinian and Honorius shared the island peaceably, both men living separately as hermits. We know no more about Honorius, but apparently Justinian and David became friends, each trying to outdo the other in austerity of living.

One story tells of Justinian's frustration at what he considered the lax life in David's monastery, which sent him in a huff over to Ramsey, at that time still a part of the St. David's headland. Determined to live in isolation on an island, Justinian took his trusty axe and hacked Ramsey away from the mainland. As his blade grew more and more blunt, the pieces hacked away got bigger and bigger. Thus is explained the origin of the treacherous rocky Bitches, jutting out from Ramsey's coast.

Justinian must have been a crusty old curmudgeon, for still another story tells of his followers murdering him by cutting off his head. Not one to let such a mishap stand in his way, Justinian picked up his severed head and swam from Ramsey over to the mainland. Once there he set his head down on top of the cliff, and from that spot a spring of clear water immediately emerged. Still flowing today, the spring is known as Justinian's holy well. Afterwards he seems to have resumed his friendship with David, although whether with or without his head does not seem to be clear.

Justinian at some point instructed David where he wished to be buried, and David complied, interring his body in Justinian's chapel as requested. Some time later, after many miracles, David had

Justinian's remains moved from the chapel to his own (St. David's) cathedral. Until very recent carbon dating proved otherwise, the mingled bones of David and Justinian were thought to be in the reliquary casket behind the high altar in St. David's Cathedral.

For anyone who cannot get to Ramsey Island itself, next best— or perhaps equally rewarding—is a walk along the Pembrokeshire Coastal Path, open any time of year. Numerous access points make it possible to cover short sections on an afternoon or a long summer's evening. If preferred, one can pack a knapsack and make it a full day's trip, taking in longer sections as inclined. The St. David's stretch includes some of the most spectacular coastal scenery to be found anywhere in Ireland or the British Isles. One of my most vivid recollections is the early morning a friend and I were walking near the St. Non's Retreat House and, looking down into a cove, saw a huge bull seal making amorous advances to his lady love, quite unconcerned at our spying. It is not at all unusual to see Atlantic seals—they are delightfully curious and often pop their wet heads up out of the water and watch you as intently as you watch them—but to see them courting was a rare privilege.

Seabirds are always soaring overhead and carpets of wildflowers are everywhere. Depending on the time of year, one can see primroses, cowslips, dandelions, oxeye daisies, foxgloves, blackberries, bluebells, ragged robin, heather, creeping thyme, gorse, St. Johnswort, willow herb, sheep bit, and countless other flowers. The riotous color of the flowers is enhanced and complemented by the range of hues in the rocks. The cliffs contain quartz and shale, and the sandstone is sometimes blue, sometimes purple, sometimes yellowish, sometimes pink. There are striations in parallel lines, almost-perpendicular sharp faults, and an endless assortment of shapes. As with Ramsey Island, one can be thankful and grateful that the Pembrokeshire Coast National Park and the National Trust own and maintain this spectacularly beautiful coastland and preserve it for all of us and for our children.

*I was overwhelmed when I saw St. David's Cathedral for the first time.
I had an emotional response that is still hard to describe: the sense of
holiness made me want to take off my shoes. At first I did not even walk
around and gape; I simply sat quietly in the back of the nave and drank
in the silence and the stillness. It was late afternoon, and I remember
being glad to be there, grateful for the opportunity to ponder, to mar-
vel. I remember the pink sandstone seeming to welcome me as though
I were a friend of many years instead of the newcomer I was. I watched
other tourists milling around, heard the muted sounds of shoppers in
the cathedral gift shop, rejoiced in the beauty of the stained glass windows and reveled in the soft light bathing the cathedral piers and rows
of cathedral chairs. The rays of the sun catching the dust motes looked
like angels. The marble statue of St. David in the pulpitum seemed to
be looking squarely at me, as though David himself was offering a particular kind of welcome. Overhead the golden Irish oak ceiling was like
a protective curtain, alive and intimate, and the intricate carvings and
the hanging pendula were incredible in their beauty—I wanted to be
able to reach up and touch them in a kind of caress. The great arches
of the nave looked like arms outstretched above me, offering both welcome and protection and also expressing an attitude of praise.*

*I felt a sense of absurdity. It was ridiculous to anthropomorphize the
cathedral in such a way. Yet truly I was over overcome by I knew not
what—only the astonishing sense that in some mysterious way, I had
come to a place of deep rest, a place called home. Jesus says, "Come to
me, all you that are weary and are carrying heavy burdens, and I will
give you rest" (Matthew 11:28). When I am tired, it's usually a physical tiredness, and rest and sleep can generally take care of it, but when
I am weary, it's a much deeper spiritual or psychological tiredness, and
physical rest may not help at all. I admit that I am a workaholic, and
sitting still is not something that comes easily to me. Is this because I
am running from something, unwilling to face up to major frustrations
in my life, or struggling fruitlessly to achieve some ephemeral,
unreachable goal? I meet many men and women in my ministry who
are tired on the inside—truly weary—and I wonder why we let this
happen to ourselves.*

*Being in a place like St. David's is wonderfully healing, where the
atmosphere itself quiets me and offers a deep peace. My time in the*

cathedral made me realize once again how important it is for
churches to be hospitable places, so that people like me can come in for
the first time, perhaps weary and heavy laden, and know that they are
welcome. As I think back on the day, I have no further recollections of
that cathedral visit other than sitting for more than an hour lost in a
peaceful contemplation and leaving with an unshakable conviction that
some day I would be back.

The next day the weather was bright and clear, so three of us toured
the Bishop's Palace. It was enormous! The bishops who lived here
weren't poor, not by a long shot. I remember studying in school about
the wealth—and subsequent corruption—of the church, and here it
was right before my very eyes. No wonder the church needed the
Reformation. Opulent as it was, I had to remember that in Wales the
church was always very poor, relatively speaking; so if this was "poor,"
how did the bishops live in far, far wealthier England? And how could
these bishops reconcile such grand living with the very clear mandate
in the gospel to identify with the poor and live simply? How is the
church different today in its attitude toward wealth and affluence?

The site custodian at the Bishop's Palace let the three of us (dare-
devils all!) climb up one of the remaining corner towers for a breath-
taking view of the sea in one direction and the imposing west front of
the cathedral in the other, to say nothing of the full spread of the palace
environs immediately below us. Fortunately I'm not uncomfortable
with heights, because the steps are very narrow and steep and it's a long
drop to the ground beneath. Once up there, though, I admit I was a lit-
tle scared, because the parapet is only about eighteen inches high, and
there was barely enough space for us who had risked the climb, but truly
it was worth it. The sea gulls were soaring around us and the rooks were
screaming their raucous cries—the wind was exhilarating—and the
view of Ramsey Island resting on the horizon in the sea was unforget-
table. The whole experience took my breath away. There is a timeless-
ness to a visit like that, and I felt very small when I realized that the
bishops of the Middle Ages, and perhaps some of their guests, had
undoubtedly climbed these very same steps, had sat on this very same
ledge, and had drunk in this very same view.

I'm glad we had some free time in St. David's, because I wanted to
explore some of it by myself. I especially wanted to go out to St. Non's

on the edge of the cliffs and then to walk part of the coastal path. The weather wasn't as good as it had been the day we went to the Bishop's Palace, but at least it wasn't raining, so I tucked a picnic into my backpack and took off. I went first to the holy well, praying especially for my friend at home with cancer. She's a great believer in prayer as well as in nontraditional medicine, so I had carried with me a small bottle to collect some of the water from the holy well to take back to her. I felt a little self-conscious doing it—was I being silly? On the other hand, have I gotten so sophisticated in my understanding of God that I can pooh-pooh the idea of water from a holy well being another God-given way of healing? Perhaps what I am wrestling with is the essence of my own faith, faith as the assurance of things hoped for, the conviction of things not seen (Hebrews 11:1). The way to total healing often cannot be seen, and we must then embrace that way by faith. I collected the water carefully and put the stoppered container in my pocket, knowing I would, with as much conviction as I could muster, take it back to her in the United States.

From St. Non's Well I walked over to the coast, only a hundred yards or so away. The wind was blowing really hard, and the sea was crashing against the cliffs with a thunderous roar. I was a little afraid to leave the path or walk very close to the edge of the cliffs. The path itself is safe, of course, with sturdy handrails along the precipitous places, but I was still pretty careful how I walked. I sat on a rocky promontory to eat my lunch in a place where I could watch the birds swooping and fishing, but it was too rough to see any seals. An elderly couple came by, walking their dog, and they called a hello to me sitting out on my rock. The lady's white hair was blowing in the wind. Wales is a friendly place, I have discovered, and part of that discovery for me relates to the Communion of Saints. I did not know those people and probably would never see them again in my life. Yet, in sharing the beauty of the seacoast and the wind and the seagulls and exchanging a wave of our hands, I felt connected both to them and to the untold thousands who have walked this same path.

I wondered if St. Non once sat on this same rock when she was pregnant, or if the young David had played here, perhaps throwing rocks at the seagulls, or if the pilgrims from the Middles Ages had rested and prayed here and enjoyed the serenity of the place just as I was doing.

*Pilgrimage to a place like St. David's is a profound experience: the wel-
come in the cathedral, the opulence of the bishops, the simplicity of
holy water, the natural beauty of Pembrokeshire, and the friendliness
of people all come together in one moving and memorable package.*

St. Winefride's Well

THE WATER AT ST. WINEFRIDE'S Well flows out with such force
that it seems to boil. Around the well proper, the water is a deep
green, green like the North Atlantic, and very dark. The well used
to produce hundreds of gallons a minute, until the Halkyn
Reservoir in the hills above the valley accidentally tapped the natural spring and the water was diverted elsewhere. Water is now
pumped into the well to recreate the original rate, and it is hard to
realize that it has been flowing like that since long before humans
stood upright and walked about.

How different it must have been before the valley was developed.
Surely the water erupted from the earth and then cascaded down a
green glen as a raging cataract with many waterfalls. It must have
foamed and rushed over huge rocks and beneath overhanging trees
as it surged toward the Dee Estuary and the sea beyond. The valley
is so steep that until one gets to the very bottom, it is hard to imag-
ine enough cleared level land where the Druids or the pre-Christian
or the Celtic peoples could have had their settlements and performed their mysterious ceremonies, as surely they must have.

Today, of course, it is all very different with the entire water
course from the well to the sea enclosed within the Greenfield
Valley Heritage Park; now there are pleasant woodland paths,
serene lakes, and pleasant gardens. The valley was not remotely
like that a hundred years ago. At that time industrialism drew heavily on the water pouring so abundantly from the well to power a
dozen mills producing copper wire, cotton, and other commodi-
ties. Along the eastern side ran a railroad line, engines spewing
smoke and cinders all over the narrow and deep valley as they

Pool where pilgrims bathe,
St. Winefride's Well
Cadw: Welsh Historic Monuments
Crown Copyright

Statue of St. Winefride
Cadw: Welsh Historic
Monuments. Crown Copyright

St. Winefride's Holy Well

huffed and puffed their way up and down the steep grade. The trains delivered raw materials down to the factories and then carried finished goods up to the main railway line at Holywell. The noise of the mills and the waste produced by them must have been horrendous. Such a paradox! Pure water flowing spontaneously from a natural spring, a holy well, was used to turn the noisy wheels and turbines of factories—industrialism at its height.

Different again was the scene in the Middle Ages, when the flow of water was used only to run the mills belonging to the Cistercian abbey of Basingwerk, situated not far from the sea on the flatlands at the bottom of the valley. At that time the woodlands on either side of the valley were undisturbed, except for the traffic of pilgrims between the well and the abbey precincts. The valley was called Maes Glas, or the "green field," from whence comes its name of Greenfield today.

Basingwerk Abbey was founded in 1131 by monks from Savigny in France, but it became Cistercian fifteen years later. In its day it was large and wealthy, for it was founded primarily to protect the hundreds of travelers visiting the well, and the alms of grateful pilgrims swelled its coffers enormously. Archaeologists have found very early Saxon building remains at Basingwerk, so it is likely to have been a settled community even earlier, possibly as far back as the Celtic or even pre-Celtic period. The Roman road between Chester and Segontium (on the outskirts of present-day Caernarfon) passed nearby, and there is every reason to believe that the Romans, too, venerated the well as a sacred place, first as pagans and later as Christians, who no doubt then used the waters for baptisms. Today Basingwerk is only an evocative ruin of red sandstone, a mute witness to its holy past, and on three sides it is surrounded by all forms of modernity: a busy roadway, British Rail tracks, a car park, shops, factories, service stations. But the valley itself, upstream from the abbey and all the way to the well, is lush and green again, preserved within the Greenfield Valley Historical Park.

Historically speaking, St. Winefride's Well is one of the most important holy sites in all of Britain, and it is the only one that can claim an unbroken tradition of pilgrimage since the seventh century. We know nothing that can be authenticated about the historical

St. Winefride, but the traditional tales about her are both ancient and revered. By the time her life was written down in the *Buchedd Gwenffrewi* (*The Life of Saint Winefride*) in the twelfth century, there was little hope of disentangling fact from fantasy. She was undoubtedly a real person, said to have been the niece of St. Beuno, who was probably the most important of the Celtic saints in the north of Wales.

Uncle Beuno lived in the early part of the seventh century and received his religious training in the south, perhaps at St. Illtud's monastery at Llanilltud Fawr, the Llantwit Major of today. He was an ardent missionary, as were so many of the Celtic saints, and Beuno's missionary activity in the north was as extensive (and as successful) as was St. David's in the south. His best-known remaining foundation today is that at Clynnog Fawr on the Llŷn Peninsula, but there are dozens of churches said to have been founded by him, and any number of others were founded by his many disciples. (See section on the Llŷn Peninsula.)

According to the twelfth-century hagiographers, Winefride was the daughter of wealthy patrician parents, and Beuno was her mother's brother. The whole family was devoutly Christian, and from Winefride's parents Beuno obtained the lands on which he built his churches in North Wales. Winefride had chosen not to marry and had received her parents' consent to become a nun. As the story goes, Winefride, said to be both beautiful and chaste, was alone in the house on a Sunday morning. Along came Prince Caradog, ostensibly asking of Winefride a cup of cool water, but in fact determined to avail himself, with or without permission, of Winefride's favors. She fled toward the sanctuary of Beuno's church and was captured by Caradog at the door. Furious at being so spurned, he drew his sword and struck off Winefride's head. Where it landed on the ground, a great gush of water flowed forth—and has flowed ever since as St. Winefride's Well. Beuno, in the meantime, disturbed at his prayers (or at his preaching, as another version goes), cursed Caradog so vehemently that the earth opened wide and swallowed him, and he vanished forever. Beuno then reverently picked up the severed head and placed it back on Winefride's body, and shortly afterward the maiden awoke, whole and sound, but showing a tiny white scar around her neck.

The tale continues with Winefride's becoming abbess of a convent at Gwytherin, in a remote mountain valley not many miles away, where eventually she died a second death (this time presumably a natural one). In 1138 her relics, according to divine direction, were transferred to Shrewsbury Abbey where, it was claimed, many miracles subsequently occurred. In spite of the "tissue of improbabilities" surrounding Winefride's story, her cult developed into a major one in the Middle Ages.

By the twelfth century the practice of pilgrimage was very widespread, and St. Winefride's Well was of prime significance. A crude drawing of the road network in early medieval Wales shows routes to the principal pilgrimage centers, and St. Winefride's Well was one point of a great pilgrimage triangle between itself, St. David's in the south, and Walsingham in the east (England). T. Charles-Edwards calls St. Winefride's Well "the most prominent star in a galaxy of pilgrimage centers which bore witness to the Age of the Saints."[38]

Throughout the Middle Ages the monks of Basingwerk Abbey kept watch over the well and cared for its pilgrims, and the well's fame and importance continued to grow. Pilgrims came by the hundreds, from as far away as the continent. By the fifteenth century, the feast day of St. Winefride (June 22) was celebrated throughout Britain, and by then the well was so famous that Henry V made a pilgrimage there in 1416 to express gratitude for St. Winefride's help at the Battle of Agincourt and to implore her continued favor. Fifty years later Edward IV made a similar pilgrimage pleading for Winefride's assistance in his Yorkist struggles. Following the Battle of Bosworth in 1485, Lady Margaret Beaufort, mother of the newly crowned Welsh (Tudor) King Henry VII, had the Holywell parish church rebuilt and a new well chapel erected above the waters. This church and chapel still stand today, and the church continues to serve the people of Holywell parish. The Beaufort Chapel and the well itself are under the watchful care of Cadw, Welsh Historic Monuments.

The lovely Beaufort Chapel is filled with the lingering aura of the medieval pilgrims. It is an architectural masterpiece, richly adorned with fascinating carvings. Many are badly worn, but visitors who look carefully can make out a number of animals, some real, like the beaver and the horse with its rider, and some mythical, like the mantichora and the griffin. One scene shows two men who seem to be fighting each other, and several angels appear here and there. Best of all are the two comic faces staring at each other across the nave, one grinning hugely and the other sticking his (her?) tongue out. Perhaps they are two pilgrims at odds with each other—or perhaps they are exhibiting different reactions to a medieval sermon.

Medieval walling encases and contains the well. The pool is five-sided, intentionally imitating of the Pool of Bethesda, a gathering place for the lame, the deaf, the blind, or the mute—for all those in need of healing. (*Now in Jerusalem by the Sheep Gate there is a pool, called in Hebrew Beth-zatha, which has five porticoes. [John 5:2]*). The water flows up, urgent and restless in the center, but around the edges it seems velvet and still. The upsurge of the main spring is too powerful to stand in, so the waters are directed to flow under a kind of retaining wall and into a channel that has been carefully laid out for those who want access to bathe. The pilgrim enters on one side of the channel, goes carefully down three stone steps into the water, and, immersed to the waist, walks through the channel to the other side and then emerges, climbing up another three stone steps. Traditionally this is repeated three times. Then, dripping and no doubt thoroughly chilled, the pilgrim stands or kneels before the statue of St. Winefride and lights a prayer candle... Lord, have mercy.

The fact that the Beaufort Chapel and St. Winefride's Well survived the destruction of the Reformation in the sixteenth century and the strong anti-Catholic feelings of the seventeenth is nothing short of miraculous. Basingwerk Abbey was dissolved by Henry VIII in 1537, and the chapel (with its income, of course) was turned over to Henry's servants. Queen Mary restored the well to the custodianship of Catholic priests, but Queen Elizabeth tried, unsuccessfully, to suppress its Catholic leanings. A Catholic priest by the name of Father John Bennett remained hidden from the royal authorities in the seventeenth century, secretly continuing to celebrate Mass and to minister to the people for half a century before he died of the plague. He is still regarded as a saint. The

Church of England's Bishop of Bangor (now in Wales) in 1625 informed his superiors in London with great dismay that pilgrims continued to visit the well in droves and that the Mass was celebrated continually, albeit clandestinely. The bishop expressed frustration that attempts to stop the pilgrims from such "papist practices" were so unsuccessful.

The significance of the well for the Catholics remained undiminished, and in time, the Jesuits became the recognized custodians. Interesting graffiti remains in the well chamber from this period, some of it apparently intentionally cryptic. We can read IC and assume that means "Jesus Christ," but we are not so sure about the several carvings of MH and TM. Some people think they may stand for "Mary Help" and "Thanks Mary," but we do not really know. What we do know is that suppression of pilgrimages to St. Winefride's Well was unsuccessful, and they have continued in unbroken tradition to this day.

As I stood there at St. Winefride's and stared at the water flowing from the well proper into the healing channel, I found I wanted to submerge myself in it also. I wanted to feel the cold (the guide says it's forty-eight degrees), and I wanted to walk through the water, feeling its resistance against my own body. I wanted to climb out dripping and light a candle and pray for my own healing. It was an unrealistic wish, of course, because I knew I would never do it—I would be too self-conscious, too sophisticated, too proud. But I watched and prayed over the well's water anyway and tried to picture myself with that kind of a simple uncluttered faith.

While I was pondering, an elderly man came into the well chamber, walking slowly and haltingly and leaning heavily on a wooden cane. He looked as if he might have been a stroke victim. His wife (I assumed it was his wife) was with him, hovering lightly at his side. With total abandon and unselfconsciousness, she helped him sit down on the bench and take off his shoes and socks. Then together, they slowly walked over to the steps and he eased his feet into the water. I watched transfixed... staring, of course, but at the same time I realized that my own body suddenly felt weak and helpless, and I identified with the man's pain. He did not stay in the water long; he stood there only long enough to bow his head and make the sign of the cross, and then just as slowly and painfully he stepped out of the water and walked over to St. Winefride's shrine. There he and his wife both knelt down and prayed for a long time, and then they lit two candles. I looked up at the statue of St. Winefride and saw her with new eyes; she seemed to be smiling.

The rest of the pilgrim group was still standing around the main well listening to the guide, and I don't think most of them even noticed. They were engrossed in his presentation. The elderly couple concluded their prayers and unobtrusively moved on. When our guide had finished talking, my group moved out into the daylight where lay the large healing pool. It is the size of a small swimming pool, and I could picture dozens of pilgrims from the Middle Ages in the water. I was still moved by the old man's simple piety and faith, and finally I knelt down at the water's edge, took off my glasses, and washed my face, three times, in the name of the Trinity. I was vaguely aware of others doing the same, but no one spoke about it and there wasn't any chatter.

Nevern

I WAS STILL VERY NEW to Wales when I first read about the Nevern cross, but I knew it was one of the Celtic sites I particularly wanted to visit. I had been in North Wales and was driving south to St. David's, planning to stop to see the great high cross on the way. Typically, the drive took much longer than I had expected, so I did not get to Nevern until quite late. Nevertheless, I parked outside the churchyard and entered the avenue of ancient yew trees in the cemetery and looked around for the cross. The dusk was so heavy I could barely see, and even though generally I am not afraid

Pentre Ifan burial chamber near Nevern

*Ancient clapper bridge across the
stream at Nevern*

The High Cross at Nevern

of cemeteries, being alone in a graveyard in an unfamiliar area in a foreign country at night was not a situation I would readily have chosen. I was determined to see the cross, though, wherever it was.

The cross was not hard to find; it stands beyond the alley of venerable yew trees only a few feet from the south wall of the church. I gasped at its size—more than twice my own height and as high as the gutters on the eaves of the church. The message it conveyed to me in the rapidly descending darkness was one of welcome, stability, comfort, and peace, and I threw my arms around the shaft, embracing it as though it were alive. I realized I was more fearful in that dark graveyard than I had thought I was. It was too dark to see much, but I explored the carvings with my fingers in the same way a blind person might, following the interlacing and knotwork with a sense of awe and incredulity. It was the Nevern cross on that evening that gave me my first realization of the intricacy of the Celtic knot, probably because I discovered it first with my fingers rather than with my eyes.

While there are many smaller carved crosses from the early Christian period, the Great Cross at Nevern is one of only three outstanding high crosses in Wales; by way of contrast, Ireland has more than one hundred of them. Nevern's sister high crosses are at Maen Achwyfan in the north (Clwyd) and at Carew in south Pembrokeshire. All three are about twelve feet high and show similar kinds of Celtic fretwork and interlaced designs.

Perhaps Nevern is my favorite of the Welsh high crosses, not because it is more impressive than the others, but simply because I saw it first. It dates to the late tenth or early eleventh century and is constructed in two separate pieces; the wheelhead at the top has a small base projecting outward rather like shoulders and sits on top of the tall shaft. The base is not stepped, such as is typical of market or preaching crosses, but rises straight out of the ground. All four sides of the shaft are filled with decorative carving. The actual cross within the wheelhead on both faces is made of interwoven knotwork, the kind of design that is a source of inspiration for many Celtic jewelry makers.

The cross is only one of the ancient and holy things at Nevern. The parish church there was originally founded by St. Brynach, an

Irish saint, sometime in the sixth century. Little is known of Brynach, although he is said to have been a friend and older contemporary of St. David, whose settlement is only about twenty-five miles to the south. According to tradition, Brynach came to the Nevern area with his wife Cymorth, the daughter of a Breconshire chieftain. Of the several settlements Brynach founded in the area, the one at Nevern (Nanhyfer in Welsh) is the most important. He used to climb nearby Carn Ingli (Mount of the Angels), where he fasted and prayed and from whose summit, on a clear day, he would have been able to see the coast of Ireland.

Many legends are associated with the foundations of the Celtic saints, and St. Brynach at Nevern is no exception. Brynach is usually pictured with a cuckoo on his shoulder; according to tradition, the first cuckoo of the spring arrives faithfully on April 7, St. Brynach's Day, and sings from the top of the Nevern cross. One year the bird was late in arriving, and the priest was loath to begin the Eucharist. The people waited and waited, until finally, near dusk, the faithful cuckoo arrived, landed exhausted on the top of the cross, sang one note, and fell to the ground dead. Regarding this tale, the chronicler George Owen said, "This vulgar tale, although it concern in some sort church matters, you may either believe or not, without peril of damnation."[39]

Although part of the church is clearly Norman with its typical squat tower, most of the walls are somewhat later, dating from the fifteenth and sixteenth centuries. The interior was greatly altered during the nineteenth century and is now unmistakably Victorian. However, there are several older stones in and around the church that clearly indicate a very early foundation, most likely from the Celtic period. The Maglocunus stone, set in the window ledge of the Trewern-Henllys (south) chapel is probably even earlier than Brynach himself, for the carving is bilingual, in both Latin and *ogham* (an early form of Irish writing), which suggests a date of 450 to 500. The inscription indicates a memorial to Maelgwn, son of Clutorius, about whom we know nothing.

Even more interesting in the companion window of the same chapel is the Cross Stone, date uncertain but generally accepted to be pre-Norman, perhaps of the Celtic period. Incised in this stone is a Celtic cross, about five feet long but with arms only a foot wide. According to the church's guide booklet, the cross has some unusual features. It seems to be made of rope strands that intersect in such a way that a Celtic cross is formed from a Celtic knot. Variations on this knot-rope-cross are often seen in modern Celtic jewelry, but there seem to be no other similar crosses from this early period, either in Wales or anywhere else, making it all the more unusual.

The cross on this stone is one of my favorites, for depending on where you stand in the church to look at it, the cross transmits different messages. Because it is mounted horizontally beneath the window itself, it is reminiscent of a recumbent knight, and the two rope-like extensions in the base of the cross resemble spurs. When the morning sun streams in through the window, the dark lines in the carving become darker and the knot-like aspect becomes more pronounced. When the cross is drawn and shown flat on a piece of paper, upright like other typical crosses, the jewelry-like quality is immediately apparent.

Outside the church and near the entrance is the Vitalianus Stone, also thought to be fifth century. This, too, is a bilingual memorial stone, with an inscription in Latin as well as in *ogham*. Most experts think it is dedicated to a Roman soldier. Sometimes it is easy to focus on Celtic Christianity and forget that in all likelihood it was the Romans who brought Christianity to this part of the world in the first place, so Celtic artifacts and Roman artifacts need to be studied together. Who was Vitalianus? Was he a soldier from Caerleon, the huge Roman fortress only a hundred miles or so away? What brought him to Nevern? And who was he, or what did he do, to have a memorial stone erected in his honor? Sadly, none of these questions can be answered.

The avenue of yew trees in the cemetery, the ones under which I walked on the night of my first visit, are decidedly ancient—some experts estimate them at about 1000–1200 years old. There must be six or seven trees on each side, but one tree on the east side has its own inexplicable uniqueness: it constantly bleeds. At eye level, from only one particular branch on that one particular tree is a steady oozing of blood-red sap. Although many suggestions have been offered as to why this happens—the tree is weeping for the crucifixion, it is weeping for the dead in the graveyard, or it is weeping because of some pragmatic botanical reason—no fully satisfactory explanation has yet been given. As with the story of the cuckoo, we can make of it what we will.

A modern churchyard surrounds the church and climbs up the hillside to the north. A walk behind the church leads up to the crumbling remains of an early Norman castle. On the way, the path crosses the small river over an ancient clapper bridge, a bridge made from an enormous single slab of stone. The stream seems gentle, a storybook type gurgling merrily on its way, but a few years ago during a huge storm it became a raging torrent. At that time it not only caused the ancient clapper bridge over it to collapse (it has since been repaired and restored), but it also undermined part of the church foundations and tore out the roadway bridge, causing untold damage.

Nevern Church is situated very strategically where this unpredictable little stream empties into the Nyfer River. Some people speculate that this is the exact pilgrims' route that connected important sites in the north, particularly St. Winefride's Well, with St. David's in the south, but experts disagree about this. If it is true, however, then Nevern was probably the final stopping point before the last stage of the journey to St. David's. Thus it would have been a sizeable foundation, probably with a hospice and a number of pilgrims' huts, as well as a church. Unfortunately archaeologists have not found remains of any early buildings, so again we are faced with a story like that of the cuckoo: make of it what you will. Small sections of the route thought to be the Pilgrims' Way remain in isolated segments, but the longest section, the part in best condition, is near Nevern.

Only a few hundred yards from the church is a section reputed to be the original walkway, perhaps two miles long, still in good condition and maintained as a signposted footpath. Leaving the macadam roadway at a sharp bend a little beyond the church, a visitor enters the woods, walks a hundred yards or so, and stops at the Pilgrims' Wayside Cross, carefully cut out from the bedrock. It is deeply worn, adding to its sense of ancient sanctity. A small ledge

projects out at about knee level, and the pilgrim can kneel on this
and reach up to grasp the lower edge of the cross itself. I never miss
an opportunity to stop and pray here, and invariably, as my chest is
pressed hard again the cool stone and my head is turned sideways
and I can smell the freshness of the moss covered rock, I hear in my
head the lines from the hymn: "In my hand no price I bring; simply to thy cross I cling."[40] And cling I do, for it is a place that I find
extremely numinous and life-giving. I typically experience a kind
of spiritual tongue-tiedness, for words do not come, other than
those lines from the hymn. I do not question even momentarily,
however, the authenticity of the experience or the validity of my
prayer. Every cell in my body recognizes that I am praying where
untold thousands have prayed before me, and my inarticulate
prayer mingles with all those other prayers that have gone before.

A few years ago, a flurry of articles in the Welsh newspapers
reported that two Welsh historians and an American clergyman
had become convinced that, hollowed out behind the bedrock, was
St. Brynach's hermit's cell from centuries back, and that in it was
very possibly the True Cross of Christ, brought back to Britain by
Helena in the fourth century. By inserting a slender rod between the
layers of rock below the cross, the men had determined that the
area behind was hollow, and subsequent explorations with a sonar
device had demonstrated that an open space of some size does
indeed exist. Naturally there was a great burst of interest and
excitement. Public opinion was loud and insistent, with some people feeling it a great sacrilege to disturb such a holy site and others
decidedly eager to investigate further, but Cadw (Welsh Historic
Monuments), which holds all such historic sites in its meticulously
watchful care, put an end to the explorations. Without the funding
to excavate thoroughly and carefully, using only the most sophisticated techniques, Cadw felt it wisest to let well enough alone. So
the site remains as it has been for centuries. If St. Brynach's hermit
cell is indeed behind the rock and the True Cross with it, so be it:
surely this possibility only adds to the holiness and sacred mystery
of the place.

A few yards beyond the Pilgrims' Cross, the path climbs up a
short but steep incline. Cut deeply into the bedrock are unmistakable

steps shaped like footprints, said to have been worn into the rock by the feet of the ancient pilgrims. Carved into the heel of each of these footprints is a tiny cross. Cadw has fenced off this section, so that pilgrims can no longer actually walk in the footprints, but we can put our hands in them, trace the heel crosses, and experience the palpable presence of the Communion of Saints.

The path continues for another mile or so, following the edge of the Nyfer River, passing through some lovely woods thickly carpeted with bluebells and across a field or two before it emerges on a paved country lane in front of a modern cottage. This lane, now accessible to automobiles, wanders on toward Newport, where the original Pilgrims' Way is once more obliterated by modern developments.

When I took my first pilgrimage group to Nevern, back in 1992, I met some of the people who live in the tiny village and who today worship in St. Brynach's church. I remember well one of the first letters I received saying how glad they were that I would be bring-ing a pilgrimage group to visit them. Pilgrimage is a strong part of Nevern's history, and yet in many ways the modern world has passed Nevern by. "We're so terribly isolated," said one of the church members, "and when pilgrims come today, it brightens our lives and strengthens our Christian faith. For," she continued, "where would any of us be without Christian community?"

I was deeply moved by the incised cross beside the highway. We had left St. David's and were on the way to Nevern for a day of reflection, but we stopped first where there was an ancient incised Celtic cross set into the stone wall at the side of the road. I was amazed. A carved cross just stuck in a stone wall? Only five or six feet from the highway? We got off the bus one by one, still in silence, and stood there with the traffic whizzing by while we read some poetry and said some prayers. The world rushing by made no difference whatsoever—it simply passed us by. Then one by one we stooped down, traced the cross and its circle

with our fingers, then made the sign of the cross on ourselves. The stone was pleasingly cool, rough to the touch, but unexpectedly smooth in the groove where the cross was inscribed. I was struck by the contrast— the roughness of the natural stone as against the incised cross, which had been worn smooth and deep by who knows how many fingers over who knows how many centuries.

I've often thought of our lives like rocks in a rock tumbler—we are tossed into the tumble of life with all our irregularities and roughness, but the relentless grinding of stone upon stone gradually wears away the rough places and we become softer and smoother. This cross in the wall was rather like that, the rough places in the natural stone had been made smooth, only instead of a rock tumbler doing the smoothing, it was thousands of fingers. I thought about my years in religious community, where the constant interpersonal interactions help smooth off our rough edges of personality. I thought about how privileged I am to be shaped and smoothed by the tolerance and patience of my sisters as I try to grow more loving and compassionate. I thought about how my life is still like the rough stone in the wall, and it is not only the actions of those who love me, but also my being willing to stand still and let the finger of God trace the cross on me throughout my life that will continue to make my own rough places smooth.

After this, everybody got back on the bus—and all in a reflective silence. Here we were, modern pilgrims in a modern bus with modern traffic roaring by, but we had had a moment of deep peace in the midst of all that hoo-ha. Truly the cross beside the road had an eloquent message—for me personally and also for our world. I never did find out why it was there, but I continue to ponder how different our lives might be if we could touch the cross and openly claim its power in our lives without self-consciousness or shame as the busy world races unconcernedly by.

I was still thinking about the smooth cross in the rough stone when we got to the church at Nevern, and I was grateful for the opportunity to go off by myself. I walked along the ancient Pilgrims' Way past the Pilgrims' Cross and eventually found myself in a large pasture. There I stretched out full length on the grass and looked up at the sky. The weather was pleasant and I lay there, completely at peace, basking in the sun. I was basking in the awareness of how over the years many *loving touches from those around me have helped me to smooth out some of my rough edges and to grow and mature. I rejoiced at the inexpressible joy of knowing that I am loved and valued, in spite of all my imperfections and shortcomings, and at the growing I have yet to do. The warmth of the sun filled me with the warmth of God's love, and I slept.*

Patrisio

PATRISIO IS NOT a church you would stumble upon by accident. You need a map, and even armed with that, you must be aware that the place is spelled a variety of ways: your map might call it Patricio, or Partrishow, or Partrisiw, or Patrisw, or Parttrissw, or any of several other variants. The Church in Wales, in whose care Patrisio is, seems to agree on Patrisio. If, however, you are looking it up in the National Library of Wales in Aberystwyth, you need to look under Patrisw. If you are reading an English rather than a Welsh source (including the official Ordnance Survey maps), it is spelled Patricio; and one reference to it in a tour guide published by the Wales Tourist Board spells it Partrishow. The patron saint's name is equally tricky: he is St. Issui, or Ishow, or Ishaw, or Isho, or Is-something else. What is generally agreed, however, regardless of spelling, is that Patrisio is a very early church on a Celtic foundation dedicated to St. Issui the Martyr.

After you have located Llanfihangel Crucornau, a little north of Abergavenny, on your map, then you need a car with enough horsepower to climb a fairly steep country lane, or, if you haven't got a car, you need a good pair of sturdy legs and a sturdy heart to go with them. If you're trying to get to Patrisio by coach, you can only go so far, and after that it is necessary to walk. The grade isn't too steep for the coach, of course—that's not the problem—but it can't make the sharp bends in the lane and it's too wide for the stone bridge part way up the mountain. This bridge, the Pontyresgob, or Bridge of the Bishop, gets its name because Bishop Baldwin, Archbishop of Canterbury, and the renowned historian

Patrisio Church

St. Issui's Holy Well, Patrisio

*Statue of St. Issui
at Patrisio*

Giraldus Cambrensis (Gerald of Wales) came through here in the twelfth century preaching the Third Crusade.

Issui is another of those Celtic saints about whom we know next to nothing, and he is not listed in the usual books of saints. Theophilus Jones, a local historian at the turn of the century, told Issui's story, describing him as a holy man living a solitary life in the secluded valley. Issui had a small hut beside Nant Mair, the stream flowing down from the mountain. Nearby was his well, lined with stone and containing small niches where gifts could be left. Tradition tells us that an ungrateful traveler who had received welcome and hospitality from Issui turned on the monk, murdering him and stealing the offerings that had been left in the well.

Because St. Issui had a reputation for great sanctity, soon after his murder his hermit cell became a place of pilgrimage. Over the intervening years, many pilgrims have left gifts at Patrisio. In the early eleventh century, it seems, a certain pilgrim from France was cured of his leprosy at St. Issui's Well, and in gratitude he left a gift of a sack of gold. With that gold was built the earliest part of the church, which still stands today, and the little niches in the walls of the well continue to receive gifts of coins or flowers or other mementos from grateful pilgrims. When I saw the well for the first time, the niches were filled with the gold of newly picked daffodils.

Inside the church, visitors find a bright yellow leaflet serving as a guide to the church. It contains the following paragraph:

> Country churches have a smell of their own. Dampness contributes much to it, but here at Patrisio, as we walk into the church, we are welcomed with what must be the smell of history. Here we touch hands with forgotten ages, shrouded in the mists of time.

There is more than just the smell of history at Patrisio; a visit here is like turning back the clock several centuries. The pilgrim's gold from so long ago went toward the building of a very small chapel, still standing, located behind the west wall of the main church. The age of this chapel can be fairly accurately dated to the eleventh century, because the *Book of Llandaff*, compiled about

1150, tells us that Herewald, Bishop of Llandaff, consecrated the church of Merthyr Issui (the Martyr Issui) some time between 1056 and 1103.

For many years the chapel served as a storeroom, but a few years ago it was refurbished and rededicated as a place for prayer. Some scholars think that when the main church was built, most likely in the fourteenth century, the chapel then served as lodging for the priest, who had been living in an even tinier loft above the west end of the already tiny chapel. Others speculate that at some other time in its history, the chapel was the dwelling place of a hermit.

Inside the little chapel are an altar, a squint (an opening in the interior wall), and a niche for a statue. The altar is unusual in that it has on it six carved consecration crosses, rather than the usual five. Nobody seems to be sure why this is. Peering through the squint, the resident hermit could see the altar in the church and hear Mass being celebrated, while in the niche would be his favorite saint. The original statue in the chapel niche disappeared centuries ago, probably during the Reformation. However, thanks to the recent restoration, a beautiful modern cast aluminum statue of St. Issui, with a bag of gold at his feet, is now in the niche. Once more pilgrims can pray quietly in this holy place. History has come full circle.

The crowning glory of Patrisio, though, is in the main church, which was probably built about three hundred years later than the chapel, sometime during the fourteenth century. Here is found a magnificent carved Irish oak screen. The workmanship is superb, showing minute details of a dragon, the symbol of evil, trying to consume the vine, the symbol of good: "I am the vine, you are the branches," says Jesus (John 15:5). At one time, prior to the Reformation, a large cross (rood) would have risen above the screen, symbolizing the ultimate triumph of Christ over all. Only the screen itself remains today, though, and the fact that it does is a small miracle. Such magnificent carvings were thought by iconoclastic reformers to be of the devil, and most such screens were destroyed in the sixteenth or seventeenth century.

Behind the screen is a loft, again miraculously saved, which can be reached by climbing the fifteenth-century stone steps set in the north wall of the church. All across the rail in the loft above the screen are sockets for candles. On special occasions, such as Christmas—when all the candles are lit, the fragrance of wax mingles with the fragrance of freshly cut holly, and the smell of cedar replaces the smell of dampness—the church is filled with a warm glow and is breathtakingly beautiful.

The chancel is Elizabethan and has not been modernized. Resting in a glass case in the chancel is a rare 1620 Welsh Bible. The Bible was not translated into Welsh until 1588, and its presence in such a tiny rural church probably means it was there not only for worship services but also as an aid in the teaching of literacy.

An unusual and fascinating aspect of the church of Patrisio church is its three stone altars. In addition to the main altar in the sanctuary, there is a stone altar on either side of the chancel arch on the nave side. All three of them have the usual complement of five consecration crosses. Both Edward VI and Elizabeth I ordered the destruction of all stone altars, believing that a simple wooden table was more appropriate, but somehow Patrisio escaped such vandalism, and its three stone altars remain in their original locations.

The font at Patrisio is also noteworthy. Inscribed in Latin around its rim are these words, translated here from medieval Welsh into English: "Menhir made me in the time of Genillin." Genillin was Prince of Powys and Lord of Ystrad Yw just prior to the Norman Conquest (1066), so the font can be accurately dated to the eleventh century, where no doubt it stood in the tiny original chapel built with the pilgrim's gold. It is one of the oldest surviving fonts in Wales.

Like many churches from the Middle Ages, Patrisio has some fine medieval wall paintings. One in particular is on the west wall, depicting "Father Time" as a daunting skeleton in red and ochre and black, holding his hour glass and scythe. One can picture the priest gathering his still illiterate congregation around the painting and reading to them from the big Welsh Bible, teaching them that our days on this earth are few but the rewards in heaven following a life well lived are great (Psalm 39). On the south wall is a list of the Ten Commandments, and it is apparent that much painstaking labor went into its production. Reading it very carefully today, one can see where the painter struggled to correct his (or her) omissions and spelling mistakes.

Patrisio was electrified only within our own day; formerly, candles were the sole source of interior light, other than that which came through the windows. Until very recently, the electricity in the church was activated only when visitors put a coin in the meter behind the font. Then the light lasted for just so many minutes before the meter required another coin! There was no heat at all.

There is almost as much of interest outside the church as there is inside. The lych-gate through which visitors enter the churchyard is modern, built early in this century. The churchyard is filled with graves, many very ancient and many quite recent. Presumably St. Issui's bones are there, too, although we have no idea where they might be.

Outside the south side of the church, with the mountains stretched across the valley as a backdrop, stands a tall preaching cross. A strong but undocumented tradition holds that when Bishop Baldwin and Giraldus Cambrensis were in the area, they preached at the Patrisio cross to a large congregation. The top part of this cross was destroyed in the sixteenth century, but a relatively modern new section was added later, showing on its four sides carvings of the Crucifixion, St. Mary, St. Issui, and Bishop Baldwin preaching. The stepped base of the cross is original, and near that is a not-very-old rickety wooden lectern for the preacher's notes.

Listeners would sit on the long stone bench built against the south wall of the chancel section of the church, not far from the preaching cross. Such a bench is an unusual architectural feature. Sitting on it today, even if not listening to a sermon, you can admire the splendid cross and the splendid view. If the weather is clear, you can see for miles up and down the valley; but if the mist is heavy, you feel as though you are above the clouds, or within them, and your ears absorb more than do your eyes. You can hear the omnipresent sheep, the sound of the water flowing in Nant Mair, the birdsong, and the wind. It is easy to be reminded of Elijah's coming out of his cave and hearing the sound of "sheer silence" (1 Kings 19:12) that is the voice of God. Patrisio, in any weather, is a place of sheer silence.

Just below the church, in a tree-shaded glen, is St. Issui's Holy Well and the place where Issui is said to have had his hermit hut. At the entrance to the well area, set in the ground is a flat stone, which has inscribed on it a small Maltese cross. Tradition associates this cross, too, with Bishop Baldwin and Geraldus; perhaps they baptized new members of the church or preached another sermon here.

St. Issui's well is not spectacular to look at; its holiness comes from its history, its location, and its association with sanctity. There is room for only one person at a time to get to the water, which at times may be very low. However, the well's location at the side of burbling Nant Mair, with ferns arching gracefully on the bank, bright green moss carpeting the rocks, overhanging trees, and blooming wildflowers, is a place of extraordinary charm. For people who come to Patrisio on foot, stopping at the well to wash hands and face is a gloriously refreshing experience.

Patrisio, perched on its hillside on a shoulder of Crug Mawr in the Black Mountains and high above the Grwyne Valley, is a place of restful and overwhelming beauty. That in and of itself inspires reverence and enhances its holiness. Perhaps that is the reason St. Issui selected the spot so long ago. Local people, both in the parish and further afield, continue to offer financial and prayerful support to this holy place. And pilgrims—at least the ones who can find it—continue to come.

We piled on the bus headed for Patrisio and wound along country lanes, finally turning onto an extremely narrow and steep road. Tree branches brushed both sides of the bus in the wooded areas, and sometimes from my window I couldn't see the edge of the road at all, which I confess made me a wee bit nervous. I was grateful for our driver— thank goodness for his obvious skill and confidence behind the wheel. Eventually we stopped and got off and met the vicar, who was waiting for us at a farm gate. He looked the part of the vicar—he was wearing

his black robes!—but he had a wonderful friendly smile and welcomed us warmly.

We received little pilgrimage booklets and said some prayers, and then we all put a pilgrimage token around our necks. The token was only a little piece of cardboard, not particularly elegant, but it was a tangible reminder of where we were and what we were doing: we were pilgrims undertaking a journey in search of the Holy together. A number of people were smiling in anticipation.

Then we began the walk, at a slow and gentle pace. We were on a farm lane, very straight, with gorgeous blooming hedgerows on either side, and while the road went up and up and up, it wasn't particularly steep, just an unrelenting rise. After about two hundred yards or so we stopped at a particularly attractive spot, actually level, with a gate on either side of the lane, and we could look around in all directions. We rested there, and because everybody was quiet, we could hear the sound of the sheep in the pastures, water rushing in a stream somewhere, and birds calling to one another. My heart was pounding because of the climb, and I realized in a new way the importance of my body—its incredible capability and the importance of keeping it in fit condition. We stayed there a long time and had some prayers that focused on the beauty of the earth—and it indeed was beautiful. We had a chance to appreciate such beauty because we had all slowed down and stopped talking.

It was also a magic moment, because I realized I had gotten into the true spirit of pilgrimage. We were walking in a way that enabled even those least fit to keep up, and more than once when the going seemed a bit rough, one of us pilgrims was quick to help another. After all, a real pilgrimage means a certain amount of effort; it means walking and feeling the ground underfoot and smelling the earth and breathing deeply, and it means being willing to both give and receive assistance.

We stopped for prayers several times, and then entered a sheep pasture complete with dozens of sheep and young lambs. There we listened to the gospel passage about the Good Shepherd.

I am the good shepherd. The good shepherd lays down his life for the sheep. The hired hand, who is not the shepherd and does not own the sheep, sees the wolf coming and leaves the sheep and runs away—and the wolf snatches them and scatters them. The hired hand runs away because a hired hand does not care for the sheep. I am the good shepherd. I know my own and my own know me, just as the Father knows me and I know the Father. And I lay down my life for the sheep. I have other sheep that do not belong to this fold. I must bring them also, and they will listen to my voice. So there will be one flock, one shepherd. (John 10:11–16)

It was all so true—we did frighten the sheep and they did run away because they did not know us. At the same time, they remained as one flock. Would that we humans could do that also—not be like uniform peas in a pod, all thinking alike and believing the same things (God forbid!), but honoring one another's diversity at the same time we acknowledge and respect the "one-flock-ness" of all human-ity. Nearly everyone lives in a "flock" of some kind, whether it is a family unit or some kind of intentional community. Always the same challenge is there to confront us: to live together in peace and amity, trying hard to respect each one's individuality and to rejoice in our God-given diversity.

What also impressed me was the incredible beauty of the place, how everyone seemed so willing to help everyone else, and how the physi-cal exertion was so much a positive part of the total experience. I real-ized, too, how seldom I really stop and take in the beauty of this world. And how I often don't appreciate the wonder of my body and how out of condition I have allowed myself to get.

It was a special moment to look up and see that incredibly beautiful tiny church perched on the side of the hill above us. When I did this—and I know it sounds silly—all I could think of was that the church was totally unselfconscious. It was just there. No architectural splendor, no pretense, nothing spectacular. Just a simple country church that had been witnessing to the Christian presence for a thousand years.

We continued along a little farther to the holy well, and I put my spray of wild foxgloves into one of the well's niches, built intentionally to receive pilgrim offerings. Other people had put bits of fern, or blue-bells, or some yellow flowers whose name I don't know, and it was lovely—a moment to treasure. We had a short service of Renewal of our Baptismal Vows, and then each of us, one by one, knelt down to

*wash our faces in the water. After that climb, the water was delicious-
ly clean and cool, and the new life promised by Baptism felt very real.*

*We then walked up to that lovely little church, singing "Guide me,
O Thou great Jehovah," would you believe! We had plenty of time to
wander around outside the church, and we could see for miles down the
valley. The sound of the sheep was like a symphony, and it was all so
peaceful that I finally could not keep the tears back any longer. Part of
me wanted to stay outside, to remain an insignificant speck in the beauty of God's world, but the pull toward our Eucharist was stronger.*

*I don't remember the walk back down the hill to the bus very well,
but I remember that nobody talked much. I think the whole experience
of walking, praying, baptism, and Eucharist in that ancient holy place
was so profound that we needed the time to take it all in. Once we got
to the pub, though, everybody was happily chattering; we knew we
had bonded together as pilgrims in a very special way.*

Bardsey and Llŷn

JUST OFF THE WESTERN TIP of the Llŷn Peninsula in northwest
Wales and pointing toward the south coast of Ireland lies Bardsey
Island, called the Island of 20,000 Saints. The island and the peninsula together are an area of indescribable charm, and both are
steeped in history. Bardsey, or Ynys Enlli, as it is known in Welsh,
was an early Celtic foundation, and during the Middle Ages it was
among the best known of the pilgrimage sites in Britain. Today
Bardsey calls to pilgrims as loudly as ever, and there is a great resurgence of interest in walking the old pilgrimage route along the Llŷn
to get there.

The Pilgrims' Way

Part of the challenge of traveling the Pilgrims' Route along the Llŷn
Peninsula, en route to Bardsey Island, is that no one knows just
exactly where the actual paths were. We know the general routes

Bardsey Island from the end of the Llŷn Peninsula

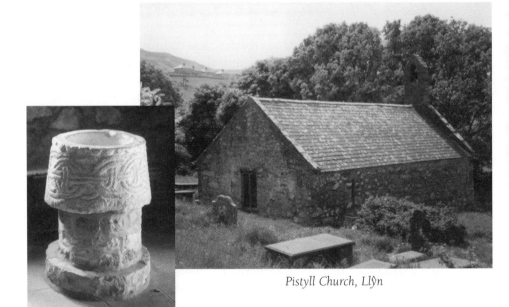

Pistyll Church, Llŷn

*The medieval font in Pistyll
Church, Llŷn*

because of the string of holy wells, cross-inscribed stones, grave markers, shrines, and small churches, all from the Middle Ages or earlier, but we can only postulate where the pilgrims actually walked. Further, medieval pilgrims left almost no records. We do know, however, that it was an important and well-traveled pilgrimage route, because Pope Calixtus II declared generous indulgences for those undertaking it; he proclaimed that three pilgrimages to Bardsey were equal to one pilgrimage to Jerusalem.

We also know that those undertaking a pilgrimage to Bardsey and approaching from the north foregathered at St. Beuno's Church at Clynnog Fawr, not far from present-day Caernarfon. From Clynnog Fawr they would walk the twenty-five or thirty miles to Aberdaron, where they would hope to find a boat to take them the last lap across to Bardsey itself.

Clynnog Fawr

St. Beuno is a sixth-century Welsh saint, one of the enthusiastic and peripatetic Celtic *peregrini* who founded a number of churches and monasteries. As a missionary, Beuno is as important to the north of Wales as St. David is to the south. According to his fourteenth-century *Life*, Beuno was actually born in the south, somewhere in present-day Herefordshire, where the village of Llanfeuno, meaning Beuno's settlement, still exists. His main work, however, as well as that of his disciples, was farther north, and we find foundations bearing his name in both Powys and Clwyd. His largest and best-known foundation was at Clynnog Fawr at the eastern end of the Llŷn Peninsula. Beuno was said to be the uncle of St. Winefride, and his story is closely associated with hers. (See the chapter on St. Winefride's Well.)

Clynnog Fawr was actually founded around the year 616, when Beuno built for himself a small chapel beside a stream. That small chapel grew into a thriving monastic settlement, the center of Beuno's cult; Beuno died and was buried at Clynnog. His grave immediately became a holy shrine, and those who were sick bathed in the waters of his nearby holy well and then were laid on top of his tomb for the night. If the shivering patient was able to sleep, a cure was assured; if not, the patient patiently moved farther along the Pilgrims' Way to the next place of healing and presumably prayed for better things.

The Celtic monastery founded by Beuno continued in existence as a *clas*, or collegiate church, until it was taken over by the Normans. At that time it became a "portionary" church, meaning that it was served by a number of different clergy. This status of being a cross between a parish church and a college, rather than a monastery, enabled Clynnog Fawr to escape being dissolved by Henry VIII. It became the largest, wealthiest, and most important church in this section of Britain.

Beuno's chapel, a separate building from the main chuch, is warm and welcoming, with bright light streaming through the clear-glass east window. The chapel, originally much smaller than it is now, was the site of Beuno's tomb until 1796. Leaning against the wall near the walkway between this chapel and the main church is Beuno's Stone, dated to the fifth century. Traditionally, pilgrims kneel before the stone, trace the outline of a cross with fingers or thumb, and then make the sign of the cross on themselves. Centuries of such a practice have marked the stone deeply with a dark cross, not incised or carved out, but formed only by the repeated action of praying fingers.

In the sixteenth century the present large airy church was built to offer shelter and service to the increasingly vast crowds of pilgrims. This church, built on top of an earlier building, is connected to Beuno's earlier chapel by a covered walkway. The walkway is interesting in its own right, having served various functions over the years, including that of parish prison. The main church, unusually large for a church of this type, has a truly fine museum-type exhibit of the Pilgrims' Way to Bardsey Island, and it would be easy to spend an hour or two reading it and poring over the many photographs.

The church offers other items of great interest. In the chancel is a fifteenth-century screen and carved misericords, and above the nave is an especially fine wood ceiling. On the wall in the south transept is a set of dog tongs, used by medieval "dog whippers" to separate fighting and snarling dogs. Near the entrance to the nave is St. Beuno's chest, now preserved in a glass case. According to custom, money from the sale of certain calves and lambs was placed in it, along with "sin offerings": "Here I offer to God four pence for my private sins on which account the Almighty is now punishing me," says the carved inscription.

Llanaelhaearn

Moving on from Clynnog and heading farther out along the peninsula, pilgrims next pass the village of Llanaelhaearn, the church of the St. Aelhaearn, the Saint of the Iron Eyebrow. Because it is only five or six miles from Clynnog, this was the next halt for the sick and weary on the Pilgrims' Way toward Bardsey. Aelhaearn's little church of today (like so many others, built upon an earlier foundation) stands in a roughly circular, yew-treed churchyard, where several Celtic stones and grave markers remain. Close beside the highway, in a stone housing, is Aelhaearn's holy well. Most medieval pilgrims would have stopped here, knowing that just ahead of them lay a strenuous and steep climb over the high rocky shoulder of Yr Eifl. Once that difficult part was behind them, pilgrims would find a welcome break at the monastery and hospice at Pistyll.

Pistyll

The tiny church at Pistyll is truly a gem. Also founded by St. Beuno in the fifth century, in importance it stands in the shadow of Beuno's more impressive foundation at Clynnog Fawr. Visitors who go on pilgrimage today to seek the Holy, however, may well find it more readily at St. Beuno's Pistyll than at St. Beuno's Clynnog. At some time in the distant past—no one seems to know exactly when—the little church resumed the practice of celebrating Lammas (meaning "loaf") Sunday near the first of August. The custom itself is very ancient, deriving no doubt from the Celtic harvest festival of Lughnasa, but Lammas Sunday as we know it today is more Anglo-Saxon than Celtic. On that day, the harvest began and the first grain was picked, ground, and made into ceremonial loaves that were brought to the church for Eucharist. It was a time of great feasting and celebration, praying for and anticipating a successful harvest.

Lammas Sunday is still celebrated at Pistyll, and the little medieval church is decorated with all kinds of symbolic breads. The floor is strewn with rushes cut from the surrounding hillsides; the church is gloriously fragrant with local herbs and flowers. Botanists always have a field day; usually they can find bulrushes, chamomile, cow parsley, fennel, grasses, heather, red-berried rowan branches, sea holly, wild hops, and wormwood—to name only the most easily recognized. Mosses in small cups surround the lip of the ancient font with its Celtic-style interlace, and reeds grace the window ledges. The borders of the wall painting on the north wall are edged in ferns, the pulpit has huge sprays of dried flowers on either side, and the intricately decorated lammas breads grace the altar. The vicar is quick to point out that it is not unusual to have small, four-footed furry members present in his congregation, and six-legged ones with their webs tend to come also, but all creatures great and small are welcome.

Pistyll church probably was built in the twelfth century and lies nestled in a grassy hollow beside a swift flowing stream, remaining essentially unchanged for eight hundred years. The church has only a few medieval artifacts, and its very simplicity is part of its charm. On the north wall of the chancel are the remains of a medieval wall painting of St. Christopher, patron saint of travelers. The font inside the church is particularly interesting. The overlapping circles carved in relief around the basin, the scalloped rim, and the double row of beading make it tempting to assume that the font is Celtic in origin, but experts assure us that it is no earlier than the late twelfth century. The design, however, is appealing and attractive, regardless of its original provenance. A graceful hand-painted sign stretches across the east wall above the altar, saying in Welsh, "SING TO THE LORD A NEW SONG."

Growing on the hillsides in the surrounding valley are the offspring of the same herbs and medicinal plants that grew there during the Middle Ages, when the site was a pilgrim hospice for the sick. Some are common plants used as familiar remedies, but many are rare or endangered species of considerable historic significance. Where these live and grow is a closely kept secret. The placid fish-pond of today is the remains of a mill pond from the last century, but it is generally thought that some kind of a dammed pond was in that same spot in medieval times, providing fish for the hospice community. Slightly upstream from the fishpond is the fresh spring that is Pistyll's holy well.

Llangwnnadl

From Pistyll, the pilgrims would have moved still farther down the peninsula. Again, we do not know exactly by which route, but many of them surely would have stopped at Llangwnnadl. This is another extraordinary church, with three naves and three altars. Its foundation also goes back to the sixth century, when St. Gwynhoedl arrived with his extended family and built a church. He is one of the few saints we can verify, because his burial place in the church is marked by a stone carved in late medieval Latin. The place was a good one to establish a church because it was near the sea—the interstate highway of the early centuries—and on a fair-sized river that provided water for living and for baptism. St. Gwynhoedl was one of the earliest saints of the Llŷn, being some-what older than St. Beuno, although Gwynhoedl's cult did not spread or ever reach the importance that Beuno's did.

During restoration work on the church in 1940, a large stone with a Celtic cross was found when plaster was removed from the interior of the south wall. Traces of red paint in the cross not only tell us that the cross was originally painted, but they enable a fairly accurate dating to about 600. Also dating from the same time is a bronze bell, one of the very few surviving in Wales. The original is in the National Museum of Wales in Cardiff, but an excellent repli-ca is in the church and can be rung—or perhaps "clunked" might be a more accurate description of the sound it makes.

Llangwnnadl, like Pistyll, was a stopping place of major impor-tance on the Pilgrims' Way. Not only did the convenience of the river have appeal, but the location near broad fertile fields also made it attractive. The field adjacent to the church is still called Cae

Eisteddfa, which means "the place of sitting and resting." As was
true with Clynnog Fawr, the popularity of this site for hundreds of
pilgrims over a long period of time necessitated several enlarge-
ments of the church. Because it was situated with its back to a hill
and its front to the river, there was no room to expand the church
in length, so each enlargement expanded laterally instead. Thus
Llangwnnadl today has its three naves.

The triple-nave arrangement gives Llangwnnadl a special feel, in
that its width is considerably greater than its length. It is almost
like three attached churches, and each one has its particular charm.
Cae Eisteddfa outside may indeed have been the place of sitting and
resting for medieval pilgrims, but today this lovely church is an
inside place of sitting and resting. Its peace and sense of sanctity is
palpable; it is a church in which it is therefore unusually easy to
pray. Without ostentation or distraction, this is a place where one
can be still and know the presence of God.

Aberdaron

Aberdaron was and still is more or less the end of the line for those
hoping to go to Bardsey Island. Situated on a gracefully curving
beach, in the last sheltered area at the westernmost end of the Llŷn,
it was the final waiting place for travelers on the Pilgrims' Way. Even
today crossing to Bardsey on a given day cannot be guaranteed, as
the tidal race between the island and the mainland is very swift, and
a delay is not at all unusual. During the Middle Ages, pilgrims often
had to wait weeks for the right combination of weather and tide.
Aberdaron was thus a heavily populated place with a monastery,
several chapels, inns, local dwellings, and St. Hywyn's Church.

St. Hywyn's, located at the very edge of the sea, is undoubtedly
monastic in origin, a church that grew from a very early Celtic foundation. Like Clynnog Fawr, it became a *clas*, or collegiate church, of
considerable importance, sometimes referred to as the "Cathedral of
Llŷn." The gathering of hundreds of pilgrims waiting to cross to
Bardsey meant it was indeed of cathedral prominence, albeit without a bishop. The medieval church with its lovely Norman doorway
has suffered greatly with the passage of time; at one point it was

nearly washed into the sea. At another more recent time, St. Hywyn's was abandoned in favor of a new Victorian building, but so unattractive and unpopular was this new building that the people refused to "relocate" and returned to medieval St. Hywyn's. Still more recently, within the last few years, another major storm once again tried to pull the church into the sea, but the combined efforts of the Church in Wales, Cadw, and the British government have saved it by building a sturdy and presumably permanent breakwater.

Only a hundred yards or so from the church is Y Gegin Fawr (translated from the Welsh to mean "The Big Kitchen"), which serves an excellent tea and unforgettable scones. This simple whitewashed building dates back to the fourteenth century, when it provided pilgrims with a simple bed and board. The two local hotels, The Ship Inn and Ty Newydd, both boast a venerable age, although not quite as venerable as Y Gegin Fawr. They both still serve the same function as their earlier predecessors did: they provide food, fellowship, and shelter for pilgrims waiting to cross to Bardsey.

Aberdaron, at the far end of the Llŷn Peninsula, is thus about survival and waiting, St. Hywyn's being a symbol of a people determined to remain constant to God and grounded in their faith. Today all the parishes along the Pilgrims' Way are very small, but the congregations and their vicars are dedicated and faithful. Anyone who chooses to follow the Pilgrims' Way today along the Llŷn in search of the Holy is very likely to find it.

St. Mary's Chapel and Holy Well

If the weather seemed likely to remain unfavorable for some time, medieval pilgrims very possibly walked from Aberdaron across the steep heather and gorse-clad slopes of Uwchmynydd to St. Mary's Chapel, now totally ruined, where they could spend part of their waiting time and look expectantly across to Bardsey, called during the Middle Ages the Isle of 20,000 Saints. The island is not visible from Aberdaron itself, nor from Porth Meudwy, still the traditional embarkation point. From St. Mary's Chapel, though, one can see the siren island and long for the day when a crossing would be possible. There is essentially nothing left to see of St. Mary's Chapel today. Even the foundations have been dug out in places, but from above, from the top of Uwchmynydd, the outline of the chapel, its surrounding buildings, and surrounding wall are easy to pick out in the grass. When the light is right, one can also still see traces of the field ridges left from the days when the immediate area was a seventeenth-century farm. Today it is undeveloped National Trust property, a peaceful green pasture for sheep, covered in early June with a mass of purple foxgloves.

Tucked in the cliffs below St. Mary's Chapel, and immediately across from Bardsey at the point where the island is closest to the mainland, lies one of the most magical and mystical of all the holy places: St. Mary's Well. It is steeped in lore and legend because of its unusual location right at the high tide line. When seasonal changes or storms bring in very high tides, this fresh water spring is overwhelmed by the salt water of the sea, but once the tides have receded to normal levels, the spring sweetens itself to fresh water again.

Getting to this particular well is a challenge; the trip is not for the feeble or fainthearted. The path goes down stone steps hewn out of the bedrock at the side of a steep gully, then it swings around onto rough rocks under the cliffs, and then continues onto a very narrow rock ledge perilously close to the water. If the waves are heavy and the sea is heaving, you can't get all the way to the well, but at those times when you can, having braved the slippery rocks and sea moss-covered ledge, you are more than rewarded. The water seeps out of the cliff rock into a natural triangular rock basin, crystal clear and edged with brilliant green moss and algae. It is one of the few wells from which we can safely drink, and surely it is the sweetest water one has ever tasted. St. Mary's Well is not called one of the holiest of the holy wells for nothing.

The Welsh poet R. S. Thomas, long time resident and great lover of the Llŷn, wrote his poem *Ffynnon Fair* about this well:

> They did not divine it, but
> they bequeathed it to us:
> clear water, brackish at times,
> complicated by the white frosts
> of the sea, but thawing quickly.

Ignoring my image, I peer down
to the quiet roots of it, where
the coins lie, the tarnished offerings
of the people to the pure spirit
that lives there, that has lived there
always, giving itself up
to the thirsty, withholding
itself from the superstition
of others, who ask for more.[41]

In many ways, I think, this poem represents not just St. Mary's Well, but the whole of Llŷn. Here is an area that has been bequeathed to us so that we might reclaim an aspect of our lives long lost. Are there not many people today whose world has become a "tarnished offering," tightly circumscribed by economic bondage? The spirit of unspoiled and unsophisticated Llŷn, nearly surrounded by the sea, will give itself up to those who can turn away from endless self-gratification and possessiveness and who thirst for a simpler life.

The southern route

The route described above is the one usually followed by pilgrims headed to Bardsey from the north. Those coming from the south would likely have foregathered somewhere near Llangybi, although we can only guess exactly where. At Llangybi, however, besides St. Cybi's church, there is Ffynnon Gybi, or St. Cybi's Well. This was a major center for healing, and it is of such historical importance that it is now in the care of Cadw: Welsh Historic Monuments. Cadw maintains the medieval causeway leading to the well itself, tends the surrounding area, and keeps the water itself reasonably free from debris and pollution. Pilgrims can visit the well, sit on one of the original stone seats, and bathe in the healing waters; then they can stop for a prayer in St. Cybi's church just at the top of the slope, before moving on. Undoubtedly this is exactly what the early pilgrims did also.

After leaving Llangybi, pilgrims passed the church of Aberech, popularly supposed to indicate the resting place of those who did not make it to Aberdaron, much less to Bardsey, but died en route. This church may have been the foregathering place for pilgrims from the south. Again, we do not know; nor do we know the exact route they would have followed, for it is likely that all the little churches and chapels had resting places and accommodations for weary pilgrims, as well as holy wells to aid in their comfort and healing. After Aberech, pilgrims could have passed Deneio (another church dedicated to St. Beuno), Penrhos, Llanbedrog, Llangian, Llanengen, Llandygwnning, Rhiw, and finally arrived at Aberdaron. All of these little churches were established during the sixth and seventh centuries by Celtic saints, and their foundations, even though now replaced by medieval buildings, bear a strong silent witness to those Celtic evangelistic missionaries.

Bardsey Island

Bardsey Island, the goal of the Llŷn pilgrims, is truly a special place with a history all its own. It lies just two miles across from Uwchmynydd, the headland at the westernmost tip of Llŷn. Islands to the west, lying in the path of the setting sun, figure strongly in Celtic legends and myths, where they are usually seen to be "dwelling places of the blessed dead." Given the Celtic people's great attraction to the offshore islands, Bardsey most probably has its share of pre-Christian artifacts, but since systematic archaeological studies have not been undertaken, we cannot be sure.

Bardsey is steeped in history and legend, although much of its documented history from the early centuries has been lost—most likely during the destruction by the Vikings. The earliest building remains are the several hut circle foundations on the southern slope of Bardsey's mountain, Mynydd Enlli, which were probably footings for dwelling places of the Celtic monks. Little remains of them today; in fact, the outlines of the foundations can be seen only in the winter or early spring before the bracken has come up. They are situated in a reasonably sheltered position on a level plateau with a breathtaking view of the sea in three directions. These foundations are reminiscent of the monastic remains still standing on Ireland's Skellig Michael. Since they have never been excavated, though, we can only guess at their date. They could be as old as the sixth century or as recent as the twelfth.

Bardsey is said to have been founded, at least in Christian times, by St. Cadfan and his followers who had come over from Brittany sometime during the fifth century. Cadfan also founded the church at Tywyn, on the coast, another convenient point of departure for Bardsey. Both sites claim to be the burial place of Cadfan. In the Tywyn church, a stone bears the inscription: "Beneath a similar mound lies Cadfan, sad that it should enclose the praise of the earth. May he rest without blemish."

The Celtic monastery on Bardsey Island, of which there are no remains other than possibly the beehive huts on the mountain, is still credited to Cadfan, with or without his burial place. His cult was strong and widespread, and there are many churches and places bearing his name in mid Wales: Llangadfan, Pistyll Gadfan, Eisteddfa Gadfa, Llwbyr Gadfan among them. Cadfan's holy well near the churchyard at Tywyn continued to attract large numbers of pilgrims even after the Reformation and up until the very end of the nineteenth century, when it was finally closed. Its waters were said to cure skin diseases and rheumatism.

The island's importance did not diminish during the Middle Ages, rather it undoubtedly increased. We do not know for sure why it came to be called "The Isle of 20,000 Saints" (and it is highly unlikely that such is numerically true), but one reason may be that by the twelfth century and following, it was a very popular place for burial. Those who could not afford the long pilgrimage to Rome, burial place of the Apostles Peter and Paul, instead followed the pilgrimage to Bardsey, the burial place of the Apostles to Wales—Cadfan, Deiniol, Dyfrig, and all the others.

The eleventh and twelfth centuries were times of great monastic reform. Both Clynnog Fawr and Aberdaron had remained *clas* churches, that is, their Celtic monastic organization had continued. But the Normans insisted on "regularizing" all monastic foundations, so gradually all the *clas* churches were converted to continental models. Aberdaron and Bardsey both became Augustinian. We know this had occurred by 1094, because there is a record of the canons having provided a boat for Welsh Prince Gruffydd ap Cynan ab Iago to escape to Ireland. Naturally this transition did not occur without resistance and hostility, but ultimately the Augustinians became dominant and remained so until the sixteenth century and the Dissolution under Henry VIII. The present ruined tower on Bardsey dates from this period.

There is a record of King Edward I and his wife Eleanor, with all their court, visiting the island in 1294, soon after Edward's triumphant conquest of Wales. Obviously at that time it would have been necessary to have a sizeable establishment to house such a large entourage. We can wonder about Edward's visit; did he come in an attitude of penitence (in spite of his territorial aggression, both in Wales and in Scotland, he was said to have been a very devout man); or was he on a triumphal march through his newly conquered lands? Or perhaps he was just curious about the famous island? Who knows?

After the Reformation, when pilgrimage was strongly discouraged, the island became an outpost for bandits and pirates and gradually declined in importance. By the time Lord Newborough bought it in the middle of the nineteenth century, it was a simple farming and fishing community of fewer than a hundred people. Only the ruined tower stood as a reminder of the island's former glory. The present sturdy farm houses and outbuildings were built by Lord Newborough as a "model" farming community that remained such for just under a century. Gradually, however, the community dwindled, the school closed, and people moved to the mainland where life was much less harsh than on a wind-swept sea-girt island.

The importance of Bardsey, however, especially to those interested in ecclesiastical history, natural history, or ecology did not diminish. In the 1950s the Society of St. Francis began to take an interest in the island, and at about the same time Bishop J. C. Jones of the Diocese of Bangor organized a major pilgrimage along the Llŷn to Bardsey.

Forty-two years later, Bishop Cledan Mears, also of the Diocese of Bangor and nearing retirement, organized a similar pilgrimage. The original red wooden Pilgrimage Cross from Bishop Jones's 1950 pilgrimage had the date 1992 added to it, and various groups gathered either at Aberech on the south of the peninsula or at Clynnog Fawr in the north. An enormous crowd took part, walking behind the great red cross, talking and singing together. At Uwchmynydd,

atop the headland overlooking Bardsey Sound and across to the
island, Bishop Mears addressed the assembled modern-day pilgrims:

> It is expedient on an occasion like this that we look back,
> remembering the pilgrimages of the past: the pilgrimage of the
> Jews as they walked to Jerusalem to celebrate the great feasts of
> the Passover, and the Tabernacles; the pilgrimages of the early
> Christians as they flocked to sacred sites associated with the
> birth, death and resurrection of their Lord, and later to Rome
> where the apostles Peter and Paul were martyred; and nearer to
> home the pilgrimages of our forbears from the Celtic period to
> the Middle Ages as they turned their faces towards St. David's,
> Holywell and Bardsey Island. Today is an opportunity to give
> thanks for the faith, the vision, the courage and the persever-
> ance of those saints and to ask God for strength to follow their
> good example and to walk in their steps.

> But we are not assembled here today as some sort of histori-
> cal or archaeological society to trace our ancestry, our family
> tree, or dig into the roots of our Celtic past; but in order to
> renew our faith and to rekindle the fire of that primeval
> vision and calling that inspired Christians in the first place.

> What we are doing today as we walk together is a sign, a
> parable of, and a testimony to the world that the life of a
> Christian from beginning to end is a pilgrimage. We have
> here no abiding city, no permanent dwelling place. Our real
> home lies beyond the brief span of life on this earth.[42]

In the time between these two major pilgrimages, the future of
Bardsey was threatened by its possible sale to outsiders who wanted
it for commercial development. A group of determined individuals
banded together in the mid-seventies to form the Bardsey Island
Trust, which immediately set about raising enough money to buy
the island. It was a tough struggle, but with a lot of hard work,
prayer, and perseverance, funding was eventually found, and in
1979 the Trust purchased the island. The Trust now has full

responsibility for it and maintains it as a place for religious and spiritual renewal and a center for ornithology, marine biology, and other natural sciences. Today it is inhabited by only one family but still is farmed, in a way that balances sensitive ecological and environmental goals with modern farming techniques.

A full-scale archaeological investigation of the island has never been undertaken, and perhaps that is just as well: Bardsey is silent about most of its history. Remembering that in the Middle Ages the abbey had been under the protection of St. Mary, Donald Allchin's words are singularly appropriate:

> In the gospels Jesus' mother says very little. She is silent at Bethlehem, silent at the foot of the cross. But St. Luke tells us that she treasured up all the things that had happened and pondered them in her heart (Luke 2:19, 51). So in its silence Bardsey, too, seems to keep and ponder on the things which have happened, on the secret of Christ's death and resurrection, on the mystery of the deep things of God.[43]

Bardsey remains a hauntingly holy place, and we do not need archaeological or historical records to prove it.

I was on the way to Bardsey for the first time, and I was not sure exactly what to expect. We were to be there a week, and I had been warned that there was no electricity, no running water, no heat, and no flush toilets—each of us would have to take turns dealing with the one chemical toilet in a privy behind each house. I was also warned that because of the weather, we might be delayed in getting to the island, so I was prepared to pay for an extra night (or two or three) in Aberdaron. Similarly, we might be delayed in getting back to the mainland, so I was also prepared to stay on the island longer if need be. I was very excited about going, though, and thanks to help and advice from the

sisters at Tymawr convent, where I was staying at the time, I managed to pack the right things.

On the Saturday morning we were due to cross, the weather was kind. We made our way to the secluded cove of Porth Meudwy, and one by one each of us, wearing warm sweaters and raincoats and well-shod in waterproof boots, stepped into the water and climbed into a rubber dinghy about the size of a large bathtub. Then, in a kind of back-and-forth shuttle service, we were taxied out to the waiting Bardsey Island Trust boat. All our gear was tightly wrapped in black plastic garbage bags, and it was immediately apparent why. The crossing was a normal one—and all of us got drenched by flying waves and sea spray. Far from being frightened, I found myself exhilarated. We couldn't see the island at first because the rocky promontory of the edge of the peninsula was in the way, but once we rounded that, we could see the rock of Bardsey rising out of the sea, waiting for us.

Once on the island I was assigned to Ty Capel, meaning Chapel House, and I more or less settled in. There were about fifteen in our group, and we were there for a week of meditation, reflection, and silence—and for most of us, a period of rest. It was a truly sacred time in a sacred place.

I have two vivid memories of that first trip. The first came about midway through the week, when several of us decided to get up about 3:00 A.M. or so and climb the northern shoulder of the mountain to watch the shearwaters come in to feed their young. I had heard their weird haunting cry during the previous nights, a sound like no other, and I was thrilled at the opportunity to actually see the huge birds at close range. Shearwaters spend most of their days skimming the waves of the Atlantic and feeding; they come in at night and dig burrows in the ground of offshore islands to lay a single egg. Once the chick is hatched, the parents come in, night after night, to regurgitate food into its open mouth. It was this process we were getting up to watch. The birds are enormous—they have a wingspan of about three or four feet—and when scores of them arrive all at once, the noise is truly the sound of a mighty rushing wind. Some of the people in our group had powerful flashlights and shone them on the birds as they landed. I was transfixed by the birds' huge eyes. They went straight to their work of feeding their young, and seemingly they all finished at the same time, because suddenly they all took off together as though God had rung a special shearwater bell. To this day I can see the huge wings of those birds and their glowing eyes and hear their mysterious whooping calls.

The second vivid memory was the day I was in the deep silence of retreat. I had just gone for a long solitary walk around the circumference of the island. When I climbed the mountain and got to the area of the hut circles, I was tired and decided to take a nap, so I stretched out on the grass inside one of the circular foundations, using—like Jacob— a rock for a pillow. It was a brilliant day, and warmed and lulled by the sun's warmth and sheltered from the wind, I was soon asleep in that sacred space. I didn't dream of angels, or of wool-clad Celtic monks in their beehive huts—in fact I didn't dream at all—but when I awoke, I had an experience as mystical as I have ever had. Still stretched out on the grass, as I opened my eyes, I saw within the semicircle of my relaxed hand a small frond of bracken just emerging from the earth. It was still curled over, with its delicate fiddle head well tucked under—the epitome of the vulnerability of emerging new life. I could not move; I simply stared at the innocent young plant, so protected by the shape of my hand, and thought of the way each one of us is similarly surrounded and encircled by God's love. With each new venture we undertake, each new risk we accept, God's hand is always there, guarding us and keeping us safe as we grow.

I also thought about "this fragile earth, our island home,"[44] and how all of us human beings need to place our hands around the gifts of creation and protect our natural world from the destructive ravages of commercialism, greed, and contempt. It was a sacred moment in a sacred place, an experience beyond time. Surely I was surrounded by the angels and the whole host of heaven, and I remembered the evening a friend said to me, "Bardsey is that island of solitude where we are least alone."[45]

I have no idea how long I lay there, mesmerized by the mystery of it all. When I did finally get up, the sun was low in the sky, the chilly evening mist was descending, and I was much too late for supper. I went to bed that night fully aware that I had been in touch with the Holy.

I had been to Iona, and I had been to Lindisfarne, or Holy Island, in Northumbria (England) a few years previously. Both of those islands are well known and have hundreds of visitors, and certainly they are

sacred places. But for me there is something about Bardsey that is dif-
ferent. Bardsey is isolated, being off the tip of a backwater of Wales—
truly the most Welsh part of Wales, where the first language of most
people is Welsh, not English. Here there are no large cities, the primary
economy is sheep farming, and the air is pure and unpolluted. There
are no ferries to the island, as to Iona, and no highways, as to
Lindisfarne. There is no electricity, no modern sanitation, no piped
water. What there is instead is silence, a silence obtainable only when
we are removed from our technology-driven civilization. At night the
stars are overwhelming in their brilliance, and the wind and the sea
make a symphony of sound together. The haunting song of the seals in
the harbor, the mewing of the seabirds, and the bleating of the sheep
replace the sounds of automobiles, televisions, telephones, and door-
bells. The joy of human laughter sounds wonderfully different against
such a background, and even the sound of one's feet walking across the
stony paths is a kind of music.

I thought about the medieval pilgrims—what a struggle they must
have had to get here. A walk of how many miles over how many
months... and a wait at Aberdaron for how many weeks... and a sea-
sick crossing over a choppy sea... Yet the pilgrims kept coming. They
endured the rigors of the pilgrimage because to them Bardsey held out
a promise, the promise of the place of their Resurrection. For them, it
would be good to die on Bardsey, the Isle of 20,000 Saints.

From the top of Mynydd Enlli, where I went one morning to watch
the sun rise, I tried to put myself in the place of those pilgrims who had
made it. In the bitter cold of the predawn I snuggled deeply into my
thick wool blanket and leaned against a sheltering rock. I was com-
fortable in my wool sweater and sturdy boots and grateful for a ther-
mos of hot coffee at my side. When the sun exploded above the sea,
sending brilliant cataracts of color across the sky, I suddenly found
myself in tears. I felt a part of God's world in a way I never had before.
Away from the complexities of a technological civilization, I was truly
at one with the mountain, the sea, the seagulls, the gorse, even the very
rock against which I was leaning. I felt like I was holding God's hand
even as I felt myself being held by God's hand, and I was humbled to
realize that countless other pilgrims before me had undoubtedly par-
ticipated in that same glory, rejoicing in the arrival of a new today.

Afterword

THE WORD CELTIC by itself is difficult enough to define, but when combined with spirituality it becomes a somewhat confusing term for which few can formulate an agreed meaning. In her Introduction, Cintra rightfully warns against its improper application. At the same time, she admits to using it in the absence of any better phrase. It is up to each of us to create our own interpretation, and so, with echoes of Humpty Dumpty's famous phrase, "When I choose a word, it means just what I choose it to mean," my own vision links Celtic spirituality inextricably with the poetic expression of the Celtic holy person's communion with God through the medium of nature.

The couplets penned on manuscript margins a thousand years ago reflect the joy of being close to the birds and bees—their song and their hum—together with the mundane gyrations of the more earth-bound cats and mice. Joy in being a part of God's world is raised to the level of an ecstatic lyric exercise.

Comparing the vivid imagination and freshness of approach of the ancient Celtic literature to its contemporary material elsewhere in early medieval Europe, the Scottish philologist Kenneth Jackson, in his *Celtic Miscellany,* said that it was "as if every poet, gifted with a high degree of imaginative insight, re-discovered the world for himself." Jackson also points out that this literature "did not belong at all to the common culture of the rest of Europe." Indeed, this precocious vernacular phenomenon of the Celtic poets can be said to proclaim its outpourings as the uncommon culture of Europe, representing merely one aspect of the highly unusual and individualistic position of Britain and Ireland during the first millennium of the Christian era.

Another aspect we rightly associate with the Celtic Christian period is that of an unusual church organization. The episcopal diocesan system, with the Pope at the top of a pyramid resting on a solid four-square base below, was the norm throughout much of Christendom. In the Celtic islands, however, it was the monasteries—which sprang up like fairy rings throughout the countryside—and not the episcopal sees that blossomed into the spirited centers of Christian culture and devotion. Sometimes these monasteries formed groups, such as those associated with St. Columba, but others seem to have lived a gloriously independent existence. They all acknowledged fealty to a far-distant pontiff in Rome as the representative of Christ on earth, but there were those who, like St. Columbanus, stridently disagreed with him whenever they felt it necessary.

The common use of Latin as a means of communication between monk and Pope did not prevent Ireland and the other Celtic countries from developing their own separate literature and culture. The scribes and craftsmen of those islands of northwestern Europe quickly learned to distance themselves from their forbears in the declining Roman Empire of the fifth century. Thus unshackled, they went on to create a clearly anti-classical abstract art that set Britain and Ireland apart from the rest of Europe. This art revitalized and gave new Christian meaning to the spiral motifs of the La Tène art of the very early pagan Celts.

It was only when the Hildebrandine reforms of the eleventh and twelfth centuries swept across Europe that the independence of insular monasticism was finally curbed, and the ecclesiastical structure was made to conform with the rest of Europe. The Roman pyramid triumphed, and the four archbishoprics created in Ireland could each appropriately be said to have formed its supporting sides. The same could be said for Wales, Scotland, the Isle of Man, and the Celtic parts of England.

During the six centuries before such changes, however, it was this "otherness," this distancing from the classical and institutional norms of Rome, along with the development of a vivid and dynamic literature and art—owing little to Mediterranean inspiration—that helped to give these insular Celtic monasteries their own particular character.

It was to these same Celtic monasteries, both large and small, that the faithful have gone on pilgrimage from at least the seventh century onwards. Many reasons have been adduced for the practice: people wanted to be cured of an illness, or to atone for sins committed, or perhaps they were hoping to obtain a higher place in heaven. Regardless, the real intention of these pilgrim devotees was to get closer to God. To help them achieve their aim they went to venerate the relics of some local saint who, they hoped, would intercede for them at the feet of the Almighty. The pithy ninth-century phrase that Cintra quotes: "To go to Rome, much labor, little profit," shows the Celtic churches advising their adherents not to cross the seas to reach the throne of Peter, but rather to make their pilgrimage at home. Countless thousands, less joyfully literate than Cintra is here, must have answered that call down the centuries. Pilgrims still throng to such places as Croagh Patrick and Lough Derg in Ireland, to Iona in Scotland, and to Bardsey Island in Wales—and for the same reason: to get closer to God.

The interest that Cintra and her fellow pilgrims evince when following in the footsteps of their forbears in visiting the holy sites could be interpreted as a vote of confidence in the same celebration of nature by the ancient Celts on both sides of the Irish Sea. Perhaps these modern pilgrims, too, reflect current thinking that increasingly equates God and the environment (sometimes almost even replacing God with it) and turns away from an over-institutionalized church toward an active crusade to preserve nature as God made it.

In her own spiritual way, Cintra's soulfaring (lovely title, that!) is a joyous identification with the beautifully moving spirit of Celtic poetry and its glorifying praise of God's bounty. Perhaps soulfaring today is her—and our—generation's response to Wordsworth's call to "return to nature" and the yearning to feel with Browning that "God's in his heaven, all's right with the world," despite all our best efforts to destroy nature for mammon and lucre.

To sit and muse and pray with Cintra and her soulfaring friends (as I have done) in rarely frequented sites of early Celtic monasteries, or at the island tomb of an ancient hermit, or on the edge of holy wells (surely our most tangible link with the nature-root of the Celts, both pre-Christian and Christian), is to be refreshed and rekindled—as we are in this book—with the charisma and joy of God's creation. Here we are invited once more to enjoy the perennial peace and calm that such places provide, like a spiritual oasis, on the margins of our troubled world.

PETER HARBISON

Endnotes

1. Geoffrey Chaucer, "Prologue," *Canterbury Tales* (London: Grafton, 1965), p. 13.

2. Simon Coleman and John Elsner, *Pilgrimage Past and Present in the World Religions* (Cambridge: Harvard University Press, 1995), p. 196.

3. Michael Rodgers and Marcus Losack, *Glendalough: A Celtic Pilgrimage* (Dublin: Columba Press, 1996).

4. Ian Bradley, *Columba: Pilgrim and Penitent* (Glasgow: Wild Goose, 1996), p. 78.

5. Noel Dermot O'Donoghue, "The Angels Keep Their Ancient Places: A Spirituality of Place," lecture presented at Celtic Soul Conference, December 1, 1995, Minneapolis, Minnesota, sponsored by the College of St. Catherine.

6. Oliver Davies, *Celtic Christianity in Early and Medieval Wales* (Cardiff: University of Wales Press, 1996), p. 61.

7. Aubrey Burl, *A Guide to the Stone Circles of Britain, Ireland and Brittany* (New Haven: Yale University Press, 1995).

8. John Finney, *Recovering the Past: Celtic and Roman Mission* (London: Darton, Longman & Todd, 1996).

9. Eleanor Duckett, *The Wandering Saints* (London: Collins, 1959), pp. 27–28.

10. Ibid., 27–28.

11. Tim Severin, *The Brendan Voyage* (London: Abacus, 1978), Appendix I, pp. 265–273.

12. Ibid. Severin's book documents the trans-Atlantic journey.

13. Quoted in Desmond Forrestal, *Columbanus* (Dublin: Messenger Publications, 1992), p. 18.

14. E. G. Bowen, *Saints, Seaways and Settlements* (Cardiff: University of Wales Press, 1977).

15. John Marsden, *Sea-Road of the Saints* (Edinburgh: Floris, 1995).

16. J. G. Davies, *Pilgrimage Yesterday and Today* (London: SPCK, 1988), p. 1.

17. Ibid., passim.

18. John O'Riordan, *A Pilgrimage in Celtic Scotland* (Dublin: Columba Press, 1997), p. 105.

19. Shirley du Boulay, *Pilgrimage to Canterbury* (London: Harper Collins, 1994).

20. For information on visiting the Center for Healing at Pennant Melangell, write the Reverend Evelyn Davies, Iscoed, Pennant Melangell, Llangynog nr Oswestry, SY10 0HQ, Wales.

21. Madeleine Gray, "Penrhys: the Archeology of a Pilgrimage," *Morgannwg XL* (Cardiff: Cadw: Welsh Historic Monuments, 1996), pp. 10–32.

22. The Sacred Land Project, Press Information, 1997.

23. Coleman and Elsner, *Pilgrimage Past and Present*, p. 6.

24. Ibid., p. 216.

25. T. S. Eliot, "Little Gidding," *Four Quartets* (New York: Harcourt Brace Jovanovich, 1943, 1971; London: Faber and Faber, 1942, 1944), lines 39–51.

26. Peter Harbison, *Guide to the National and Historic Monuments of Ireland* (Dublin: Gill & McMillan, 1970, 1992), p. 263.

27. Liam de Paor, *Saint Patrick's World* (Notre Dame: University of Notre Dame Press, 1993), p. 222.

28. Geoffrey Moorhouse, *Sun Dancing* (London: Phoenix, 1997), pp. 99–101.

29. Ibid.

30. Averil Swinfen, *Kilfenora Cathedral* (Kilfenora: Lilliput Press, 1986, 1995), p. 7; see also Harbison, *Guide to Monuments*, p. 64.

31. Alannah Hopkin, *The Living Legend of St. Patrick* (London: St. Martin's Press, 1989), photo caption following p. 64.

32. R. P. C. Hanson, "The Mission of St. Patrick," *An Introduction to Celtic Christianity*, ed. James P. Mackey (Edinburgh: T. & T. Clark, 1989), p. 24.

33. Harry Hughes, *Croagh Patrick: An Ancient Mountain Pilgrimage* (Westport, Co. Mayo, 1991), p. 24.

34. Ibid., p. 35.

35. O'Donoghue, lecture.

36. Charles Thomas. *Whithorn's Christian Beginnings* (Whitehorn: Whitehorn Trust, 1992).

37. Nona Rees, *St. David of Dewisland* (Llandysul: Gomer, 1992), p. 33.

38. T. Charles-Edwards, *St. Winefride and Her Well: The Historical Background* (Holywell: W. Williams & Sons, undated), p. 4.

39. Quoted in the guidebook to the Church of St. Brynach, Nevern (Cardigan, 1950, 1993), p. 7.

40. *The Hymnal 1982* (New York: Church Hymnal Corporation, 1982), No. 685, "Rock of Ages," v. 2.

41. R. S. Thomas, "Ffynnon Fair," *Laboratories of the Spirit* (London: Macmillan, 1975), p. 45.

42. *The Link, Bangor Diocese Quarterly Newsletter 13* (Bangor: 1992) pp. 2–3. Used with permission.

43. A. M. Allchin, *Bardsey: A Place of Pilgrimage* (Aberdaron: University of Wales Press, 1991), p. 13.

44. *Book of Common Prayer* (New York: Church Publishing Incorporated, 1977), p. 370.

45. Mary Chitty, long-time devotee of Bardsey, quoted this to me at dinner on Bardsey Island in 1995. She attributed it to her husband, the theologian Derwas Chitty.

Appendix

IRELAND
Irish Tourist Board
Baggot St Bridge
Dublin 2
IRELAND
Phone: 003531 679 1977; Fax: 003531 602 41000

The Burren
Ennis Tourist Information Office
Clare Road, Ennis, County Clare, IRELAND
Phone: 00353 65 28 366; Fax: 00353 65 28 350
Map: Ordnance Survey: Ireland Discovery Series No. 51

The Burren Centre
Kilfenora, County Clare, IRELAND
Phone: 00353 65 88030; Fax: 00353 65 88102

Croagh Patrick
Tourist Information Centre, Westport
The Mall, Westport, County Mayo, IRELAND
Phone: 00353 98 25711; Fax: 00353 98 26709
Map: Ordnance Survey: Ireland Discovery Series No. 31

The Dingle Peninsula
Cork/Kerry Tourism
Grand Parade, Cork, County Cork, IRELAND
Phone: 00353 21 273 251; Fax: 00353 21 273 504
Map: Ordnance Survey: Ireland Discovery Series No. 70

Kells
Midlands-East Regional Tourism
Dublin Road, Mullingar, County Westmeath, IRELAND
Phone: 00353 44 48761; Fax: 00353 44 40413
Map: Ordnance Survey: Ireland Discovery Series No. 42

Kildare
Midlands-East Regional Tourism
Dublin Road, Mullingar, County Westmeath, IRELAND
Phone: 00353 44 48761; Fax: 00353 44 40413
Map: Ordnance Survey: Ireland Discovery Series No. 55

Brigidine Sisters, 14 Dara Park
Kildare, County Kildare, IRELAND
Phone: 00353 45 22890

Tobar na Mult
Cork/Kerry Tourism
Grand Parade, Cork, County Cork, IRELAND
Phone: 00353 21 273 251; Fax: 00353 21 273 504
Map: Ordnance Survey: Ireland Discovery Series No. 71

SCOTLAND
Scottish Tourist Board
23 Ravelston Terrace
Edinburgh EH4 3EU
SCOTLAND
Phone: 0131 332 2433
Web: www.holiday.scotland.net

Iona
Argyll and the Isles Tourist Board
Department SOS, 7 Alexandra Parade
Dunoon, Argyll PA23 8AB, SCOTLAND
Phone: 01369 701 000; Fax: 01369 706 085
E-mail: info@Scottish.Heartlands.org.uk
Map: Ordnance Survey: Landranger Series No. 48

The Iona Community, The Pearce Institute
840 Govan Road, Glasgow G51 3UU, SCOTLAND
Phone: +44-1414-454-561; Fax: 44-1414-454-295
E-Mail: info@dgtb.demon.co.uk

Whithorn
Dumfries and Galloway Tourist Board
64 Whitesands
Dumfries DG1 2RS, SCOTLAND
Phone: +44-1387-245-550; Fax: +44-1387-245-551
Web: www.galloway.co.uk
Map: Ordnance Survey of the United Kingdom, Landranger Series
    No. 48

The Whithorn Trust
Whithorn Visitor Centre and Museum
Whithorn, Newton Stewart, Wigtownshire DG8 8NS, SCOTLAND
Phone: +44-1988-500-508

Kilmartin
Kilmartin House Trust
Kilmartin, Argyll PA31 8RQ, SCOTLAND
Phone: +44-1546-510-278; Fax: +44-1546-510-330
Web: www.kht.org.uk
E-Mail: museum@khouse.demon.co.uk

ISLE OF MAN
IOM Department of Tourism
Ferry Terminal
Douglas IM1 2RH, ISLE OF MAN
Phone: +44-1624-686-766
Web: www.gov.im
E-mail: dotl@gov.im

Maughold
Maughold Parish Church
Maughold Vicarage, Kirk Maughold IM7 1AS, ISLE OF MAN
Phone: +44-1624-812-070; Fax: +44-1624-817-875
Map: Ordnance Survey of the United Kingdom, Landranger Series
    No. 95

WALES
Wales Tourist Board
c/o British Tourist Authority, 7th Floor
551 Fifth Avenue
New York, NY 10176-0799
1-800-462-2748 or 212-986-2200
Web: www.usagateway.visitbritain.com
E-mail: travelinfo@bta.org.uk

Bardsey Island and the Llŷn Peninsula
The Llŷn Peninsula
Tourist Information Center
Station Square, Pwllheli, Gwynedd LL53 5HG, WALES
Phone: +44-1758-613-000
Map: Ordnance Survey of the United Kingdom, Explorer Series
   Nos. 12 and 13

The Bardsey Island Trust
Coedanna, Nenharon
Pwllheli, Gwynedd LL53 8PR, WALES
Phone +44-1758-730-740

Nevern
Nevern Parish Church, c/o Ty'r Ysgol
Nevern, Newport, Pembrokeshire SA42 0NB, WALES
Phone: +44-1239-820-855
Map: Ordnance Survey of the United Kingdom, Landranger Series
   No. 145

Patrisio
The Rectory, Llangenni
Crickhowell, Powys NP8 1HD WALES
Phone: +44-1873-810-348
Map: Ordnance Survey of the United Kingdom, Landranger Series
   No. 161

St Davids
Pembrokeshire Coast National Park Centre
City Hall, St David's, Pembrokeshire SA62 6SB, WALES
Phone: 01437 720 392; Fax: 01437 720 099
Map: Ordnance Survey: Landranger Series No. 157

St David's Cathedral
St David's, Pembrokeshire SA62 6RH, WALES
Phone: 01437 720 202; Fax: 01437 721 885

St Winefride's Well and Basingwerk Abbey
Greenfield Valley Heritage Park
Holywell, Clwyd CH8 7QB, WALES
Phone: 01352 714 172; Fax: 01352 714 791
Map: Ordnance Survey: Landranger Series No. 116

Bibliography

General Works

Bamford, Christopher, and William Marsh. *Celtic Christianity: Ecology and Holiness*. Lindisfarne: Lindisfarne Press, 1982.

Baring-Gould and Fisher. *Lives of the British Saints*, 4 volumes. 1907–13.

Bowen, E.G. *Saints, Seaways and Settlements*. Cardiff: University of Wales Press, 1977.

Bradley, Ian. *The Celtic Way*. London: Darton, Longman & Todd, 1993.

Burl, Aubrey. *A Guide to the Stone Circles of Britain, Ireland and Brittany*. New Haven: Yale University Press, 1995.

Cooper, J.C. *Illustrated Encyclopedia of Traditional Symbols*. London: Thames and Hudson, 1978.

Davies, Oliver and Fiona Bowie. *Celtic Christian Spirituality: An Anthology of Medieval and Modern Sources*. London: SPCK, 1995.

de Waal, Esther. *Every Earthly Blessing*. Harrisburg, PA: Morehouse Publishing, 1999.

Du Boulay, Shirley. *The London Road to Canterbury: A Modern Pilgrimage*. London: Harper Collins, 1994.

Duckett, Eleanor. *The Wandering Saints*. London: Collins, St. James's Place, 1959.

Eade, John and Michael Sallnow, eds. *Contesting the Sacred: Anthropology of Christian Pilgrimage*. New York: Routledge, 1991.

Farmer, David, ed. *Oxford Dictionary of Quotations*. Oxford: Oxford University Press, 1995.

_____. *Oxford Dictionary of Saints*. Oxford: Oxford University Press, 1997.

Finney, John. *Recovering the Past: Celtic and Roman Mission*. London: Darton, Longman & Todd, 1996.

Green, Miranda. *Dictionary of Celtic Myth and Legend.* London: Thames and Hudson, 1992.

Jöckle, Clemens. *Encyclopedia of Saints.* London: Alpine Fine Arts, 1995.

Joyce, Timothy. *Celtic Christianity: A Sacred Tradition, A Vision of Hope.* Maryknoll: Orbis, 1998.

Leathem, Diana. *The Church Defies the Dark Ages: Story of Celtic Christianity.* Wallington, Surrey: Religious Education Press, 1955.

Mackey, James P., ed. *An Introduction to Celtic Christianity.* Edinburgh: T&T Clark, 1989.

Marsden, John. *Sea Road of the Saints.* Edinburgh: Floris, 1995.

McNeill, John T. *The Celtic Churches: A History A.D. 200 to 1200.* Chicago and London: University of Chicago, 1974.

Newell, J. Philip. *Listening for the Heartbeat of God: A Celtic Spirituality.* New York: Paulist Press, 1997.

Ó Maidín, OCR, Uinseann. *The Celtic Monk: Rules and Writings of Early Irish Monks.* Kalamazoo: Cistercian Publications, 1996.

Patterson, Andrew. *Whithorn, Iona and Lindisfarne.* Edinburgh: Saint Andrew Press, 1991.

Pennick, Nigel. *Celtic Sacred Landscapes.* London: Thames and Hudson, 1996.

_____. *Leylines: Mysteries of the Ancient World.* London: Weidenfield & Nicholson, 1997.

Sellner, Edward C. *Wisdom of the Celtic Saints.* Notre Dame, Indiana: Ave Maria Press, 1993.

Sharp, Mick. *Holy Places of Celtic Britain.* London: Blandford, 1997.

Sheldrake, Philip. *Living Between Worlds: Place and Journey in Celtic Spirituality.* London: Darton, Longman & Todd, 1995.

Thomas, Charles. *Celtic Britain.* London: Thames and Hudson, 1986.

Turner, Victor, and Edith Turner. *Image and Pilgrimage in Christian Culture.* New York: Columbia University Press, 1978.

Versluis, Arthur. *Sacred Earth: The Spiritual Landscape of Native America.* Rochester: Inner Traditions International, 1992.

Walsh, Michael, ed. *Butler's Lives of the Saints.* Tunbridge Wells: Burns & Oates, 1985.

Pilgrimage

Clift, Jean and Wallace Clift. *The Archetype of Pilgrimage: Outer Action with Inner Meaning*. New York: Paulist Press, 1996.

Coleman, S. and J. Elsner. *Pilgrimage Past and Present in the World Religions*. Cambridge: Harvard University Press, 1995.

Davies, J. G. *Pilgrimage Yesterday and Today*. London: SCM Press, Ltd., 1988.

Harbison, Peter. *Pilgrimage in Ireland*. London: Barrie & Jenkins, 1991.

Jones, G. Hartwell. *Celtic Britain and the Pilgrim Movement*. London: Honorable Society of Cymmrodorion, 1912.

Nolan, Mary Lee, and Sidney Nolan. *Christian Pilgrimage in Modern Western Europe*. Chapel Hill: University of North Carolina Press, 1989.

Palmer, M. and N. Palmer. *Sacred Britain: Guide to Sacred Sites and Pilgrim Routes of England, Scotland, & Wales*. London: Judy Piatkus, 1997.

Platten, Stephen. *Pilgrims*. London: Fount (HarperCollins), 1996.

Sugden, Keith. *Walking the Pilgrim Ways*. Newton Abbot, Devon: David & Charles, 1991.

————. *In the Footsteps of the Pilgrims*. Andover, Hants: Pitkin, 1997.

Sumption, Jonathan. *Pilgrimage: An Image of Medieval Religion*. London: Faber & Faber, 1975.

Westwood, Jennifer. *Sacred Journeys: Paths for the New Pilgrim*. London: Gaia Books, 1997.

Ireland

Barrow, Lennox. *Irish Round Towers*. Dublin: Eason & Son, 1985.

Bord Fáilte, Irish Tourist Board. *Ireland Guide*. New York: St. Martin's Press, 1993.

Boylan, Henry. *The Boyne: A Valley of Kings*. Dublin: O'Brien Press, 1988.

Brenneman, Walter and Mary. *Crossing the Circle at the Holy Wells of Ireland*. Charlottesville: University Press of Virginia, 1995.

de Paor, Liam. *Saint Patrick's World.* Notre Dame: University of Notre Dame Press, 1993.

de Paor, Maire and Liam. *Early Christian Ireland.* London: Thames & Hudson, 1958.

Dunne, John J. *Shrines of Ireland.* Dublin: Veritas, 1989.

Flanagan, Donal, ed. *The Meaning of Knock.* Blackrock, Co Dublin: Columba Press, 1997.

Forristal, Desmond. *Columbanus.* Dublin: Messenger Publications, 1992.

Harbison, Killanin and Duignan. *The Shell Guide to Ireland.* Dublin: Gill & Macmillan, 1995.

Harbison, Peter. *National and Historic Monuments of Ireland.* Dublin: Gill and Macmillan, 1970, 1992.

_____. *Pre-Christian Ireland: From the First Settlers to the Early Celts.* London: Thames and Hudson, 1988.

_____. *Irish High Crosses.* Drogheda: Boyne Valley Honey Co., 1994.

Hopkin, Alannah. *The Living Legend of St. Patrick.* New York: St. Martin's Press, 1989.

Hughes, Harry. *Croagh Patrick: An Ancient Mountain Pilgrimage.* Westport: privately printed, 1991.

Hughes, Kathleen. *The Church in Early Irish Society.* London: Methuen, 1980.

Keane, Maryangela. *The Burren.* Dublin: Eason and Son, 1983.

Kirby, Michael. *Skelligside.* Dublin: Lilliput Press, 1990.

Lavelle, Des. *The Skellig Story: Ancient Monastic Outpost.* Dublin: O'Brien Press, 1993.

Logan, Patrick. *The Holy Wells of Ireland.* Gerrards Cross, Bucks: Colin Smythe, 1980.

MacDonogh, Steve. *The Dingle Peninsula.* Dingle: Brandon, 1993.

Manning, Conleth. *Early Irish Monasteries.* Dublin: Country House, 1995.

McNally, Kenneth. *Standing Stones and Other Monuments of Early Ireland.* Belfast: Appletree Press. 1988.

Moorhouse, Geoffrey. *Sun Dancing.* London: Phoenix (Orion), 1997.

North Kerry Archaeological Survey, (entry 914. Tubrid More).

O'Brien, Jacqueline, and Peter Harbison. *Ancient Ireland from Prehistory to the Middle Ages.* London: Weidenfeld & Nicholson, 1996.

O'Connell, J. W. and Korff, A., eds.. *The Book of the Burren.* Galway: Tír Eolas, 1991.

O'Meara, John, trans. *The Voyage of Saint Brendan.* Gerrards Cross, Bucks: Colin Smythe, 1976, 1991.

Paterson, John. *Kildare: Cathedral Church of Saint Brigid.* Kildare: Kildare Cathedral, 1982.

Richardson, H. and J. Scarry. *An Introduction to Irish High Crosses.* Dublin: Mercier Press, 1990.

Rodgers, Michael and Marcus Losack. *Glendalough: A Celtic Pilgrimage.* Dublin: Columba Press, 1996.

Roe, Helen M. *The High Crosses of Kells.* Kells: Meath Archaeological and Historical Society, 1988.

Severin, Tim. *The Brendan Voyage.* London: Abacus (Little, Brown), 1978.

Swinfen, Averil. *Forgotten Stones: Ancient Church Sites on the Burren.* Dublin: Lilliput Press, 1992.

Scotland

Ashmore, P. J. *Neolithic and Bronze Age Scotland.* London: Batsford, 1996.

Ashmore, Patrick. *Calanais: The Standing Stones.* Stornoway: Urras nan Tursachan, 1995.

Bradley, Ian. *Columba: Pilgrim and Penitent.* Glasgow: Wild Goose, 1996.

Brooke, Daphne. *The Medieval Cult of Saint Ninian.* Whithorn: Whithorn Trust, 1987.

_____. *Wild Men and Holy Places: Ninian, Whithorn and the Medieval Realm of Galloway.* Edinburgh: Canongate Press, 1994.

Clarke, Amanda. *Whithorn 7: Report on the 1995 and 1996 Excavations at Whithorn.* Whithorn: Whithorn Trust, 1997.

Fenton, Alexander. *The Island Blackhouse (No. 42, Arnol).* Edinburgh: Historic Scotland, 1995.

Ferguson, Ronald. *Chasing the Wild Goose: Story of the Iona Community.* Glasgow: Wild Goose Publications, 1998.

Finlay, Ian. *Columba*. Edinburgh: Chambers, 1979.

Hill, Peter. *Whithorn and St. Ninian*. Whithorn: Whithorn Trust, 1998.

MacArthur, E. Mairi. *Iona*. Grantown-on-Spey: Colin Baxter, 1997.

Marsden, John. *The Illustrated Life of Columba*. Edinburgh: Floris, 1995.

Ó Ríordáin, John J. *A Pilgrim in Celtic Scotland*. Blackrock, Co Dublin: Columba Press, 1997.

Pringle, Denys, ed. *The Ancient Monuments of the Western Isles*. Edinburgh: Historic Scotland, 1994.

Ritchie, Anna. *Iona*. London: Batsford, 1997.

Ritchie, Anna and Graham. *Scotland: An Oxford Archaeological Guide*. Oxford: Oxford University Press, 1998.

Ritchie, Graham and Mary Harman. *Argyll and the Western Isles*. Edinburgh: HMSO, 1996.

Stell, Geoffrey. *Dumfries and Galloway*. Edinburgh: HMSO, 1996.

Summers, Gilbert. *Explorer Scotland*. Basingstoke: AA Publishing, 1995.

Thomas, Charles. *Whithorn's Christian Beginnings*. Whithorn: Whithorn Trust, 1992.

Wales

Allchin, A. M. *Praise Above All: Discovering the Welsh Tradition*. Cardiff: University of Wales Press, 1991.

_____. *Bardsey, A Place of Pilgrimage*. Aberdaron: privately printed, 1991.

_____. *Pennant Melangell: Place of Pilgrimage*. Pennant Melangell: Gwasg Santes Melangell, 1994.

_____. *God's Presence Makes the World*. London: Darton, Longman & Todd, 1997.

An Inventory of the Ancient Monuments in Caernarfonshire. Royal Commission on Ancient and Historical Monuments, 1964.

Avent, Richard. *Criccieth Castle, with St. Cybi's Well*. Cardiff: Cadw: Welsh Historic Monuments, 1989.

Bowen, E. G. *Settlements of the Celtic Saints in Wales*. Cardiff: University of Wales Press, 1956.

Burnham, Helen. *Guide to Ancient and Historic Wales: Clwyd and Powys*. London: HMSO, 1995.

Charles-Edwards, T. *St. Winefride and Her Well: The Historical Background*. Holywell: W. Williams & Sons, undated.

Chitty, Mary. *The Monks on Ynys Enlli: Part I c. 500 A.D. to 1252 A.D.* Aberdaron: W. Alun Jones, 1992.

The Church of St. Brynach, Nevern, Pembrokeshire (unsigned). Cardigan: E. L. Jones & Son, 1960.

David, The Rev. Christopher. *St. Winefride's Well: A History and Guide*. Holywell: privately printed, 1971.

Davies, Oliver. *Celtic Christianity in Early and Medieval Wales*. Cardiff: University of Wales Press, 1996.

Evans, J. Wyn. *St. David's Cathedral*. Andover: Pitkin, 1991.

_____. *St. David's Bishop's Palace, with St. Non's Chapel*. Cardiff: Cadw: Welsh Historic Monuments, 1991.

Gray, Madeleine. "Penrhys: Archaeology of a Pilgrimage" *(Morgannwg XL pp10–32)*. Cardiff: Journal of Glamorgan History, 1996.

James, David W. *Twice to St. David's*. Llandysul: Gomer, 1995.

Jones, Francis. *The Holy Wells of Wales*. Cardiff: University of Wales Press, 1992.

Jones, Peter and Thomas, R. S. *Between Sea & Sky: Images of Bardsey*. Llandysul: Gomer, 1998.

Kenrick, Eddie. *I Came To Llŷn*. Hillside, Edern: E. Kenrick, 1935?

Kightly, Charles. *A Mirror of Medieval Wales: Gerald of Wales and His Journey of 1188*. Cardiff: Cadw: Welsh Historic Monuments, 1988.

Lynch, Frances. *Guide to Ancient and Historic Wales: Gwynedd*. London: HMSO, 1995.

Marriott, H. *St. David's Cathedral*. London: Pitkin, 1973.

Meyrick, Thomas. *Life of St. Wenefred*. Llanerch, Felinfach: Llanerch Facsimile Reprint (1996), 1878.

Nash-Williams, V. E. *The Early Christian Monuments of Wales*. Cardiff: University of Wales Press, 1950.

O'Malley, Brendan, ed. *A Welsh Pilgrim's Manual*. Llandysul: Gomer, 1989.

Rees, Nona. *St. David of Dewisland*. Llandysul: Gomer, 1992.

_____. *The Medieval Shrines of St. David's Cathedral*. St. David's: St. David's Cathedral, 1998.

Rees, Sian. *Guide to Ancient and Historic Wales: Dyfed*. London: HMSO, 1992.

Rees, William. *Historical Atlas of Wales*. London: Faber & Faber, 1959.

Robinson, David M. *Heritage in Wales: Guide to Ancient and Historic Sites in the Care of Cadw*. London: Macdonald, Queen Anne Press, 1989.

_____. *Basingwerk Abbey*. Cardiff: Cadw: Welsh Historic Monuments, 1996.

Sharkey, John. *Pilgrim Ways: The Grand Pilgrimage to St. David's*. Glanrhyd, Cardigan: Ancient Landscapes, 1994.

_____. *Celtic High Crosses of Wales*. Llanrwst: Gwasg Carreg Gwalch, 1998.

Thomas, Roger. *Llŷn: A Special Place*. Llandudno: The National Trust, 1998.

Victory, Siân. *The Celtic Church in Wales*. London: SPCK, 1977.

Watney, John. *Celtic Wales*. Andover: Pitkin, 1997.

Other

Bebe, The Venerable. *Ecclesiastical History of the English People*. Edited and translated by Colgreve, B. and Mynors, R. A. B. Oxford: Oxford University Press, 1969.

Chaucer, Geoffrey. *Canterbury Tales*. Modern prose rendering by David Wright. London: Grafton (Harper Collins), 1965.

Cubbon, A. M. *Ancient & Historic Monuments on the Isle of Man*. Douglas, IOM: Manx National Heritage, 1973.

_____. *The Art of the Manx Crosses*. Douglas, IOM: Manx National Heritage, 1983.

Eliot, T. S. *Four Quartets*. New York: Harcourt Brace Jovanovich, 1943, 1971.

Gallyon, Margaret. *The Early Church in Northumbria*. Lavenham, Suffolk: Terence Dalton, 1977.

Guide to Maughold Parish Church. (unsigned and undated).

Hume, Basil. *Footprints of the Northern Saints.* London: Darton, Longman & Todd, 1996.

Kelly, Eamonn P. *Sheela-na-Gigs: Origins and Functions.* Dublin: National Museum of Ireland, 1996.

Macdonald, Iain. *Saints of Northumbria.* Edinburgh: Floris, 1997.

Mackay, Shiela. *Lindisfarne Landscapes.* Edinburgh: Saint Andrew Press, 1996.

Taylor, Thomas. *Celtic Christianity of Cornwall.* London: Longmans, Green and Co., 1916.

Thomas, R. S. *Laboratories of the Spirit.* London: Macmillan, 1975.

Ward, Benedicta. *The Venerable Bede.* Harrisburg: Morehouse, 1990.

Warner, Martin. *Walsingham: An Ever-Circling Year.* Oxford: Oxford University Press, 1996.

Young, G. V. C. *A Brief History of the Isle of Man.* Peel, IOM: Mansk-Svenska Publishing, 1983.

About the Author

SISTER CINTRA PEMBERTON (Cintra Shober Austin), a religious sister in the Episcopal Order of St. Helena, has been designing, organizing, and leading spiritual pilgrimages since 1992.

Before entering the convent, Sister Cintra was married and raised a family. She has a daughter, Pemmie Austin Sheasby, and a son, John Brander Austin, Jr., and four grandchildren.

A native of New Orleans, she currently lives in New York City. With an M.A. degree and an academic background in history and music history, she has many years' experience in teaching, having served on the faculties of St. Martin's Episcopal School and Louisiana State University in New Orleans. She is a skilled photographer and studied at the International Center for Photography in New York City.

She is now recognized nationally for conducting retreats, quiet days, various spiritual programs, and workshops in Celtic spirituality. She has studied and traveled extensively throughout both Britain and Ireland and is certified by the British Tourist Authority, the Irish Bord Fáilte, and the Wales Tourist Board as a qualified leader of specialized travel programs.

For more information:

Sister Cintra Pemberton, OSH
Pilgrimages: Explorations of Celtic Spirituality
134 East 28th Street
New York, NY 10016-8156
Phone 212-725-6435; fax 212-779-4009
e-mail cintra@ix.netcom.com
web site: www.osh.org/pilgrimages